Remediating Reading Difficulties

Remediating Reading Difficulties

Fifth Edition

Sharon J. Crawley
Florida Atlantic University

King Merritt

McGraw-Hill
Higher Education

Boston Burr Ridge, IL Dubuque, IA New York San Francisco St. Louis
Bangkok Bogotá Caracas Kuala Lumpur Lisbon London Madrid Mexico City
Milan Montreal New Delhi Santiago Seoul Singapore Sydney Taipei Toronto

The McGraw·Hill Companies

McGraw-Hill
Higher Education

Published by McGraw-Hill, an imprint of The McGraw-Hill Companies, Inc., 1221 Avenue of the Americas, New York, NY, 10020. Copyright © 2009, 2004, 2000, 1996, 1991. All rights reserved. No part of this publication may be reproduced or distributed in any form or by any means, or stored in a database or retrieval system, without the prior written consent of The McGraw-Hill Companies, Inc., including, but not limited to, in any network or other electronic storage or transmission, or broadcast for distance learning.

1 2 3 4 5 6 7 8 9 0 DOC/DOC 0 9 8

ISBN: 978-0-07-313109-2
MHID: 0-07-313109-1

Editor in Chief: *Michael Ryan*
Publisher: *David S. Patterson*
Sponsoring Editor: *Allison McNamara*
Marketing Manager: *James Headley*
Development Editor: *Marley Magaziner*
Editorial Assistant: *Sarah Kiefer*
Production Editor: *Carey Eisner*
Manuscript Editor: *Jennifer Bertman*
Cover Designer: *Ashley Bedell*
Text Designer: *George Kokkonas*
Production Supervisor: *Richard DeVitto*
Composition: *10/12 Times Roman by Laserwords Private Limited*
Printing: *45# New Era Matte Plus, R. R. Donnelley & Sons*

Front Cover: © Ryan McVay / Getty Images
Back Cover: © Comstock/PictureQuest

Library of Congress Cataloging-in-Publication Data

Crawley, Sharon J., 1946–
    Remediating reading difficulties / Sharon J. Crawley, King
Merritt.—5th ed.
        p.   cm.
    Includes bibliographical references and index.
    ISBN-13: 978-0-07-313109-2
    ISBN-10: 0-07-313109-1
    1. Reading—Remedial teaching.   I. Merritt, King, 1933– II. Title.
LB1050.5.C7   2009
372.43—dc22

                                                         2008002057

www.mhhe.com

CONTENTS

UNIT VI: STUDY SKILLS   185

UNIT VII: AFFECTIVE AREAS   203

UNIT VIII: SPECIALIZED APPROACHES   223

PREFACE

According to the title of an aptly named publication by the American Federation of Teachers, "teaching reading is rocket science"; that is, teaching reading is an important undertaking that requires significant preparation. To illustrate just how important an undertaking, consider the following: if children have difficulty learning to read in the early grades, this difficulty can continue through middle school, high school, and into adult life. Also consider the number of children facing these difficulties: it is estimated that

- About 20 percent of elementary students nationwide have significant problems learning to read.
- At least 20 percent of elementary students do not read fluently enough to enjoy or engage in independent reading.
- The rate of reading failure for African American and Hispanic children, limited-English speakers, and poor children ranges from 60 percent to 70 percent (American Federation of Teachers 1999, p. 7).

As an educator involved in literacy instruction, your goal is to help students with reading challenges succeed. To do so, you strive to organize your classroom teaching based on your students' needs. You use explicit instruction in teaching skills and strategies to your students and provide many reinforcement opportunities. Because you know your students' reading strengths and weaknesses through observation and testing, you work toward giving them successful experiences to develop their independence and confidence in reading.

You know that it is one thing to identify students' literacy strengths and needs, but quite another to do something about these needs. Some solutions for teaching will come to mind quickly. For other solutions, however, a comprehensive reference source, with practical teaching ideas specifically designed for handling literacy needs, will be a "welcomed friend." *Remediating Reading Difficulties* is meant to be your "welcomed friend."

This book is designed as a concise, easy-to-read, easy-to-use guide with suggestions for teaching and remediating aspects of a student's literacy needs that are diagnosed through an experienced teacher's observations and, more specifically, through the use of an Informal Reading Inventory (IRI) or Reading Running Records. It is also a handy reference for teaching and reinforcing skills needed by any students in your class; this includes students who are speakers of other languages or who have limited English proficiency.

The Contents

Now, turn to the Table of Contents. You will notice that most chapters begin with a semantic map, a brief introduction, and a description of major terms and concepts. This is followed by explicit teaching of the featured skill, which involves telling students what they are going to learn, using specific steps in teaching, and providing opportunities to practice and reinforce the skill. During explicit teaching students should always be given the opportunity to read narrative or expository materials in which the skills are utilized.

After the explicit instruction strategies, you will find a variety of applicable classroom-tested reinforcement activities. Please remember that your selection of teaching strategies should be based on your students' age, maturity, and reading ability. Because the numerous ideas presented cover a broad spectrum, your selection for appropriateness is, of course, important. Also, it is extremely important to have your students apply these skills in context; children's books have been listed throughout the chapters to help you do just that.

Unit I focuses on the emergent/beginning reader. This is included because students may not have sufficient grasp of concepts of print, letter identification, or phonemic awareness and, thus, may experience difficulty engaging in the reading process.

Unit II, Word Analysis Skills, emphasizes the basic decoding skills of sight word recognition, picture clues, phonic analysis, and syllabic analysis.

As we move from decoding to comprehension, vocabulary development becomes the focus of Unit III. Vocabulary forms the foundation for comprehension. Graphic organizers, morphology, context clues, word relationships, and activities for extending vocabulary are presented in Chapters 8 through 12.

Fluency has been given separate recognition in Unit IV. Without developing fluency, students have difficulty chunking materials into meaningful units. Chapter 13 presents major fluency strategies, and Chapters 14 and 15 are directly related to examiner notations and observations of student reading behaviors. The easy-to-follow chapter formats make it simple to quickly retrieve teaching suggestions.

Unit V focuses on comprehension. It has been reorganized into preparing students to read, organizational structures, elaborative structures, questioning structures, and teaching structures. The unit moves from building background and setting purposes in Chapter 16 to organizational patterns or structures in Chapter 17. Elaborative structures in Chapter 18 extend the student's interaction with the text.

Chapter 19 presents specific questioning structures that assist students in generating and answering questions. Finally, Chapter 20 presents teaching structures or frameworks for instruction.

Unit VI, Chapters 21 through 23, addresses study skills that relate to oral and silent reading. These include adjusting reading rate, study strategies and memory aids, and listening.

Units VII through IX are devoted to establishing and even extending the element of success in literacy. The old adage "Nothing succeeds like success" is never more critical than for your classroom students, especially those who are speakers of other languages (ESL/LEP) and those who have experienced failure in previous school years. Therefore, we have included chapters on improving self-concept, developing interests, suggestions for parents, specialized approaches to assist struggling readers, and suggestions for working with ESL students.

Appendixes A through C supplement information for sight word and word analysis strategies. Appendix D discusses how to develop a teaching kit, and notable children's books are identified in Appendix E. Appendixes F through H relate to trade materials suitable for remedial programs and literacy classrooms. Specific commercial materials, kits, and multimedia, including games, software, and writing activities, are included in these appendixes. These will benefit anyone interested in the wide variety of material for teaching literacy. Appendix I presents a listing of publishers and how to contact them.

This Fifth Edition

There have been several changes to this fifth edition that are worth noting:

- **Discussion of environmental print, book walks, shared reading, and a chapter on preparing students to read have been added.** Language Experience and chapters on comprehension also have been expanded.
- **Over 70 new activities have been added to the fifth edition.**
- **The text is accompanied by a book-specific Web site that includes templates for strategies discussed in the text.** Twenty-six strategy-specific templates are included. The case studies, interest inventory, and parent interview questionnaire are still included in this Web site.
- **Appendixes E–H have been fully updated and Appendix E has been expanded to include more award categories.** These new awards relate to picture books and/or books specific to diverse cultures. Students who are reluctant readers might be more motivated to read about their own cultures. The new awards include the Boston Globe–Horn Book Award, E. B. White Read Aloud Award, Theodor Seuss Geisel Award, Schneider Family Book Award (focusing on the theme of disability experience), American Indian Youth Services Literature Award, The Pura Belpré Award (Latino culture), and the Sydney Taylor Book Award (Jewish experience).

Although the title of this book is *Remediating Reading Difficulties,* the strategies and reinforcement activities suggested can be used in many literacy programs. You may choose to build on some of these suggestions with ideas of your own to further tailor your instruction. If you do, then the true value of this book will have been realized.

We wish you the wonders and joys of success as you encounter the challenge of meeting your students' literacy needs.

Sharon J. Crawley
King Merritt

Acknowledgments

Joyce Armstrong
King's College

Cynthia Bowden
College of Notre Dame of Maryland

Karen Bromley
Binghamton University

Cathleen Doheny
State University of West Georgia

Lee Dubert
Boise State

Susan Fisher
Indiana Wesleyan University

Paulette P. Harris
Augusta State University

Ellen Jampole
Cortland College

Louise Kaltenbaugh
Southern University at New Orleans

Linda Lilienthan
University of Northern Colorado

Linda Marley
Oakland City University

Joanne Ratliff
University of Georgia

Lori Tullis
California State University

Deborah Tidwell
University of Northern Iowa

Sally C. Wedge
Keuka College

Joseph E. Zimmer
St. Bonaventure University

Emergent/Beginning Literacy Skills

Concepts of Print

Letter Identification

Phonemic Awareness

Unit Introduction

Emergent or beginning literacy skills . . . are the skills that form the foundation of speaking, reading, and writing and develop into conventional or traditional reading and writing. The following map presents the major categories of these skills.

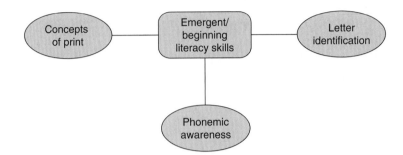

Students who perform poorly in your classroom or on an informal reading inventory or reading running records might have a weakness in one or more of the emergent/beginning reading skills areas. It is advisable to assess students' knowledge of emergent literacy skills if they are having difficulty reading.

Parents, siblings, or significant others may not have read to students. Books may not be in the home. Students may not have had preschool experiences where emergent literacy skills were emphasized. Languages other than English may be spoken in the home and by students. Students may not have developed phonemic awareness. "All babies are born equal. Not one can speak, count, read, or write at birth, but by the time they go to kindergarten they are not equal"(Trelease 2001, p. 36).

Concepts of Print

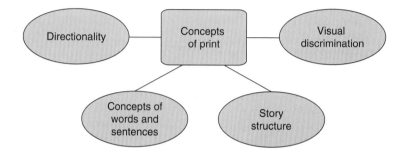

Description

Neuman and Celano (2001) write that many children have very limited experiences with print. This is also true of adults coming from countries of poverty. As a result, they have not developed concepts of print. Specific instruction is needed in order for children to learn letters, sounds, and story structure. (Reutzel, Fawson, Young, Morrison, & Wilcox, 2003).

Children develop concepts of print through exposure to print. Adults point to and read the names on boxes and signs. They read stories while pointing to words. They talk about the stories and ask children about them. They provide many writing materials (pencils, crayons, markers, paper) for children to use in writing.

Concepts of print . . . the foundational, or emergent literacy, skills involved in how to hold a book and turn the pages, identifying a word or sentence, where to begin and end reading a page, having the eyes move in the correct direction, retelling a story, or relating the author's ideas to one's own experiences. The **graphemic,** or written, form of each language is read in its own unique manner.

Directionality . . . moving one's eyes in the correct direction for reading the printed form of a language. Hebrew is read from right to left. In English, students must develop the skills of moving their eyes from left to right, and from the top to the bottom of the page. They must also recognize where to begin and end reading a page.

Story structure . . . the ability to identify the characters, plot, and setting of a story. Students initially will orally retell the story by identifying the characters, what happened in the story, and where the story took place. These abilities will become evident in a student's writing.

Visual discrimination . . . the skill of seeing likenesses or differences among objects, pictures, letters, numbers, or words. Students learn to recognize the differences between the graphemes *b* and *d* and the words *bad* and *dab*.

Words and sentences . . . identifying the individual words and sentences on a page, identifying that sentences are made up of words, and recognizing that these words and sentences contain meaning are important concepts of print.

The best way to teach students concepts of print is to provide many experiences with books and writing. Provide numerous activities in which you and others read and write with students.

Explicit Instruction: Reading Big Books

1. When reading a children's big book or writing a story, point from left to right and top to bottom as you read or write. Be sure your pointing is a smooth movement and you do not lift your finger from the page while pointing to individual words. You want students to develop smooth eye movements and not develop the habit of fixating on each word in a sentence. (See Chapter 4 for guidelines on using big books.)
2. Ask students where to begin reading. Ask a student to come to the big book and point to the first word that should be read.
3. Encourage students to frame individual words in the story with their hands.
4. Have students count the individual words in a sentence by starting at the left and moving to the right.
5. Encourage students to trace over individual letters or words in sentences.
6. Encourage students to read along as they become familiar with the story.
7. Encourage students to write their own stories, or use language experience with students. (See Chapter 30 for guidelines on using language experience.) The same activities that are used with reading big books can also be used with language experience stories or students' individual writing.

Environmental Print

The print that surrounds us is an excellent source for teaching students that they can be successful in reading. Students can easily identify many of the symbols and can feel successful as "readers." Typical environmental print categories of packaging, logos, and labels (words) include: traffic or safety signs (stop, yield, railroad crossing, fire exit, school, speed limit), fast food restaurants (McDonald's, Taco Bell, Arby's, Burger King, Wendy's, Domino's Pizza), stores (Target, Wal-Mart, Toys "R" Us, Circuit City), cookie and cracker packages (animal crackers, graham crackers, Wheat Thins, Ritz crackers, Oreos, Chips Ahoy), peanut butter jars, candy wrappers (M&M's, Hershey's Kisses), cereal boxes (Wheaties, Cocoa Puffs, Froot Loops,

Frosted Flakes), soup cans (Campbell's tomato, chicken noodle), toys/games (Chutes & Ladders, checkers, Uno, dominoes, Barbie dolls, Matchbox cars), pet foods, juice boxes, soda cans, entry tickets, signs in grocery store aisles, and so on.

Explicit Instruction: Environmental Print

1. Select one or two areas of environmental print for discussion. Examples might be cookies and crackers or safety signs. Read a book to the students that encompasses the theme. For cookies you might read *If You Give a Mouse a Cookie* (L. J. Numeroff 1985), *Mmm, Cookies!* (R. Munsch and M. Martchenko 2002), *Pee Wee Scouts: Cookies and Crutches* (J. Delton 1988), *Who Took the Cookies from the Cookie Jar?* (B. Lass, P. Sturges, and A. Wolff 2000); for signs you might read *I Read Signs* (T. Hoban 1987), *Signs in Our World: Spot the Signs All Around You!* (J. Searcy 2006), or *Signs on the Road* (M. Hill 2003).
2. Show students the samples and encourage them to identify as many as they can. (These samples must be collected prior to teaching the environmental print category.)
3. Ask students how they are able to "read" the signs. (Some might remember the logos, some the TV advertisements, others might know the letters or actual words.)
4. Have students bring in actual signs or pictures of signs. Post these signs with labels around the room or put them onto a word wall.
5. Expand the activity to include other categories of environmental print. Have students identify the signs, label the signs, and put the signs up around the room with labels.
6. As the list grows and more categories are added, the pictures can be sorted or categorized by students.
7. Students can make their own environmental print books. These books can be for a specific category of environmental print or a page for each category studied. They can read them individually, in pairs, place them in the book center, and so on.

Reinforcement Activities: Environmental Print

1. Trace the environmental print words and write them on index cards.
2. Use magnetic letters or three-dimensional letters to create the environmental print words.
3. Have students create word banks with their logos and labels.
4. Ask students what letters they see in the different words. Have them frame or point to the letters.
5. Discuss the initial sounds in words. What sound do you hear at the beginning of the word? What other words do we know that have the same sound?

6. Have students create books with their environmental word pictures and label the pictures.
7. Have students write sentences to go along with the logos and labels.
8. Students can read their books in pairs or place them in book centers.
9. Let students take their books home to read to parents, grandparents, and caregivers.
10. Count the number of letters in words.
11. Count the number of environmental print words they have.
12. Look at environmental word configurations. Match pre-made word frames with the environmental words.
13. Identify and circle a specific consonant or vowel on a package or box.
14. Categorize environmental print logos as circles, ovals, triangles, squares, rectangles.
15. Sort labels by beginning sound.
16. Match picture logos with labels.
17. Make a bingo game. Logos can be placed on the bingo cards, and the teacher calls out the name. Students place a marker on the correct logo. Or, at a more advanced stage, written words (or labels) can be placed on the bingo game and the teacher calls out the word.
18. For a word wall, try to locate an environmental print example for each letter of the alphabet.
19. Students (depending upon age and achievement) can alphabetize and create a pictionary of the environmental print words.
20. Create rhyming words to match the "rime" of environmental print words.
21. Students can create their own environmental print words.
22. Students can make their own collage of environmental print words.
23. Create a missing memory game from environmental print labels or words. Show the students three (gradually increase the number) labels. Cover the labels, remove one, and have the students guess which was removed.
24. Create an order memory game from environmental print labels or words. Show the students three (gradually increase the number) labels. Cover the labels, change their order, and have students rearrange them into the correct order.
25. Students can sort the environmental logos by shape and then count to find out which shape is used most often. If you align similar shaped logos you could create a picture graph.
26. Create a concentration game. Start with eight word or logo pairs and gradually increase the number. Put the eight words or logos on index cards. Place the index cards face down in mixed order. Students select two cards at a time and try to find a match. If the cards match, they keep them. If the cards do not match, they are placed face down in their original position.

ENVIRONMENTAL PRINT WORD LIST

address
airport
ambulance
automatic door
baggage claim
bake
bank
baseball
basketball
beach
beans
beef
beware of dog
bicycle
bike route
biohazard
boil
book
box(es)
bread
buckle up
bump
bus stop
buy
cake
camping
car
car rental
car wash
cashier
caution
caution: slippery when wet
cell phone
checkout
cheeseburger
chicken
city
closed
coffee
computer
construction ahead
crackers
customs
danger
danger: hard hat area
date
deer crossing
deli

dentist
detour
direction
directory
doctor
do not enter
don't litter
drive
east
elevator
employees only
end construction
enter
escalator
exit
fire exit
fire extinguisher
fire station
fish
fishing
flammable
flour
flowers
food
football
fries
fruit
fry
gas (gasoline)
grand opening
gravy
ground transportation
hamburgers
handicapped parking
hard hat area
help wanted
horseback riders
horses
hospital
ice cream
in
information
interstate highway
juice
lane closed
library
lifeguard
lighthouse

littering is unlawful
lodging
lost and found
marina
meat
men's restroom
miles
milk
movies
name
neighborhood crime
   watch
no cell phones
no dogs
no dumping
no fishing
no left turn
no littering
no loitering
no parking
no parking any time
no passing
no pedestrians
no right turn
no smoking
no soliciting
no swimming
no throwing trash
no trespassing
no U-turn
north
now hiring
oil
open
open house
out
paper
paramedic
park
passenger pickup
pencils
pens
phone
physician
picnic area
picnic tables
pizza
playground

(continued)

plumber	school bus	taxi
poison	school crossing guard	tea
police	self checkout	telephone
popcorn	shirts must be worn	telephone number
pork	shoes must be worn	ticketing
post office	slow: children playing	tickets
preowned cars	soap	toys
pull	soccer	train station
purchase	soda	truck crossing
push	sorry we're closed	turkey
push button to walk	soup	used cars
railroad crossing	south	vegetables
recycle	speed limit	waste disposal
restaurant	spices	west
restroom	state	will return
road closed	steak	winding road
road work ahead	stop	women's restroom
salad	sugar	zip code
sale	supermarket	
sandwiches	swimming	

Language Experience

Language experience provides an authentic learning experience for students. It helps students understand that the printed word carries meaning. Students engage in (or use) a personal experience, talk about the experience (use oral language), write about it (or someone else writes what they say), and read what they have written. It is an effective method for learning about concepts of print. It is most often used with beginning readers, but can be successfully used with adults learning to read, and secondary students in content areas. Roach Van Allen (1968) and Russell Stauffer (1970) provide thorough discussions of the Language Experience Approach. Hoffner (2003–2004) provides insight into the Language Experience Approach with secondary students in content areas. Allen (1968) summarized language experience in the following way:

> What I think about, I can talk about.
> What I can say, I can write down.
> What I can write, I can read.
> I can read what others write for me to read.

Explicit Instruction: Language Experience

1. Plan an activity in which students participate. This might be making a puppet, popping popcorn, guessing the contents of a mystery box, going

on a listening walk, doing an experiment or field experience, making something with clay, playing with a stuffed animal, or having a class party. Direct purposeful activities are best at the beginning stages and with English language learners. Direct purposeful activities serve to immerse students in meaning.

2. Lead and have students participate in the activity. Engage students in discussion as they are participating in the activity. The discussion helps direct students' thinking, builds vocabulary, and develops oral communication skills.

3. Use leading questions to help students generate a story. Initially, try to keep the story limited to about eight sentences.

4. Have students dictate one sentence at a time related to their drawings and participation in the activity.

5. Write students' contributions on a chart, thus creating a chart story. Write what students say, as they say it. Do not change or edit the words. (Students will use incorrect speech with print connections.)

6. Reread the story aloud to the students. You may want to read the story aloud several times, depending upon your students. Be certain to point to each word and emphasize the left-to-right movement and return sweep. Be careful to move your hand smoothly under the words to avoid numerous eye fixations.

7. Have students engage in repeated readings of the story, either individually or chorally. The number of repeated readings used will depend on the individual or the group of students.

8. Some teachers type and duplicate the story and give each student a copy. At this stage some teachers make very *minor* changes to the story for clarity, but only minor changes should be made. Some people say that changes should never be made in a language experience story.

9. Extend the story with related activities (matching words, matching phrase cards, sequencing sentence strips, sequencing words, or engaging in phonics activities.)

Other topics for language experience:

emotions (time when I felt happy or frightened)
foods (favorite recipes, holiday foods)
how to play a game or instrument
a favorite place you like to visit
a favorite place you like to go to play
your favorite sport
your favorite friend
what you did over the weekend
important events in your life

family members

an unusual shopping experience

your garden or favorite flower

a fear you have

a place you visited

an unusual visitor at home, at school, or at a club

what you do on your favorite holiday

camping trip or vacation

favorite book

what you would like to be when you become an adult

classroom, school, or personal news events

school field trips

favorite pet

something that happened at school

something constructed with blocks

personal (digital) photographs

favorite music

a play or cultural event that was attended

something you really do well

an unexpected or unexplained event

a special wish

a local, state, national, or international news event

Reinforcement Activities: Language Experience

1. Locate capital letters.
2. Locate specific letters (capital or lower case).
3. Match individual words.
4. Locate words that begin with a specific sound (e.g., the sound that Marie's name begins with).
5. Create a bingo game from words in students' stories.
6. Have students locate a specific word they know in the story. Write the word on an index card for the student to bring home and/or put into an individual word bank.
7. Have students look for (spy) words they used in their stories in other sources—magazines, posters, papers, and so on.
8. Ask specific comprehension questions related to the story (who, what, when, where, how).
9. Write individual sentences from the story on sentence strips. Have students reorganize the sentence strips to tell the story.

10. Cut sentence strips into individual words. Students then reorganize the words to form the sentence.
11. Make word walls of words from the story.
12. Play concentration using words from students' stories.
13. Provide different pointers (a variety of back scratchers work well) for students to use as they reread their stories and point to the words or read words on the word wall.
14. Students can enact their stories or create accounts of the story by using clay, paints, and so on.
15. After singing a song such as Raffi's "Down By the Bay," have students illustrate their own verses and write the jingle that goes along with them.
16. Students might read their stories to music.
17. Stories can be saved onto a computer in Powerpoint format. These can be posted online to be read by parents.
18. Use magnetic letters to form words from the story.
19. Write special words from the story in shaving cream (be careful students are not allergic to the shaving cream).
20. Play "musical word bag." Write words from students' stories on individual index cards and place them in a cloth bag or fancy container. Play music. When the music stops the student holding the bag must reach into the bag, select a word without looking, and then read the word.

Books for Children

Wordless Picture Books

The following wordless picture books are excellent for oral language development and as a basis for writing stories.

Alborough, J. *Hug*. Cambridge, MA: Candlewick Press, 2000.

Alexander, M. *Bobo's Dream*. New York: Dial, 1970.

Day, A. *Good Dog, Carl*. La Jolla, CA: Green Tiger Press, 1985.

dePaola, T. *Pancakes for Breakfast*. San Diego, CA: Voyager Books, 1990.

Hutchins, P. *Changes, Changes*. New York: Aladdin, 1987.

Keats, E. *Kitten for a Day*. New York: Puffin, 2002.

Mayer, M. *Frog Goes to Dinner*. New York: Dial, 1974.

———. *Ah-Choo*. New York: Penguin Group, 1993.

Ormerod, J. *Sunshine*. London: Francis Lincoln, 2004.

Turk, H. *Max the Artlover*. Natick, MA: Neugebauer Press, 1981.

Ward, L. *The Silver Pony*. Boston: Houghton Mifflin, 1973.

Wiesner, D. *Tuesday*. New York: Clarion Books, 1997.

———. *Flotsam*. New York: Clarion Books, 2006.

Big Books

The following big books can be used to reinforce left to right and top to bottom movement, develop sight vocabulary, and present reading in a natural way.

Martin, B. *Brown Bear, Brown Bear, What Do You See?* New York: Henry Holt, 1992.

————. *Polar Bear, Polar Bear, What Do You Hear?* New York: Henry Holt, 1997.

Mountain, L. *Mother Goose Tea Party.* New York: NTC/Contemporary Publishing Company, 1993.

Mountain, L.; S. Crawley; and E. Fry. *The Gingerbread Man: Heritage Readers.* Provincetown, RI: Jamestown Publishers, 1991.

————. *Goldilocks and the Three Bears: Heritage Readers.* Provincetown, RI: Jamestown Publishers, 1991.

————. *The Little Red Hen: Heritage Readers.* Provincetown, RI: Jamestown Publishers, 1991.

Raffi. *Down By the Bay.* New York: Crown Publishers, 1988.

Letter Identification

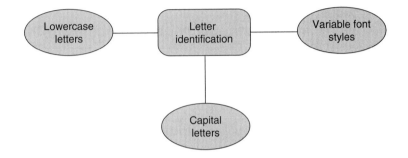

Description

Being able to identify and name the letters of the alphabet was found to be one of the best predictors of reading success by Durrell (1958). Knowing letter names assists students in associating phonemes, or sounds, with graphemes, or letters (Walsh, Price, and Gillingham 1988).

> **Grapheme** . . . the physical representation of a symbol from a standard alphabet.
>
> **Letter identification** . . . the skill of naming a graphic symbol belonging to a standard alphabet.

Explicit Instruction

1. Teach children the letters in their names.
2. With the child sitting beside you, write a desk name tag for the child.
3. Say the letters as you are writing them for the child.
4. Have the child trace the letters with his/her finger and say them with you.
5. Have the child write the letters of his/her name in the air and say the letter names as they are being formed.
6. As you teach individual letters, draw attention to distinctive features such as lines, circles, etc. Do not simultaneously teach letters with similar appearances, such as *b* and *d, p* and *q,* or *s* and *z.*

7. To reinforce the letters in the student's name:

   – Have students use magnetic letters and form their names on a magnetic board.
   – Use other three dimensional letters and have students form and trace over their names. They should recite the letters in their names as they move the letters into place or trace over them.
   – Locate the letters in their names in poems or experience stories.
   – Locate the letters in their names in books.
   – Write the letters in their names in shaving cream or sand.
   – Locate the letters in their names in the names of other students.
   – Students can count the letters in their names.
   – Students can put their names (or write their names) on a helper's chart.
   – Make a word wall with students' names.

Reinforcement Activities

1. **Identification with language experience.** Using students' language experience stories, have students circle or underline letters of their choice or letters the teacher directs them to locate. (see Chapter 1)
2. **Letter pronunciation.** As you are writing on the board or chart paper or projecting with an overhead projector, say the names of the letters as you are writing words.
3. **Simple alphabet books for students.** These books usually contain one letter per page and pictures that begin with the letter. Have students identify the letter or letters.
4. **Posted letters location.** Ask students to identify the letters in words posted around the room or in other books. Have students say the letter names aloud.
5. **Big books.** As you are reading a story to students, have them come up to the book and locate and point to the letters.
6. **People's names.** Looking at the names of people, find the letter or letters being studied.
7. **Scavenger hunt.** Using the newspaper or magazines, locate words that begin with, contain, or end with each letter of the alphabet. Underline the letter of the alphabet found. Then make a collage of these words.
8. **Elementary dictionary book race.** Students locate the section of the elementary (easy) dictionary that contains words beginning with a letter announced by the teacher. The student who first locates the letter wins the race. (This can be varied using a telephone book or any other book containing words listed in alphabetical order.)
9. **Newspaper race.** Give students a specific amount of time, such as 3 or 4 minutes, to circle or highlight as many of the letters being studied as they can locate. The student who locates the most examples of the letter wins.

10. **Sandpaper letters.** Sandpaper letters provide a tactile experience for students. Students should be directed to trace over the sandpaper letter as they say the letter name.

11. **Back tracing.** Back tracing provides a pleasant experience for students. Each student traces a letter on another student's back. Students must then guess what letter was traced on their back.

12. **Sandbox.** If a sandbox is located in your room, students might write the letters in the sand as they say them.

13. **Magic slate.** Students, using magic slates, can write a letter and pronounce its name. They can then "erase" the letter by lifting the "magic" film.

14. **Cookie letters.** Using your favorite sugar cookie recipe, cut, or better still have students cut, the dough into the letter being studied. These can be baked and eaten later.

15. **Alphabet cereal.** Direct the student to take a handful of cereal. Then ask the student to identify the letter name of each piece of cereal. If the letter is named correctly, the student can eat the piece of cereal.

16. **Chocolate-pudding finger painting.** Give each student finger-paint paper and chocolate pudding. Using the pudding as finger paint, students can form and name the letters they are learning.

17. **Finger painting.** Use the following recipe to make your own finger paint. Then encourage students to practice making and naming the letters using the finger paint. The recipe is as follows:

> 1 cup liquid starch
>
> 1 cup cold water
>
> 3 cups soap flakes
>
> powdered tempera paint (enough to color)

Using an electric mixer, mix all the ingredients together. The mixture will be stiff.

18. **Playdough letters.** Provide students with the opportunity to practice making letters using playdough. The recipe is as follows:

> 2 cups flour
>
> 1 cup salt
>
> 3 teaspoons cream of tartar
>
> 2 cups water
>
> 2 tablespoons cooking oil (100% vegetable)
>
> 3–4 drops food coloring

Mix all the ingredients and stir over medium heat until stiff. For color, add several drops of food coloring. Knead on a piece of wax paper until soft. Store the dough in a plastic bag.

19. **String letters.** On a piece of cardboard, students might form with string the letter being studied. Then, after you are certain the letter is correctly made, the student can put Elmer's glue over the string. When the glue is hardened, the student has a relief of the letter, which can then be used for tracing.

20. **Pipe-cleaner letters.** Using pipe cleaners, students can form the letters of the alphabet.

21. **String matching.** Prepare cards with uppercase letters printed on the left side and lowercase letters printed on the right side. Approximately five letters per card are sufficient. Then connect a separate string (shoelace, yarn, etc.) to each of the letters at the left, and place a hole to the left of each lowercase letter on the right. The student's task is to connect the string from the uppercase letter to the correct lowercase letter.

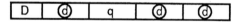

22. **Letter circle.** Prepare laminated cards with a capital letter on the left and four lowercase letters to the right. Three of the lowercase letters should match the uppercase letter; one lowercase letter should be a distractor. The student should circle all lowercase letters that correspond to the uppercase letter.

23. **Multiple response.** Pass cards to your students containing different letters of the alphabet. Each card should have one letter printed on it, although students can have more than one card. Then, as you call out the letter's name, the student who has the letter must stand up and show his/her letter card.

24. **Letter recognition checkers.** Using an old checkers game board, place letter cards on the square. (You might cut a piece of plastic the same size as the board and write the letters on that rather than on the actual board. In this way, the plastic can be removed and the checker game used for other skills.) This game is played using the same rules as for checkers, except that as students land on a square containing a letter, they must name the letter. If the student cannot name the letter, s/he must move back to the original square.

25. **Gingerbread house letter match.** Prepare a file folder game in which the student must match uppercase and lowercase letters. One game might involve a gingerbread house that has a mixture of capital and lowercase letter "cookies" on it. The student must make a double cookie by matching the cookies on the house with the corresponding uppercase or lowercase loose cookie. This is done by placing the loose cookie on top of the one already on the gingerbread house.

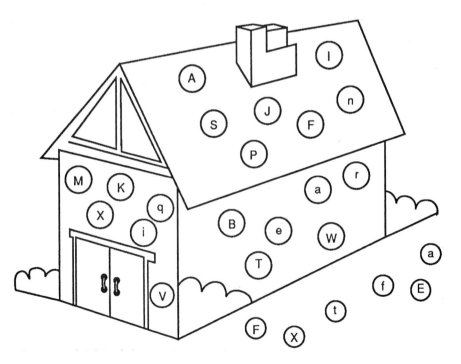

26. **Crossing London Bridge.** This is a board game in which students must cross London Bridge. They must twirl a spinner that allows them to move one or two spaces. As they land on the space, they must name the letter. If they do not name the letter, they must move back to their original space.

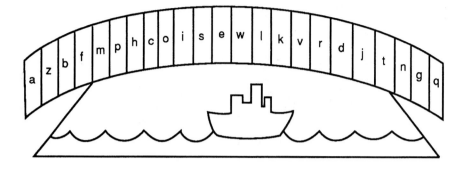

27. **Letter-recognition bingo.** This letter-recognition game is played following the same rules as regular bingo. The difference, however, is that students must locate letters rather than numbers.

B	h	g	E	f
t	z	d	i	A
p	m	H	T	c
O	e	s	a	J
F	k	G	b	u

28. **Letter-recognition dominoes.** This is played the same way as regular dominoes, except that letters are placed on the dominoes (or laminated pieces of tagboard) rather than dots. Students must match uppercase and lowercase letters.

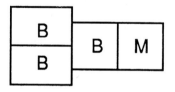

29. **Castle letter race.** A game board is provided with spaces that have letters written on them. Students twirl the spinner and move the number of spaces indicated. They then name the letter on which they land. The

first person to get to the castle wins. Naturally, there are obstacles along the path (an alligator makes you lose a turn, etc.).

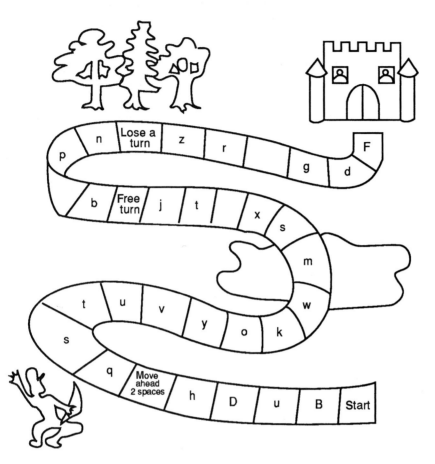

30. **Collecting headlines.** Using newspaper headlines, find 10 words that contain the letter being studied.

31. **Scavenger hunt.** Using the newspaper or magazines, locate words that begin with, contain, or end with each letter of the alphabet. Underline the letter of the alphabet found. Then make a collage of these words.

32. **Telephone book race.** Students locate the section of the telephone book that contains names beginning with a letter announced by the teacher. The student who first locates the letter wins the race. (This can be varied using a dictionary or any other book containing words listed in alphabetical order.)

33. **Newspaper race.** Give students a specific amount of time, such as 3 or 4 minutes, to circle or highlight as many of the letters being studied as they can locate. The student who locates the most examples of the letter wins.

Books for Children

Early Alphabet Books for Students

Darling, K. *ABC Dogs.* New York: Walker & Co., 2003.

Dodson, P. *An Alphabet of Dinosaurs.* New York: Scholastic Trade, 1995.

Ehlert, L. *Eating the Alphabet.* New York: Red Wagon Books, 1996.

Gag, W. *The ABC Bunny.* New York: Putnam Juvenile, 1978.

Hays, A. J. *Happy Alphabet!: A Phonics Reader.* New York: Random House, 2002.

Marsoli, L. A. *Disney's Pooh's ABC.* New York: Random House Disney, 1998.

Scarry, R. *Richard Scarry's Find Your ABC.* New York: Random, 1973.

Viorst, J. *The Alphabet from Z to A.* New York: Atheneum, 1994.

More Complex Alphabet Books

Cassie, B., and J. Pallotta. *The Butterfly Alphabet Book.* Watertown, MA: Charlesbridge Publishing, 1995.

Crane, C. *D is for Dancing Dragon: A China Alphabet.* Chelsea, MI: Sleeping Bear Press, 2006.

———. *L is for Lone Star: A Texas Alphabet.* Chelsea, MI: Sleeping Bear Press, 2002.

Herzog, B. *T is for Touchdown: A Football Alphabet.* Chelsea, MI: Sleeping Bear Press, 2004.

Pallotta, J. *The Underwater Alphabet Books.* Watertown, MA: Charlesbridge Publishers, 1991.

Ulmer, M. *H is for Horse: An Equestrian Alphabet.* Chelsea, MI: Sleeping Bear Press, 2004.

———. *J is for Jump Shot: A Basketball Alphabet.* Chelsea, MI: Sleeping Bear Press, 2005.

Phonemic Awareness

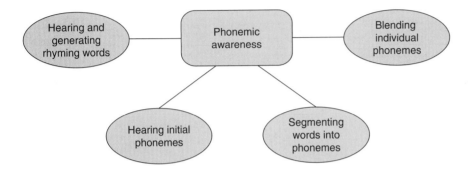

Description

The Committee on the Prevention of Reading Difficulties in Young Children (Snow, Burns, and Griffin 1998) identified that understanding the alphabetic principle was a key to learning phonics and spelling. Elkonin (1973) and the National Institute for Literacy's National Reading Panel (2000) identified phonemic awareness as an important ingredient in learning to read. Phonological awareness was found to be a better predictor of reading readiness than standard reading readiness tests (Stanovich, Cunningham, and Cramer 1984). The National Institute for Literacy (2000, 2001) in its publications of the *National Reading Panel Report* and *Put Reading First,* and the International Reading Association's summary of the *Reading Panel Report* (2002), emphasized that phonemic awareness can be taught, and it helps children learn to read and spell. Phonemic awareness and phonics are not the same.

> **Phoneme** . . . the smallest significant unit of sound in language. English has 44 sounds or phonemes represented by consonant and vowel sounds.
>
> **Phonemic awareness** . . . being cognizant of the sounds in language. Hearing and using the sounds of our language.
>
> **Phonics** . . . decoding words by using the sound value of letters and/or groups of letters. Knowing the sound(s) of a specific letter or group of letters.

Blending . . . putting individual phonemes together into a pronounceable word, either nonsense or real (/sh/ /o/ /p/ = *shop*).

Rhyming words . . . words that have similar rimes but different onsets. A *rime* is the rhyming part of the word. For example *at* is the rime in *cat, sat, fat,* and *rat.* An **onset** is the beginning or initial part of the word before the rime. The letters *c, s, f,* and *r* are the onsets in the rhyming words *cat, sat, fat,* and *rat.*

Segmenting . . . breaking a word into its individual sounds (*shop* = /sh/ /o/ /p/).

Torgesen and Mathes (1999) identify the easiest and hardest consonant phonemes to pronounce:

The easiest phonemes to extend include		The phonemes hardest to extend include	
/m/	mouse	/d/	dig
/n/	night	/b/	bottle
/f/	fire	/g/	gate
/v/	violet	/r/	rush
/sh/	ship	/j/	jack
/s/	sister	We often pronounce the *uh* sound as we make or say these more difficult sounds.	
/z/	zoo		

Hearing and Generating Rhyming Words

Explicit Instruction: Hearing Rhymes

1. Initially start by having students hear and identify rhyming words.
2. Read Mother Goose and other rhymes to students.

> Hickory, dickory, dock,
> The mouse ran up the clock,
> The clock struck one,
> the mouse ran down,
> Hickory, dickory, dock.

3. Listen to how these words sound alike: *hickory–dickory; dock–clock.*
4. Do *dock* and *ball* sound alike? Listen: *dock–clock–ball.*
5. Do *dock* and *sock* sound alike? Listen: *dock–clock–sock.*
6. Encourage students to memorize the rhymes.
7. Once students hear the rhymes, encourage students to begin generating words. Can you think of another word that sounds like *dock–clock?* (e.g., *rock, sock, mock, flock, hock.*) Accept nonsense words as long as they sound alike. (A word of caution: Rhyme should be demonstrated with young children, not explained.)

Reinforcement Activities: Hearing Rhymes

1. **Sing songs.** Sing songs such as "Row, Row, Row Your Boat" that contain rhyming words.
2. **Read any of the Dr. Seuss books.** These are full of rhymes. Students can identify the rhymes.
3. **Dictate pairs of words to students.** Use some that rhyme, some that do not rhyme. Students can hold up a picture of a happy face if the words rhyme and a sad face if the words do not rhyme.
4. **Show students pictures of rhyming words.** Use some pairs that rhyme and some that do not rhyme. Students can hold up a picture of a happy face if the words rhyme and a sad face if the words do not rhyme. (Note: Students initially say the words to themselves. If students have difficulty, pronounce the names of the pairs of pictures.)
5. **Stand Up.** Recite pairs of words to students. Some that rhyme, others that do not rhyme. If the word pairs rhyme, students should stay standing. If the word pairs do not rhyme, students should sit.
6. **Clapping.** Recite pairs or groups of words to students. Some that rhyme, others that do not rhyme. If the pairs of words rhyme, students should clap once for each word. (For example: *ball–tall,* the student would clap, clap; for *ball–tall–fall,* the student would clap, clap, clap). If there is no rhyme (*ball–box*) the student sits quietly.
7. **Nursery rhyme listening.** Read a nursery rhyme to students (for example, "The Queen of Hearts"). After you have read the nursery rhyme, tell students that you want them to listen for words that rhyme with "*arts.*" Have students hold up a stick with a smiley face each time they hear a word that rhymes with "*arts*" (*hearts* and *tarts* will occur eight times).
8. **Play concentration with rhyming words.** Show students the pictures and name them. Then place the pictures face down. Students must draw matches of rhyming words.
9. **Use dominoes with pictures.** Students match the pictures that rhyme.
10. **Create rhyming picture word walls (or picture dictionaries).** Students can bring in words that rhyme and put these on word walls or in picture dictionaries.

Explicit Instruction: Generating Rhymes

1. Read Slepian and Seidler's *The Hungry Thing* to students. Tell them to listen carefully to find out why the Hungry Thing was having problems.
2. After reading the story, discuss the problem the Hungry Thing was having. (He uses the wrong beginning sounds in words when trying to order his meal.)

3. Ask students to try to help the Hungry Thing order his meal as you read the story again. As you are reading the story the second time, ask students for a real food word that rhymes with the word the Hungry Thing is saying.
4. As students give you the "real" foods, pronounce the nonsense word and the real word together to hear the rhyme.

Reinforcement Activities: Generating Rhymes

1. **Supplying rhymes.** After reading rhymes such as "Hickory, Dickory, Dock" ask students to supply rhymes. Can you think of a word that rhymes with *clock–dock?* (Students supply a word.) Let's listen to the words *clock–dock–*(word students supply). Do these words sound alike?
2. **Rhyming riddles.** I'm thinking of a word that means "large" and rhymes with *rig. (big)* I'm thinking of a word that is a place where people live and rhymes with *mouse. (house)* I'm thinking of a word that is something you drive and it rhymes with *far. (car)*
3. **Read books** such as Seuss's *There's a Wocket in My Pocket.* Encourage students to substitute different rhyming words (There's a locket in my pocket.) The words may be real or nonsense as long as they rhyme.
4. **Rhyming names.** Have students create rhymes with their names: *Jan–ran; Joe–toe.* (Nonsense rhymes are OK as long as they rhyme.)
5. **Adding rhyming verses to songs.** A favorite is "Down by the Bay" (Raffi 1999).

> Down by the bay, where the watermelons grow
> Back to my home I dare not go.
> For if I do my mother will say,
> Did you ever see a bear combing his hair down by the bay?
> Did you ever see a bee with a sunburned knee down by the bay?

Have students make up their own verses, such as these:

> Did you ever see a cat playing with a bat down by the bay?
> Did you ever see an eagle riding a brown beagle down by the bay?
> Did you ever see a snail sailing in a pail down by the bay?
> Did you every see white mice boiling brown rice down by the bay?

6. **Rhyme hunts.** Change words in the nursery rhyme "The Farmer in the Dell." Students hunt for rhyming words.

> A hunting I will go.
> A hunting I will go.
> Hi-ho, the derry-o,
> A hunting I will go.
> I'm hunting for a word.
> I'm hunting for a word,
> That rhymes with *toe,* (teacher or student supplies word)
> And the word is *low.* (students fill in word)

Books for Children

Cameron, P. *I Can't Said the Ant*. New York: Coward, 1961.

Curtis, J. L. *Today I Feel Silly and Other Moods That Make My Day*. New York: HarperCollins, 1998.

dePaola, T. *Tomie dePaola's Mother Goose*. New York: Putnam, 1985.

dePaola, T., and S. Hale. *Mary Had a Little Lamb*. New York: Scholastic, 1992.

Druce, A. *Halloween Night*. Flagstaff, AR: Rising Moon, 2001.

Goldstein, B. S. *Birthday Rhymes: Special Times*. New York: Yearling, 1995

MacCarone, G. *The Lunch Box Surprise*. New York: Scholastic/Cartwheel Books, 1995.

———. *"What Is That?" Said the Cat*. New York: Scholastic/Cartwheel Books, 1998.

Prelutsky, J. *Tyrannosaurus Was a Beast*. New York: Mulberry Books, 1993.

Raffi. *Down By the Bay*. New York: Crown Publishers, 1988.

Seuss, Dr. *Cat in the Hat*. New York: Random House, 1957.

———. *Green Eggs and Ham*. New York: Random House, 1960.

———. *Hop on Pop*. New York: Random House, 1963.

———. *Mr. Brown Can Moo! Can You?* New York: Random House, 1996.

———. *Oh, the Thinks You Can Think!* New York: Random House, 1975.

———. *There's a Wocket in My Pocket*. New York: Random House, 1996.

Silverstein, S. *A Giraffe and a Half*. New York: HarperCollins Juvenile, 1981.

Slepian, J., and A. Seidler. *The Hungry Thing*. New York: Scholastic Trade, 2001.

Smith, J., and B. Parkes. *Gobble Gobble Glup Glup*. Barrington, IL: Rigby Education, 1984.

Hearing Initial Phonemes

Explicit Instruction

1. Listen carefully to the words I say: *ball–bear*. (Have the student say the pairs of words aloud.) *Ball* and *bear* sound alike at the beginning.
2. Does *car* sound like the beginning of *ball* and *bear*?
3. Show students pictures of words beginning with the same sound *(box, bat, bell)* and several that do not contain the same beginning sound *(lamp, house, car)*.
4. Students sort the sounds that begin alike and those that don't have the same beginning sound.
5. If students have difficulty with this task, you may need to show them how the individual sounds are made.
6. I'm going to read you a story. The story is called _____. The author is _____. Let's see if you hear any words that begin like *bear* and *ball*.

Reinforcement Activities

1. **Alliterative nursery rhymes.** Repeat, and have children join in reciting, alliterative nursery rhymes that contain the initial sound you are stressing.
2. **Songs for sound matching.** Yopp (1992) recommends using songs for sound matching. You might use the tune of "Old MacDonald Had a Farm"; substitute a different sound with each verse.

   > What's the sound that starts these words?
   > Turtle, time, and teeth. (Wait for students to give you the /t/ sound.)
   > /t/ is the sound that starts these words:
   > Turtle, time, and teeth.
   > With a /t/, /t/ here, and a /t/, /t/ there,
   > Here a /t/, there a /t/, everywhere a /t/, /t/.
   > /t/ is the sound that starts these words:
   > Turtle, time, and teeth. (p. 700)

3. **Consonant and vowel substitution.** Substitute different consonants for the letter *b* in "Apples and Bananas." Then substitute sounds for different consonants and vowels (National Research Council 1999).

   ### Apples and Bananas
   I like to eat eat eat apples and bananas.
   I like to eat eat eat apples and bananas.

   I like to ate ate ate aypuls and baynaynays.
   I like to ate ate ate aypuls and baynaynays.

   I like to eet eet eet eeples and beeneenees.
   I like to eet eet eet eeples and beeneenees.

   I like to ote ote ote opples and bononos.
   I like to ote ote ote opples and bononos.

   I like to ute ute ute upples and bununus.
   I like to ute ute ute upples and bununus.

4. **Picture sorting.** Students sort precut (preidentified) pictures into piles that begin with the same sounds.
5. **Locating and cutting pictures that start with the same sound.** Put these pictures into an "initial consonant" picture dictionary.
6. **Word listening.** Listen to sentences in which students must identify words that contain the same sounds. Read, "Mom gave Mike a glass of milk." Ask, "What words begin with the same sound?"
7. **Dominoes.** Make sets of dominoes containing pictures. Students must match the pictures on the dominoes that begin with the same sound.
8. **Picture bingo.** Use bingo cards with pictures containing different initial sounds. After you dictate a word, the student must place a marker on the picture that begins with the same sound.

9. **Name Game.**

>"My name is Beverly and I like boxes."
>"My name is Lee and I like lakes."

10. **Shopping Game.** Going "shopping," students must think of two items (or three) that they can purchase that begin with the same initial phoneme. "I went shopping and I bought mittens and mustard." "I went shopping and I bought pancakes and pins."

Books for Children

Jeram, A. *Daisy Dare.* Cambridge, MA: Candlewick Press, 1995.

Jonas, A. *Watch William Walk.* New York: Greenwillow, 1997.

McBratney, S. *Caterpillow Fight.* Cambridge, MA: Candlewick Press, 1997.

Root, P. *One Windy Wednesday.* Cambridge, MA: Candlewick Press, 1997.

Tate, S. *Tammy Turtle.* Nags Head, NC: Nags Head Art, 1991.

Segmenting Words into Phonemes

Explicit Instruction

The Elkonin boxes (Elkonin 1973) provide visual and tactile help in segmenting sounds. Here is an example using the word *sun.*

1. Place a picture in front of the child (sun).
2. Below the picture place a series of connected boxes for each sound (not letter) in the word *sun.*

3. Slowly pronounce the word /s/–/u/–/n/.
4. Have the student pronounce the word *sun* very slowly.
5. Have the student slide a counting chip into the box for each sound as the word is pronounced.
6. The box should have three counting chips (one in each box) for each of the sounds.

The following is an example for the word *ship*.

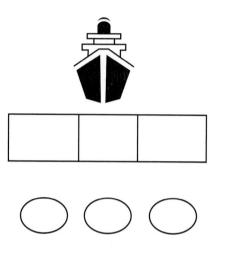

1. Place a picture in front of the student.
2. Below the picture, place a series of connected boxes for each sound in the word.
3. Slowly pronounce the word *ship* for the student.
4. Have the student pronounce the word *ship* very slowly.
5. As the student pronounces the word, she/he slides a counting chip into a box for each sound that is heard. In this instance there would be three sounds heard /sh/–/i/–/p/.

Reinforcement Activities

1. **Elkonin boxes.** Students can have Elkonin boxes and counting chips on their desks. As a picture is shown and it's name pronounced by the teacher, students can move their chips into the boxes.
2. **Clapping sounds.** Clapping for each sound in a word is a reinforcement activity involving movement.
3. **Word use.** Use words from books you have read to students. This will reinforce the concept that words we say and read are made up of sounds (phonemes).

Blending Sounds into Words

Explicit Instruction

1. Tell students you are going to need their help. They will have to be good detectives and figure out the word you are saying.
2. Tell students you are going to make sounds and their detective job is to figure out the word the sounds make.
3. Do an example with students. Listen carefully to the sounds I say in the word *bat,* /b/ /a/ /t/. What word did I make the sounds of? Listen carefully to these sounds again. /b/ /a/ /t/. What word am I saying? *Bat.*
4. Provide additional examples for students to blend into words.
5. Begin with three-phoneme words and increase your examples to four-phoneme words.
6. Consonant digraphs, of course, cannot be separated because they are one sound; for the word *chick,* you would say /ch/ /i/ /k/ (Mountain 2000, p. 74).
7. Next display the letters that make up the word. As you say the sounds, write the letters on the board. As you make the sound /b/, write the letter *b* on the board. As you make the sound /a/, write the letter *a* on the board. As you make the sound /t/, write the letter *t* on the board. Now have students read the word *bat.* (Writing the letters on the board as the sounds are being made helps establish the speech to print (phoneme–grapheme) connection.

Reinforcement Activities

1. **Use riddles or puzzles with students.** Use words in specific categories (pets, wild animals, birds, toys, children's names) and have students solve the riddle. For example, I am thinking of the name of someone in our class. The sounds in her name are /j/ /a/ /n/. What is her name? *Jan.* Have students make the sounds in Jan's name. /j/ /a/ /n/. Write the letters in *Jan* on the board as students are making the sounds. Whose name did we make with these sounds? *Jan.*
2. **Using rhymes with students.** Say the sounds of the rhyme to students and have students tell you what the word is. I have a cat who loves my /h/ /a/ /t/. Students recite the rhyme with the word.
3. **Old MacDonald's Farm.** Sing "Old MacDonald" until you come to an animal on his farm. At that point segment the name of the animal and students must blend it together.

    Old MacDonald had a farm
    E-I-E-I-O
    And on his farm he had a /p/ /i/ /g/ (students say *pig*)

UNIT

II

Word Analysis Skills

4

Sight Word Recognition

5

Picture Clues

6

Phonic Analysis

7

Syllabic Analysis

Unit Introduction

Word analysis skills . . . are the skills that students use when identifying words as they are reading. Word analysis skills are used automatically by proficient readers. This automatic use of word analysis skills allows readers to focus on comprehension—interacting with text and attaching meaning to printed symbols. The following map presents the major categories of word analysis skills. A list of word analysis generalizations appears in Appendix A.

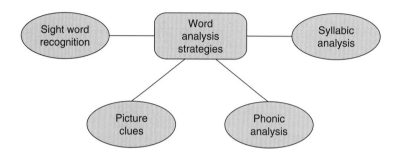

It is the goal of educators to have students who are independent in their skills of word analysis. If students have not developed sufficient skills in word analysis in the early childhood grades, they will have difficulty encountering the high density of vocabulary presented to them in grades four and above (Taylor 1996). Materials read by students in high school contain over 100,000 different words (Nagy and Anderson 1984).

Having good word analysis skills or developing automaticity in decoding words is not sufficient to be a proficient reader. It is one ingredient. This must be combined with fluency and comprehension.

Sight Word Recognition

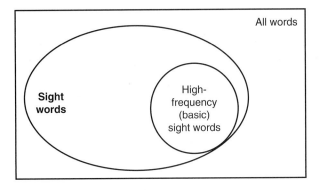

Description

Sight words . . . are words that can be recognized instantly and pronounced without resorting to the use of word analysis. *Elevator, turbo,* and *geometric* are sight words if you can read them automatically or instantly.

High frequency or basic sight words . . . are words most frequently used in written text. They are a subcategory of sight words.

Three high-frequency sight word lists are presented at the end of this chapter (see pages 38–42). The 220 "Dolch Basic Sight Words" account for approximately 70 percent of the words children encounter in grades one through three, and approximately 40 percent of the words that appear in adult text. Edward Fry's "Instant Word List" is a second high-frequency word list. The first 100 words on this list account for about 50 percent of all printed materials. The 300 words on this list account for about 65% of all printed materials. These are the words most frequently used to generate text in basal readers and other narrative materials. The "Adult Basic Word List" contains the 385 words that adults beginning to read most frequently use to generate written text. See Chapter 1 for the "Environmental Word List."

Many of these words have similar shapes or configurations that may cause confusion (like *then–than* or *went–want*). These are also low-image words; the student cannot easily picture the word in his/her mind. Finally, you may notice that many of the words do not follow regular decoding generalizations. Yet because students will use phonics in decoding them, incorrect pronunciations result.

Inadequate development of concepts of print, poor visual discrimination, and lack of phonic decoding skills may be possible causes of poor sight vocabulary. Not attending to context and word meanings is a contributing cause. Spending little time engaging in reading outside the "necessary" reading in school may also contribute to a poor sight vocabulary. Practice makes word recognition more accurate and faster.

Explicit Instruction

1. Initially present only 5 words. (Gradually add words—perhaps only one or two additional words every other week if your students are having great difficulty learning sight words.) These words should be different in configuration and begin with different initial letters (when, there, is, not, say). Begin with words students use in their writing or encounter in their reading.
2. Give students movable letters to use in spelling these words (e.g., magnetic, plastic, or wooden letters, or letters printed on tagboard), a sheet of paper, and a pencil.
3. Point to and say the word you are teaching: *there.* Spell the word aloud while pointing to each letter: *t-h-e-r-e.* Use the word in a sentence. *There are three books on the table.*
4. Have students say the word and spell it by writing in the air.
5. Have students rearrange their movable letters to spell the word at their desks.
6. Select a student to go to the board or pocket chart and rearrange the letters to spell the word.
7. Have all students say and spell the word aloud: *there, t-h-e-r-e, there.*
8. After the 5 words are learned, show students riddle sentences and have them write the answers to the riddles using the words learned. "What word did I forget to write in each of these sentences?" (Read the sentence to the students and say *blank* where the word belongs.)

   _____ are many leaves on the tree.
   _____ there any ice cream in the freezer?
   This dog is _____ very big.

9. Place these sight words on word walls or next to letters of the alphabet posted around the room.
10. Read aloud a story or big book that contains these words.

Explicit Instruction: Teaching Using Predictable Big Books

Predictable books can be used as an avenue for developing sight word knowledge. Predictable books contain phrases or sentences that are repeated. Students are able to predict a phrase or sentence because of the predictable pattern in the story.

The following steps are recommended for using predictable books:

1. Select a book that is short enough to be read in one sitting.
2. Show the student the cover of the book and read the title.
3. Have the student predict or guess what the content of the book is.
4. Read the story aloud and with enthusiasm, sliding your finger under each word as you read.
5. As the student becomes familiar with the repeated patterns, pause for the student to read along with you.
6. Read the story again, but this time stop and let the student fill in the missing words. If the student does not a know word, supply it.
7. With enough repetitions you will find that the student can read the story without help from you.

Extensions for patterned stories:

1. Print words, phrases, or sentences on large index cards, and have the student locate them in the story.
2. The student might substitute different words in the predictable pattern.
3. The student might write his/her own story using the predictable pattern.

Reinforcement Activities

1. **Environmental print.** Be sure that environmental print is displayed in the classroom.
2. **Chart stories.** Display chart stories that were written by the class. See Chapter 1.
3. **Language experience.** This approach involves providing an experience for a student, talking about the experience, having the student dictate a story about the experience, and reading the story. See Chapter 1.
4. **Introduction in context.**

    -   First, print the unknown word in a sentence on the board and have the students read the sentence with you. Follow this same procedure with three words.
    -   Print each word on a separate index card. Show students the words printed on the index cards and have them locate each word in the sentences on the board.
    -   Show students each word printed on an index card and have them make up sentences containing the word.
    -   Students next close their eyes and try to write the word from memory.

5. **Introducing through visual-motor skills.**

    -   Print each word on an index card.
    -   Tell students to look carefully at the word as you hold it up and pronounce it.
    -   The students should then close their eyes and picture the word.

- Have students try to write the word from memory.
- Show the card to the students again for comparison with the original word.

6. **Labeling objects.** Label objects around your classroom and have students attach the printed word to the object.

7. **Picture dictionaries.** Students can create dictionaries by cutting pictures from magazines and newspapers, pasting them into a book using a separate page for each letter, and then labeling the pictures. Arrange the pages in alphabetical order.

8. **Word banks.** Word banks are students' personal collections of words they have learned to recognize at sight. When a student recognizes a word, the teacher writes it on an index card. This index card is placed on a ring or in a box as the student's own personal collection.

9. **Sorting words.** Words from word banks can be sorted or organized into various categories (e.g., fruits, places to live, words with the short *a* sound).

10. **Words, pictures, flannel board.** Give students pictures and corresponding word cards that can be mounted on a flannel board. Have students match the pictures and words and mount them on the flannel board.

11. **Checkers.** Use an old checkerboard. On the black squares, print sight words right side up and upside down. The game is played like regular checkers, but every time a player lands on a square, s/he must read the word in that square. (You might print the words on pieces of plastic or clear vinyl and place the plastic over the checkerboard. That way, different words can be used with the same board.)

12. **Dominoes.** Make cardboard dominoes that contain sight words or phrases. Students must match similar words or phrases and pronounce the words correctly.

13. **Football.** Both teams and players begin at the 50-yard line. Students are shown a word that they must read. If the word is read correctly, the student moves the ball 10 yards closer to the goal. If the word is read incorrectly, the player loses 10 yards. Each time a player crosses the opponent's goal line, six points are scored. The ball goes to the opposite team after a goal is scored or if the team is unable to advance 10 yards in three tries.

14. **Fishing.** For this you need a stick with a string and piece of Velcro (or a magnet) tied to the string. This serves as a fishing pole. You also need word cards shaped like fish, with Velcro (or paper clips) fastened to the head area. Using the fishing pole, the student catches a fish and reads the word printed on it.

15. **Wordo.** Wordo is similar to bingo. However, words rather than numbers are used. When a word is called, students locate the word on their card and place a marker on it. After the card is filled, the player calls "Wordo."

16. **Locating words in newspapers.** Using a newspaper, students can underline or highlight specific words found in sentences, headings, or ads.
17. **Creating words.** Give students a specific number of letters (e.g., six). Have them create as many words as they can from these letters within a specific period of time (e.g., three minutes).
18. **Creating sentences.** Write words that can be arranged in a sentence on individual cards. Have students rearrange the cards to make a sentence.

play	Many	house	children
Many	children	play	house

19. **Completing sentences.** Locate words from the newspaper to complete sentences. The house was _____.
20. **Selecting the correct word.** Give students sentences containing a blank space and three possible choices to complete the space. _____ are three dogs barking.

Three	They	There

Books for Children

Predictable Books

Becker, J. *Seven Little Rabbits.* New York: Scholastic, 1987.

Brown, M. W. *Goodnight Moon.* New York: HarperCollins Juvenile, 1991.

Burningham, J. *Mr. Gumpy's Outing.* New York: Henry Holt, 1971.

Carle, E. *The Grouchy Ladybug.* Glenview, IL: Pearson Scott Foresman, 1996.

———. *The Very Hungry Caterpillar.* Cleveland, OH: Collins-World, 1994.

Cole, J. *This Is the Place for Me.* New York: Penguin, 1986.

Eastman, P. D. *Are You My Mother?* New York: Random House, 1960.

Flack, M. *Ask Mr. Bear.* New York: Aladdin Library, 1986.

Gag, W. *Millions of Cats.* New York: Putnam, 1996.

Hutchins, P. *Good-Night, Owl!* New York: Aladdin Library, 1990.

Krauss, R. *The Carrot Seed.* New York: HarperCollins, 1993.

Lionni, L. *The Biggest House in the World.* New York: Knopf, 1987.

Martin B. *Brown Bear, Brown Bear, What Do You See?* New York: Henry Holt, 1992.

———. *Polar Bear, Polar Bear, What Do You Hear?* New York: Henry Holt, 1997.

Martin, B., and J. Archambault. *Here Are My Hands.* New York: Henry Holt, 1998.

Rathmann, P. *Good Night Gorilla.* New York: Putnam Juvenile, 1996.

Slobodkina, E. *Caps for Sale.* New York: HarperCollins Juvenile, 1988.

DOLCH BASIC SIGHT WORDS

The following represents an approximate estimate of reading level.

0–75 words = preprimer
76–120 = primer
121–170 = 1st reader

171–210 = 2nd grade
Above 210 = 3rd grade

Words are listed by decreasing frequency of occurrence.

the	do	from	walk	soon	wash
to	can	good	two	made	slow
and	could	any	or	run	hot
he	when	about	before	gave	because
a	did	around	eat	open	far
I	what	want	again	has	live
you	so	don't	play	find	draw
it	see	how	who	only	clean
of	not	know	been	us	grow
in	were	right	may	three	best
was	get	put	stop	our	upon
said	them	too	off	better	these
his	like	got	never	hold	sing
that	one	take	seven	buy	together
she	this	where	eight	funny	please
for	my	every	cold	warm	thank
on	would	pretty	today	ate	wish
they	me	jump	fly	full	many
but	will	green	myself	those	shall
had	yes	four	round	done	laugh
at	big	away	tell	use	
him	went	old	much	fast	
with	are	by	keep	say	
up	come	their	give	light	
all	if	here	work	pick	
look	now	saw	first	hurt	
is	long	call	try	pull	
her	no	after	new	cut	
there	came	well	must	kind	
some	ask	think	start	both	
out	very	ran	black	sit	
as	an	let	white	which	
be	over	help	ten	fall	
have	yours	make	does	carry	
go	its	going	bring	small	
we	ride	sleep	goes	under	
am	into	brown	write	read	
then	just	yellow	always	why	
little	blue	five	drink	own	
down	red	six	once	found	

Source: Dolch, E. (1936, February). Dolch Basic Sight Word List. *Elementary School Journal, 36,* 458. Reprinted with permission of the University of Chicago Press.

FRY INSTANT WORD LIST

The Instant Words First Hundred

First 25 Group 1a	Second 25 Group 1b	Third 25 Group 1c	Fourth 25 Group 1d
the	or	will	number
of	one	up	no
and	had	other	way
a	by	about	could
to	word	out	people
in	but	many	my
is	not	then	than
you	what	them	first
that	all	these	water
it	were	so	been
he	we	some	call
was	when	her	who
for	your	would	oil
on	can	make	now
are	said	like	find
as	there	him	long
with	use	into	down
his	an	time	day
they	each	has	did
I	which	look	get
at	she	two	come
be	do	more	made
this	how	write	may
have	their	go	part
from	if	see	over

Common suffixes: *s, ing, ed*

Source: Fry, Edward B. (1980, December). The New Instant Word List. *The Reading Teacher,* 34(3), 284–289. Reprinted with permission of the author and the International Reading Association.

| The Instant Words
Second Hundred | | | | | The Instant Words
Third Hundred | | | |

First 25 Group 2a	Second 25 Group 2b	Third 25 Group 2c	Fourth 25 Group 2d	First 25 Group 3a	Second 25 Group 3b	Third 25 Group 3c	Fourth 25 Group 3d
new	great	put	kind	every	left	until	idea
sound	where	end	hand	near	don't	children	enough
take	help	does	picture	add	few	side	eat
only	through	another	again	food	while	feet	face
little	much	well	change	between	along	car	watch
work	before	large	off	own	might	mile	far
know	line	must	play	below	close	night	Indian
place	right	big	spell	country	something	walk	real
year	too	even	air	plant	seem	white	almost
live	mean	such	away	last	next	sea	let
me	old	because	animal	school	hard	began	above
back	any	turn	house	father	open	grow	girl
give	same	here	point	keep	example	took	sometimes
most	tell	why	page	tree	begin	river	mountain
very	boy	ask	letter	never	life	four	cut
after	follow	went	mother	start	always	carry	young
thing	came	men	answer	city	those	state	talk
our	want	read	found	earth	both	once	soon
just	show	need	study	eye	paper	book	list
name	also	land	still	light	together	hear	song
good	around	different	learn	thought	got	stop	leave
sentence	form	home	should	head	group	without	family
man	three	us	America	under	often	second	body
think	small	move	world	story	run	late	music
say	set	try	high	saw	important	miss	color

Common suffixes; *s, ing, ed, er, ly, est*

Common suffixes: *s, ing, ed, er, ly, est*

ADULT BASIC WORD LIST

a	bus	enjoy	*he	likes
*about	*but	enjoyed	head	little
after	buy	every	heart	live
again	by	everything	help	long
airplane	call	family	her	look
*all	came	fast	here	looking
alone	*can	favor	high	Lord
along	can't	favorite	him	lot
also	car	feel	his	lots
always	care	feeling	hobbies	*love
*am	chance	few	hobby	made
an	child	fire	holiday	make
*and	children	first	holidays	mama
any	Christmas	fishing	home	man
anything	church	flowers	*hope	married
*are	city	flying	hopes	math
around	close	food	house	may
as	color	football	houses	*me
ask	come	*for	how	mean
at	coming	forget	hurt	meeting
away	cook	friend	husband	memories
baby	cooks	friends	*I	met
back	could	from	if	mind
bad	country	fun	I'm	miss
ball	daddy	gave	*in	money
baseball	dancing	G.E.D.	into	more
basketball	*day	*get	*is	morning
*be	days	getting	*it	most
beach	dead	girl	it's	mother
beat	did	girls	job	mother's
beautiful	didn't	give	joy	mountain
*because	dinner	*go	July	move
bed	*do	God	just	Mrs.
been	does	*going	keep	much
before	doesn't	*good	kind	*my
being	dog	goodbye	*know	myself
best	doing	got	ladies	name
better	*don't	grade	land	need
Bible	down	great	last	needs
big	dream	had	late	neighborhood
bike	dreams	happiness	later	neighbors
blue	drive	happy	learn	never
boy	each	hard	leave	new
boyfriend	easy	has	let	next
bring	eat	*have	life	nice
brothers	end	having	*like	night

Note: Words preceded by an asterisk (*) appeared 50 or more times. Words in boldface type appeared 10 or more times. All other words were used 5–9 times.

(*continued*)

ADULT BASIC WORD LIST *(concluded)*

no	red	story	*to	**what**
not	relatives	study	**today**	*when
now	rich	summer	**together**	**where**
*of	ride	Sunday	**told**	which
off	right	supper	**too**	**while**
old	running	swimming	top	white
*on	safe	**take**	**trip**	**who**
*one	said	**talk**	trouble	**why**
only	**say**	talking	**true**	*will
open	*school	**teacher**	**try**	wish
or	**see**	team	**two**	*with
other	*she	**tell**	until	women
our	**sister**	than	**up**	**won't**
out	sitting	thanks	us	words
over	skating	*that	**used**	**work**
own	sky	**that's**	vacation	**working**
parents	small	*the	**very**	**world**
party	*so	their	wait	worries
*people	soccer	**them**	*want	worry
person	*some	**then**	wanted	worst
picnic	**someday**	**there**	wants	*would
plan	**someone**	these	*was	wouldn't
play	**something**	*they	watch	write
played	**sometimes**	*thing	**watching**	year
playing	song	**things**	**water**	years
pretty	soon	**think**	**way**	*you
put	special	thinking	*we	**your**
reach	sports	**this**	**week**	
read	start	those	weekend	
reading	stay	three	**well**	
ready	still	*time	**went**	
really	**stop**	tired	**were**	

Source: Wangberg, Elaine E., Thompson, Bruce, & Levitov, Justin E. (1984, December). First Steps Toward An Adult Basic Word List. *Journal of Reading, 28*(3), 244–247. Reprinted with permission of the International Reading Association.

Picture Clues

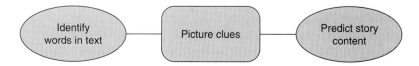

Identify words in text → Picture clues → Predict story content

Description

Picture clues . . . the use of picture clues is an emergent literacy skill that assists students in identifying words in the text and predicting story content. Picture clues are useful in developing sight vocabulary. While not all reading authorities have encouraged the use of them, Heilman makes the following observation:

> It is true that pictures may provide clues to unknown words. . . . Pictures may suggest words. In addition, they also have high motivational value and will often lure a child into reading. Pictures help focus attention on meaning; they lead into a story, and where only a limited number of words are known, pictures supplement. They serve as stimuli for oral language use in group discussions (1998, p. 27).

Initially students' books will have a picture and one, two, or three words that describe the picture. *A bird. A blue bird. A yellow bird.* The first page will contain a picture of a bird with the words *a bird* written under it. The second page will contain a picture of a blue bird with the words *a blue bird* written under it. The third page will contain a picture of a yellow bird with the words *a yellow bird* written under it. All of the words in the text can be identified by the picture clues.

Gunning (2003) identifies a second level of text and picture clues. There is a simple text that is illustrated. Most, but not all, of the words can be identified by the picture. *I can see a bird. I can see a blue bird.*

More advanced levels add more high-frequency words to the text. More of the words must be identified through sight and fewer through picture clues.

Explicit Instruction: Using Book Walks

1. Preview the text and analyze words and concepts students might need to have presented or reinforced. In the *Little Red Hen* students would need to know the meanings of *grains* and *wheat*.

2. Introduce the book to students. Help them locate the name of the author and title of the book. Have them look very carefully at the book cover. Tell them that book covers provide a lot of information about a book.

3. Encourage students to take a very close look at the illustrations on the book cover. Have them make predictions about what they think the story is about. Write their predictions on the board.

4. In early reading stages, where short books are being used, walk the students through each page and discuss the picture. Ask questions such as, "What do we see in the picture?" "Can you guess what will happen next?" Help students identify items in the picture that will help them read the text. Ask them what letters key words might begin with.

5. Read the story aloud to students.

6. After reading the story, refer back to the students' original predictions. Ask them which predictions were right. Ask students how the pictures helped them predict what the story was about.

7. Students can read their own copies of the story silently. Before reading the story, ask students how they might be able to tell what an unknown word is (using the picture, using the first letter sound, does it make sense).

Reinforcement Activities

1. **Big books reading.** Read many big books aloud to students. Engage in picture walks prior to reading the books. Ask students to supply words that can be determined from picture clues.

2. **Easy books.** Provide many easy books with pictures that students can read alone.

3. **Caption writing.** Show students pictures and have them (or someone assisting them) write captions and labels under the pictures.

4. **Menu viewing.** Bring in menus from different restaurants. Be sure the menus contain pictures (Denny's, Waffle House, Friendly's, Original House of Pancakes). As students look at the pictures, have them guess what foods the restaurant serves.

5. **Expression pictures.** Show students pictures of people with different expressions. Ask them how they think the people feel. Ask them what clues the picture gives to help them predict how the people feel.

6. **Family book jacket.** Have students think about their families. Ask them what they might put on a book jacket if they were writing a story about their families. Ask them why they chose to draw these pictures for their book jacket.

7. **Book jacket redesigning.** Have students draw another cover for a book. Present students with several books. Ask students what important information the front cover should have. Have students close their eyes and imagine what might be happening in the book. Direct students to draw new covers for the books using their imaginations.

Books for Children

Barrett, J. *Animals Should Definitely Not Wear Clothing.* New York: Aladdin Library, 1989.

Brown, M. W. *Goodnight Moon.* New York: HarperCollins, 1991.

Carle, E. *The Very Hungry Caterpillar.* Cleveland, OH: Collins-World, 1994.

Daugherty, J. *Andy and the Lion.* New York: Viking Press, 1989.

Emberly, E. *Go Away, Big Green Monster.* Boston: Little, Brown, 1993.

Hill, E. *Where's Spot?* New York: Putnam, 2000.

Johnson, C. *Harold and the Purple Crayon.* New York: HarperCollins, 1981.

Keats, E. J. *The Snowy Day.* New York: Viking Children Books, 1996.

Lionni, L. *Little Blue and Little Yellow.* New York: Mulberry Books, 1995.

McCloskey, R. *Blueberries for Sal.* New York: Viking Press, 1976.

Rey, H. A. *Curious George.* Boston: Houghton Mifflin, 1973.

Slobodkina, E. *Caps for Sale.* New York: HarperCollins, 1988.

Viorst, J. *Alexander and the Terrible, Horrible, No Good, Very Bad Day.* New York: Aladdin Library, 1987.

Phonic Analysis

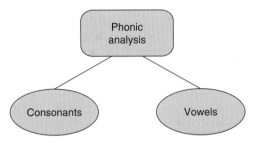

Description

Phonic analysis involves using the sounds of our language (consonant and vowel sounds) to decode words. Many of these sounds are learned through rime or other recognizable sound patterns (like *ch* or *sh*).

Phonics . . . decoding words by using the sound value of letters or groups of letters. (See Appendix A.)

Decoding . . . converting coded signals into understandable messages. Decoding may involve reader use of phonic analysis, structural analysis, or context clues in word identification.

Grapheme . . . the physical representation of a symbol from a standard alphabet. English has 26 uppercase and 26 lowercase letters.

Phoneme . . . the smallest significant unit of sound in language. English has approximately 44 phonemes, which are consonant and vowel sounds.

Rime or phonogram . . . the rhyming part of a word. For example *at* is the rime in *mat, hat, bat,* and *chat*. An **onset** is the beginning or initial part of the word before the rime. The letters *m, h, b,* and *ch* are the onsets in the rhyming words *mat, hat, bat,* and *chat*.

Although English does not have perfectly regular phoneme–grapheme (sound–symbol) relationships, there is enough consistency to warrant the teaching of phonics. Only 13 percent of our words are phonetically irregular, and over 50 percent are regular (Hanna, Hodges, Hanna, and Rudolph 1966.) Chall (1996) wrote, "Systematic and early instruction in phonics leads to better reading: better accuracy of word recognition, decoding, spelling, and oral and silent reading comprehension." The goal is not to have students memorize generalizations, but rather to apply their knowledge of phoneme–grapheme relationships and patterns. (See Appendix A for word analysis generalizations.)

Skilled readers decode words more by using patterns or rimes and less by using memorized rules (Adams 1990). Adams also noted that the use of rimes is encouraged because their grapheme–phoneme correspondence is more consistent. When teaching with patterns, begin with two-letter patterns (like -at or -in) and move to three-letter patterns (-ake, -ick) and multiletter patterns. Wylie and Durrell (1970) identified 37 consistent rimes or phonograms that make up about 500 early childhood words. These phonograms are highlighted in the list of phonograms in Appendix C. Heilman (1998, p. 133), however, cautions us that finding phonograms (or little words) in big words does not always lead to a correct pronunciation (co-at, h-on-ey, w-he-at, pot-at-o). Students should have multiple strategies at their disposal in analyzing unknown words.

The National Institute for Literacy (2000) in its publications of the *National Reading Panel Report* and *Put Reading First,* and the International Reading Association (2002) in its summary of the *Reading Panel Report,* write that systematic phonics instruction appears to make a bigger contribution to reading growth than nonsystematic instruction. However, there is no clear evidence that one systematic phonics instructional approach is better than another. Systematic phonics instruction appears to be more effective in preventing reading difficulties than nonphonics approaches.

Causes of problems related to phonics are varied. Students may experience interference from a first language other than English. The student's preferred learning modality might be visual rather than auditory. Auditory acuity (hearing loss) problems may result in not hearing certain sounds. Students may lack auditory processing (working with sounds) skills. These auditory processing skills include auditory discrimination (distinguishing likenesses or differences among sounds: bet–bit), auditory segmentation (breaking words into their individual sounds: /c/ /a/ /t/), auditory blending (combining separate sounds to form a word), and auditory sequencing memory (the ability to store information in the brain and later recall it). Faulty articulation of sounds may create confusion when students associate sounds as they pronounce them with the articulation of the sounds by others.

Teaching Consonants

Explicit Instruction: Initial Consonant, Cluster, and Digraph Sounds

(The initial consonant digraph *ch* sound pattern is used in this example.)

1. Select the phonemic element you wish to teach.
2. Work on the phonemic awareness of sounds before adding visual symbols. Use words that students already know. Initially, use words that

are in their listening vocabularies (like names of children in the class or concrete objects). Listen to the sound we hear at the beginning of *Chuck*. Which of these pictures has the same sound that we hear at the beginning of *Chuck*? *(chair, cheese, slipper, chocolate)*

3. Tell students the sound (/ch/) you will be teaching them, and write the letters that stand for it on the board. *Chuck, chair,* and *cheese* begin with the letters *ch*. Write the letters *ch* on the board. Then write the words *Chuck, chair,* and *cheese*.

   Ch ch
   Chuck
   chair
   cheese

4. *Chuck, chair,* and *cheese* begin with the /ch/ sound. Have the students read the words aloud with you as you point to them.

5. Read the story *Chicka-Chicka Boom Boom* aloud to students. Listen for the words that have the same beginning sound as *Chuck, chair,* and *cheese*. After reading, have students tell you the words that started with the sound of /ch/. Students may remember this as the sneezing or train sound.

6. Ask students to contribute additional words that contain the same sound. Write these words on the board or word wall.

7. Have students make up and write a sentence using some of the words they read that contain the /ch/ sound.

8. Provide opportunities for students to read selections that contain words that begin with *ch*.

Reinforcement Activities: Consonants and Consonant Combinations

1. **Eliminating the *uh*.** Since there is a tendency to exaggerate the *uh* when making the sounds of individual consonants, try other learning associations such as letter-picture cards for initial consonant recognition.

2. **Nursery rhymes.** Repeat nursery rhymes in which students identify words that have similar beginning sounds.

3. **Listening to sentences.** While students listen to sentences, they can identify words that contain the same sounds. The teacher says, "Mom gave Mike a glass of milk," then asks, "What words begin with the same sound?"

4. **Cutting pictures.** Provide students with opportunities to cut pictures from old magazines and mount them in picture dictionaries.

5. **Change in consonant position.** Recite words with the consonant in different places. Students must then identify whether the consonant is at the beginning, middle, or end of the word.

6. **Bingo.** Give students bingo cards with different consonants on them. As you read a word, the student covers the appropriate consonant heard at the beginning of the word. (This activity can be expanded to include consonants at the end or middle of words.)

7. **Riddles.** Following a review of the hard and soft sounds of *c* and *g* you might say, "I am thinking of something that begins with the sound of a hard *g*. It has four legs. It has horns, and it can be found on a farm. It likes to eat just about anything. What is it?" (Answer: *goat.*)

8. **Consonant holders.** Cut the tops off of empty plastic bottles that are large enough to have mounted pictures placed in them. On the front of each bottle, print the symbol for a consonant—a different consonant for each bottle. Then give students mounted pictures or actual objects and have them place the pictures or objects into the bottle that has the same corresponding initial consonant printed on it.

9. **Word wheels.** Provide students with word wheels that contain a phonogram and a circle of consonants. The student turns the consonant circle around, making different words and pronouncing them.

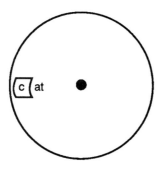

10. **Word substitution.** Orally, provide students with sentences and have them substitute words that begin with the appropriate initial consonant.

   Example: The d _____ eats meat.

   dog

   dinosaur

11. **Listing objects.** For variety, challenge students to quickly list all the objects they can think of that begin with a specific consonant combination.

12. **Tape recorder.** Read into a tape recorder a number of words that contain consonant combinations. Students must listen to the tape and write the blend or digraph they hear.

13. **Phonograms.** Substitute different consonant combinations at the beginning of phonograms.

14. **Sentence building.** Students can create sentences using as many words as possible that contain a specific consonant combination. These sentences may be tape-recorded.

15. **Other ideas.** Many of the game activities listed under letter recognition and sight words can be adapted for working with consonant elements. Use consonants on the checkerboard, dominoes, or game boards. Students supply a word that begins with the consonant sound.

Books for Children

Jeram, A. *Daisy Dare.* Cambridge, MA: Candlewick Press, 1995.

Jonas, A. *Watch William Walk.* New York: Greenwillow, 1997.

McBratney, S. *Caterpillow Fight.* Cambridge, MA: Candlewick Press, 1996.

Root, P. *One Windy Wednesday.* Cambridge, MA: Candlewick Press, 1996.

Tate, S. Nature Series. Nags Head, NC: Nags Head Art. Titles include the following:

————. *Billy Bluefish: A Tale of Big Blues.* Nags Head, NC: Nags Head Art, 1988.

————. *Danny & Daisy: A Tale of a Dolphin Duo.* Nags Head, NC: Nags Head Art, 1992.

————. *Flossie Flounder: A Tale of Flat Fish.* Nags Head, NC: Nags Head Art, 1989.

————. *Harry Horseshoe Crab: A Tale of Crawly Creatures.* Nags Head, NC: Nags Head Art, 1991.

————. *Holly from Hatteras: A Tale of Saving Lives.* Nags Head, NC: Nags Head Art, 1998.

————. *Issie Lizzie Alligator: A Tale of a Big Lizard.* Nags Head, NC: Nags Head Art, 1999.

————. *Jenny Jelly Fish: A Tale of Wiggly Jellies.* Nags Head, NC: Nags Head Art, 2001.

————. *Lucky Lookdown: A Tale of a Funny Fish.* Nags Head, NC: Nags Head Art, 1989.

————. *Mary Manatee: A Tale of Sea Cows.* Nags Head, NC: Nags Head Art, 1990.

————. *Perky Pelican: A Tale of a Lively Bird.* Nags Head, NC: Nags Head Art, 1996.

———. *Salty Seagull: A Tale of an Old Salt.* Nags Head, NC: Nags Head Art, 1992.

———. *Spunky Spot: A Tale of One Smart Fish.* Nags Head, NC: Nags Head Art, 1989.

———. *Tammy Turtle: A Tale of Saving Sea Turtles.* Nags Head, NC: Nags Head Art, 1991.

Teaching Vowels

Explicit Instruction: Short Vowels Using Analogy (Rimes or Phonograms)

(The *op* pattern is used in this example.)

1. Read a story to students that has words containing the *op* pattern. *Hop on Pop* by Dr. Seuss is a book that might be read.
2. After reading the story, write the words *hop* and *pop* on the board. Underline the *op*. Tell students that the letters *op* in the words *hop* and *pop* say /op/.
3. Have students blend the sounds together. /h/ + /op/ make *hop*. /p/ + /op/ make *pop*.
4. Tell students to listen to the sound that *o* makes. Make the /o/ sound slowly.
5. Now have students stretch out the word *hop* and say it slowly: /h/–/o/–/p/.
6. Next, tell students to listen to the sound that *o* makes in *pop*. Make the /o/ sound slowly.
7. Have students stretch out the word *pop* and say it slowly: /p/–/o/–/p/.
8. Tell students to look at the word *hop* and change one letter to make the word *cop*.
9. Now, having students use movable letters at their desks, have them change the first letter in *cop* to make the words *mop, sop, top. Mop the floor. Sop up the gravy. Spin the top.*
10. Select a word that can be used as a model for the future decoding of words that contain the *op* pattern. It is preferable to use a word that can have an illustration next to it.
11. Mix one or two previously learned patterns into the lesson. The students may have learned -*at* (key word *cat*) and -*ent* (key word *tent*). Change the first letter in *cat* to make *fat, hat, mat.* Change the first letter in *tent* to make *rent, dent, sent. Pay the rent. The car has a dent. He sent the letter.*
12. Create riddles using words from these patterns to which students will write answers. "I'm thinking of something that covers my floor" *(mat).* "I'm thinking of a word that is the opposite of *skinny*" *(fat).* "I'm thinking of a word that is the opposite of *straight*" *(bent).* "I'm thinking of a word that is the opposite of *bottom*" *(top).*
13. Read stories that contain words that use these patterns.

Explicit Instruction: Teaching Vowel–Consonant–Silent-*e* Generalization

1. Select the generalization you wish to teach. In this instance we are teaching the vowel–consonant–final-silent-*e* pattern.
2. Read the book _____ aloud to students.
3. After reading the book, make a list of the relevant words that were in the story or poem.

   _____   _____

4. Read the words aloud with students.
5. Write the following columns of words on the board that follow the short vowel, *c-v-c* pattern.

hat	strip	rid
pet	us	hop
dim	cut	mad
ton	pin	plan

6. Have students read the words aloud and listen to the vowel sounds.
7. Next to each of the short vowel words, write the corresponding word that follows the final silent-*e* generalization. Tell students to see if they can predict what will happen has you add the *e* to the end of the word.

mat	mate	strip	stripe	rid	ride
pet	Pete	us	use	hop	hope
dim	dime	cut	cute	mad	made
ton	tone	pin	pine	plan	plane

8. The students pronounce the pairs of words.
9. Have students identify what happens to the vowel sounds when the final *e* is added. Ask them what sound the *e* has.
10. Have students try to make other examples of the generalization (past–paste, cap–cape, fad–fade, rag–rage, Sam–same, stag–stage, tap–tape, bit–bite, kit–kite, hid–hide, rip–ripe, slid–slide, slim–slime, Tim–time, cod–code, not–note, rob–robe, slop–slope, cub–cube). Note. You may wish to check out related publications including word analysis by Jane Belk Moucure.
11. Select a word for the long vowel sound that will help students remember the sound pattern *(spade, tape, dime, robe)*. Put these on a word wall.
12. Have students write the following dictated sentences.

    The (note) was (not) on the table.

    Peg (cut) the (cute) bow.

    It is (time) for (Tim) to come home.

13. Encourage the wide reading of books that contain words following the generalization taught.

Explicit Instruction: Other Vowels
(Diphthongs, *r*-Controlled, Vowel Digraphs)

1. Read a story or poem to students that contains the vowel sounds and patterns you are teaching (e.g., *oi–oy, ea–ee, oo, ow–ou, er–ir–ur*).
2. After reading the selection, write the words that contain the vowel sounds (patterns) you are teaching.
3. Tell students the sounds these letter patterns contain.
4. Pronounce the words for students by blending the sounds together. Run your hand under the sounds as you make them.
5. Have students think of words that contain the phoneme you are teaching.
6. Create riddles or dictate sentences in which these sounds are used.
7. Have students read books, poems, or stories in which these sound patterns are used.

Reinforcement Activities: Vowels

1. **Auditory vowel bingo.** Make bingo cards containing pictures of objects that represent the vowel sounds your students are studying. As you call a word, students must place a marker on the picture that contains the same vowel sound.
2. **Labeled containers.** Place vowel sound labels on empty containers (plastic jugs with the tops cut off, boxes, etc.). Students put objects or pictures containing the appropriate vowel sounds into the containers.
3. **Categorizing.** Make charts for the vowel sounds your students are studying. Students should bring in pictures of objects that contain the vowel sounds. Paste the pictures on the chart and label them.
4. **Tossing bean bags.** Make a series of circles or squares on the floor or on a sheet of plastic. Write vowel sounds in the spaces. Students toss the bean bag into a space, then must give a word that contains the same vowel sound.
5. **Word-vowel bingo.** Make bingo cards that contain words and blank spaces where the vowels belong. Instead of using blank chips for markers, students use markers with vowels and vowel combinations printed on them. As a word is read, students spell the word on their cards, using the appropriate vowel or vowel-combination marker.

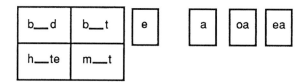

6. **Vowel checkers.** Place words containing the vowel sounds on which you are working on the spaces where students move their checkers. If a student hops over or lands on a space, s/he must think of another word that contains the same vowel sound.

7. **Phonic rummy.** This is played as regular rummy. The students, however, must match pairs of words that contain the same vowel sounds.

8. **Flip cards.** When studying words that contain the final *e* generalization, create flip cards so that students can read the short-vowel-sound word and then word with the final *e.*

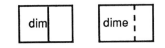

9. **Phonogram cards.** As students pull the strip with letters and blends, the phonogram remains the same. This may be adapted to have the phonogram change.

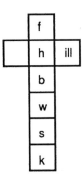

10. **Phonogram game.** Develop game boards using spinners or dice. As students move to a space on the board, they must identify another word containing the same vowel sound or read the word you have printed in the space.

11. **Building words.** Give students plastic bags containing one or more vowels and six or more consonants. (The number of vowels and consonants depends on the skills of the students.) Give students a specified amount of time to build as many different words as they can by combining different letters. (for example, the letters *c, a, h, t, s* might combine into *a, at, cat, hat, sat, chat, chats, cats, hats.*) Students should write each word they make on a sheet of paper. At the end of the specified time, the student who has made the most words wins.

Books for Children

Coxe, M. *Big Egg.* New York: Golden Book, 1997.

————. *Hot Dog.* New York: Golden Book, 1998.

Numeroff, L. *If You Give a Pig a Pancake.* New York: HarperCollins, 1998.

Syllabic Analysis

Description

Syllabic analysis . . . dividing words into syllables or pronounceable units that contain a vowel or vowel-like sound.

Gunning (2003, p. 198) identifies that a large percentage of words read by students are polysyllabic. Twenty percent of proficient readers omitted one or more syllables in polysyllabic words. This ranges from 30 percent in second grade to over 80 percent by sixth grade. Students learn the pronunciation of longer words more easily by dividing them into syllables or pronounceable units, or through analogy and identifying patterns. Mastery of dictionary syllabication should not be the goal. Instead, words should be divided so they can be pronounced. The use of syllabication should also be related to content instruction and not done in isolation.

Explicit Instruction: Consonant + *le* Is a Syllable Generalization

1. Students should be able to discriminate auditorily the syllables in words before teaching specific generalizations. Clapping (bouncing balls, tapping pencils) for syllables in words *(ta-ble, clock, door, pro-ject-or, Jack, Jan-et)* provides a basis for learning syllabication.
2. Write examples of words depicted in the generalization on the board.

fa-ble	ti-tle	kin-dle	ma-ple	an-kle
tum-ble	man-tle	bri-dle	un-cle	crin-kle

3. Read the words aloud with the students.
4. Have students listen to the syllables and draw a line between the syllables (or if you have a magnetic board, use tagboard and cut the syllables apart).
5. Encourage students to contribute words that follow this pattern (kettle, battle, bottle, pebble, rumble, stable, single, angle, giggle, fiddle, saddle, purple, sample, puzzle).
6. Read books, poems, and other materials that contain words following the generalization.

Explicit Instruction: Using Pattern/Analogy

Here is an example using *relentless.* (You will want to adapt words to your grade level.)

1. Is it a compound word? (No)
2. Do you see a prefix? *(re)*
3. Do you see any suffix? *(less)*
4. We still have *relent* left. If I know how to pronounce *bent,* then how do I pronounce *l-e-n-t?*
5. What word do we know that starts with *re? (Re* sounds like the beginning of *redo.)*
6. Let's put it together. *Re + lent = relent.*
7. *Relent + less = relentless.*
8. *Un + relentless = unrelentless.*

Here is an example using the word *uncollected.* (Choose words for your grade level.)

1. Is this a compound word? (no)
2. Do you see a prefix? (*un.* It is like *unknown.*)
3. Do you see a suffix? *(ed)*
4. Do you see two letters together that are the same? (*l-l. Lect* is like *elect.*)
5. *un-col-lect-ed.*

Reinforcement Activities

1. **Everyday words.** Use words students encounter in their everyday reading assignments.
2. **Auditory discrimination.** Direct students to listen for the number of syllables in words pronounced orally. Students might bounce a ball, clap, or hop for each syllable they hear in the word.
3. **Magazine pictures.** Provide opportunities for students to cut out magazine pictures of words that have one, two, three, or four syllables.
4. **Weekly vocabulary.** Prepare a set of index cards with vocabulary words from the week on them. Pronounce each word for the students and have the students repeat the word. Then direct the students to clap for each syllable they hear.
5. **Reading words divided into syllables.** Heilman (1998) recommends having students practice reading as quickly as possible words that have been divided into syllables. (It is best to use words from materials students are reading in class.) Students become familiar with the patterns of these syllables *(re-mark, con-vec-tion, re-turn-ing, un-dis-closed).*

6. **Building words.**
   - Initially take index cards that each contain a separate syllable from a word. Students match the index cards to make words following the syllabication pattern being taught *(can-dle)*. Pronounce each word with the students. Then direct students to clap for the syllables heard.
   - Take a word from a unit of study that contains a common prefix. Prepare index cards on which different roots and suffixes are written. Also prepare several cards that contain the same prefix. Students rearrange the cards to create different words that begin with the same prefix. Have students brainstorm other words containing that prefix. Using the prefix *dis* ("not" or "opposite of") and the following: *approve, appear, continue, arm, ing,* and *ed.*

7. **Team dividing.** Prepare a list of words that follow the syllabication generalizations taught. Write the words on index cards. Divide the class into teams. A member from each team comes to the board, takes the word at the top of the pile, writes the word, and divides it into syllables. The team with the most divided words at the end of a specified time wins.

8. **Words and descriptions.** Prepare a word list and a corresponding list of descriptions or definitions for the words. Divide the class into teams. Read a description of the word. The first team to give the correct word and its correct syllabication gets a point. The team with the most points at the end wins.

9. **Using songs.** Students will enjoy writing the words to their favorite songs. They should then syllabicate the song's words.

UNIT

Vocabulary

Graphic Organizers

Morphology

Context

Word Relationships

Extending an Interest in Vocabulary

Unit Introduction

Vocabulary . . . as defined in Webster's *New World Dictionary,* is all the words of a language. Naturally, each of us does not know all the words in our language. However, our knowledge of words and our ability to use them are essential to comprehension. "Reading instruction that focuses on the growth of children's vocabulary results in enhancing their abilities to infer meanings and to better comprehend what they read" (Rupley, Logan, and Nichols 1998–1999). Students read words that are part of their listening and speaking vocabularies more easily than those with which they are not familiar. The following map represents the major categories of vocabulary we are presenting.

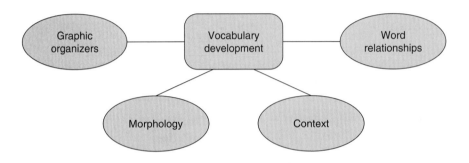

The basic vocabulary of 6th-grade students is estimated to be about 32,000 words, and that of 12th-grade students is estimated to be about 47,000 (Smith 1991). Graves (1986) estimated that the listening vocabulary of first-grade students is 10,000 words. This is quite remarkable.

During the 1990s little attention was paid to the development of vocabulary in professional journals such as *The Reading Teacher* (Rupley, Logan, and Nichols 1998–1999). Reviewing earlier research, three guidelines can be applied. Traxler (1938), McKeown et al. (1983), and Carney et al. (1984) identified the importance of direct instruction over incidental learning. The importance of the categorization of words is supported by organizational memory theorists such as Manis (1966), Asch (1969), Rundus (1971), and Reynolds and Flagg (1977). Graphic organizers provide a means of categorizing words for establishing meaning. Finally, Pavio (1971), Wolpert (1972), Reynolds and Flagg (1977), and Jiganti and Tindall (1986) provided research supporting the promotion of mental imagery in learning words.

An extensive review of the literature on vocabulary led Blanchowicz and Fisher (2000) to identify four main principles of instruction. Students should be actively involved in learning new words. They should make personal connections to new words. They should be surrounded—immersed—in learning words. And they should see the words in multiple contexts and have many repeated exposures to them.

Inadequate vocabulary may be the result of a limited background of experiences and intellectual stimulation. This may be caused by a lack of oral stimulation in the home, limited experiences with print (such as not being read to as a child), no books in the home for independent investigation, or no desire to read recreational materials. Speech defects or hearing difficulties may also contribute to slow or weak language development. Mental development is also a contributing factor to poor vocabulary development.

The goal of vocabulary instruction is not to have students memorize a list of words and write definitions. Rather, it is to provide opportunities for students to understand and use words. Wide reading provides many opportunities for students to encounter new words in multiple contexts beyond the classroom. Provide real and vicarious experiences about which students may talk. Treasure and honor interesting words students use or locate in their reading.

We have indicated that students and adults analyze words by identifying patterns. Compound words, contractions, and other morphological units such as prefixes, suffixes, and root words provide patterns to use in analyzing words.

Graphic Organizers

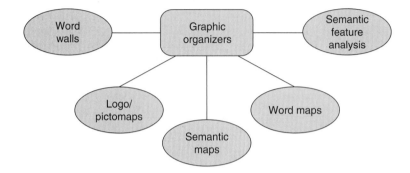

Description

Graphic organizers . . . provide a visual representation of the relationships among words. Usually geometric shapes and lines are used to show these relationships. Graphic organizers (such as word walls, logo/pictomaps, semantic maps, word maps, and semantic feature analysis) provide opportunities for students to develop a more thorough understanding of words by seeing relationships and being active in the learning process (Blanchowicz and Fisher 2000). This unit begins with graphic organizers because they can be used in teaching morphology, word relationships, and comprehension skills.

Definition word maps . . . help students see visual representations of definitions (Schwartz and Raphael 1985). The concept is presented, and students organize information into the category to which the concept belongs, its properties or attributes, and examples or illustrations of the concept. The definition word map presents a visual representation of a word's definition.

Logo and pictomaps . . . at the emergent literacy stage, students may not have developed the skills needed to decode words. In an effort to facilitate their learning and understanding, pictures or logos may be used in combination with words when developing a word wall or any other type of map. A pictorial representation of the words and their relationships is presented.

Semantic feature analysis . . . is a grid that assists students in identifying similarities and differences among concepts that are related to each other. The grid organization helps students make comparisons. Pluses or the word *yes* and minuses or the word *no* are placed in grid boxes.

Semantic maps . . . are a diagrammatic way of showing relationships among concepts, ideas, and examples by using circles and lines. Very simple semantic maps are often called *concept maps*. Words are organized or categorized using a semantic map.

Word walls . . . have been defined as "working bulletin boards" (Rasinski and Padak 2001). A word wall is a chart with a theme or focus determined by the teacher (or students). These charts of words are posted around the room and used as a way of studying word patterns and word relationships.

Graphic organizers are presented at the beginning of this unit because they provide many opportunities for categorization and student involvement with words. The skills included within morphology and word relationships can be taught and reinforced by using graphic organizers.

Word Walls

Explicit Instruction

Word walls can be created for any topic or skill being studied in class. Possibilities include student's names, high-frequency sight words, commonly misspelled words, rhyming words, phonic analysis skills, word relationships, prefixes and suffixes, content area words, thematic words, or words related to a story being studied. The use of word walls is limitless.

1. A topic is decided on by the teacher or students.
2. Words are written on chart paper, sticky notes, poster board, sentence strips, or a special white board in your classroom. The important point is that the words must be easily seen by students in the class. (If you want to manipulate the words, sticky notes might be better to use.)
3. The students or teacher may add words to the word wall each day.
4. As words are added to the word wall, it is important that the teacher direct students' attention to the words, say the words, talk about the meaning of the words, and have students use the words.

Reinforcement Activities

1. **Alphabetizing.** Alphabetize words on the word wall.
2. **Categorizing words.** You can use these words to create the graphic organizer listed later in this chapter.
3. **Riddles.** Use the words to answer riddles.
4. **Cloze activities.** Create modified cloze activities that use the word wall words.
5. **Rhyming words.** Collect words that rhyme with words on the word wall.
6. **Sentence construction.** Dictate sentences using words on the word wall. Students listen to a sentence. Repeat or reread the sentence. Then students write the sentence.

7. **Word sorts.** Provide 10–20 words from the word wall. These should be written on index cards or sticky note for students (or depending upon age, students can write their own). Direct students to sort the words into different categories according to their characteristics. After giving their rationales for sorting, you may find that students sort the words into different categories.

Logo and Pictomaps

Explicit Instruction

1. Create a logo or pictomap the same way you would a map using words only.
2. With a logo or pictomap, use pictures and words.
3. In the center circle, write your central theme (such as transportation).
4. In circles outside the center, write your subtopics (land, sea, air).
5. The specific ways (or details) we travel by land, sea, and air go out from the subtopics as details. Give students pictures of ways to travel on land, on water, or in the air.
6. Ask students, Who has a picture of a way we can travel on land? (Put the picture on the chart and write the word under it.) Who has another picture of a way we can travel on land? Who has a picture of a way we travel on water? Who has a picture of a way we travel in air? Be sure to write the words under the pictures.
7. Students might draw pictures of other ways to travel on land, sea, and air to add to the map.
8. An example of a pictomap appears here.

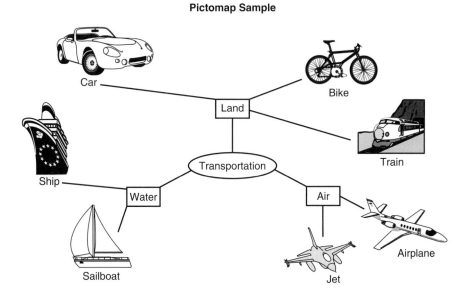

Pictomap Sample

Reinforcement Activities

1. **Class book.** Students can make a class book, "Our Book of Transportation." These can contain students' pictures of a way they use transportation and a sentence telling about it.
2. **Locating pictures.** Have students locate other pictures related to the topic and place them on the map.
3. **Word banks.** Print words from the map on cards for students' word banks. These words can be used for future writing.
4. **Classification.** Remove the words and pictures from the pictomap and have students classify them.
5. **Analogies.** Have students complete puzzles (analogies) based on the map. *If a plane travels in the air, then a boat travels _____. (in the water)*

Semantic Maps

Explicit Instruction

1. You or the students identify a central theme or concept. This theme is placed in a circle (or other geometric shape) at the center of your chart.
2. As a class, have students brainstorm words that are related to the theme or concept. Group these words into categories (without identifying labels for the categories).
3. Next, have students brainstorm individually and think of as many words as possible that are related to the topic. Have students categorize these as they are writing them.
4. After brainstorming individually, students contribute these during class discussion and add them to the class map.
5. After words are added to the map, check to see if other important words students need for the topic study are added. If they have not been identified, add them. Explain how they relate to the other words.
6. Have students identify labels for the categories.
7. Note: Sometimes students find it easier to see relationships if the main idea is one color (like yellow) and subcategories or classifications are another color (like green) or if different shapes are used.
8. The following are examples of semantic maps.

Semantic Map Example: Manatees

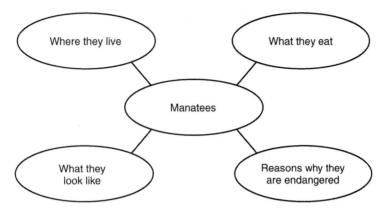

Semantic Map Example: Reptiles

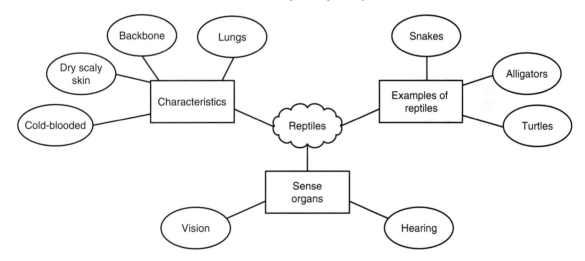

Reinforcement Activities

1. **Summarize.** Students can write summaries or essays based on the map. The center becomes the theme or main idea of the essay. Each subcategory becomes the topic of a paragraph, and details from the subtopics become details to add to the paragraphs.
2. **Word location.** Have students locate additional words related to the topic and place them on the map.
3. **Word banks.** For younger students, print words from the map on cards for students' word banks. These words can be used for future writing.
4. **Categorizing 1.** Have students write the words from the map on small pieces of paper or index cards (or use the words from their word banks). Have them rearrange the words under the proper categories.
5. **Categorizing 2.** Have students try to arrange words from the map in ways different from the arrangement completed in class. Be sure they can justify why they were arranged this way.
6. **Puzzles.** Have students complete puzzles or analogies based on the map.
7. **Maps for science.** Select a specific type of reptile (snake, turtle, alligator). The main topic would be the type of reptile. Subcategories might be where they live, what they eat, and different kinds.
8. **Maps of stories.** Read a story on a topic you will study in class. After students have finished listening to the story, create a map detailing the topic being studied in class.

Definition Word Maps

Explicit Instruction

1. Have students work individually or in small groups (no more than three).
2. Use chart paper or a transparency. Remember to model the procedure with an easy word that your students will readily identify with.
3. For example, place the word *pie* in the center box. Ask students, "What is cake?" In the "what it is" box, write *dessert.*
4. Ask students to tell you some examples of different types of pie (apple, pecan, peach, chocolate). Write these examples in the "examples" boxes.
5. In the "what it is like" boxes, students contribute words describing pie (sweet, crust, filling).
6. You may add a box for an antonym (opposite) meaning word.
7. When students understand the concept of the definition word map, they can move on to defining more advanced words related to content (such as pollution, reptile, capitalism, triangle, or polygon).

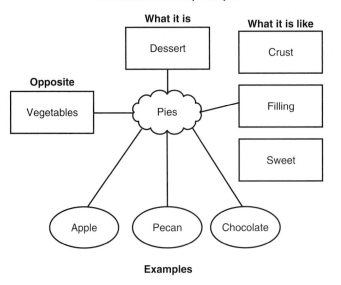

Definition Word Map Sample

What it is

Dessert

What it is like

Crust

Opposite

Vegetables

Pies

Filling

Sweet

Apple Pecan Chocolate

Examples

Reinforcement Activities

1. **Create written definitions.** Have students create written definitions using a definition word map.
2. **Word walls.** Create word walls using words from a definition word map.
3. **Analogies.** Use words from these to create analogies:

   pie:_____::broccoli:vegetable (dessert)
   crust:_____::pot:soup (filling)

Semantic Feature Analysis

Explicit Instruction

1. Write the topic on the board (for example, fish).
2. Prepare a grid that contains places for types going vertically down the left column. Then place characteristics horizontally along the top of the grid.
3. Have students brainstorm different types or examples of fish (such as bluefish, flounder, jellyfish, and salmon).
4. Place the names of these fish vertically on the grid.

5. Have students identify features or characteristics of this topic (fins, eyes, scales, gills, cold-blooded, bones).
6. Place these characteristics horizontally across the top of the grid.
7. For each example, students work across the grid and indicate whether it has the characteristic. If the example has the characteristic, place a plus sign (+) or the word *yes*. If it does not have the characteristic, place a minus sign (−) or the word *no*. If you are unsure, place a question mark (?).
8. Students read to confirm their answers. The answers are corrected if necessary.
9. Semantic feature analysis may also be used as a follow-up after studying a topic.

Semantic Feature Analysis Sample

	Fins	Eyes	Scales	Gills	Bones	Cold-blooded
Jellyfish	−	+	−	?	−	?
Bluefish	+	+	+	+	+	?
Flounder	+	+	+	+	+	?
Salmon	+	+	+	+	?	?

Reinforcement Activities

1. **Hold up.** Have students use the grid to play the game "hold up." Ask a question. *Do jellyfish have backbones?* Using the grid, students hold up the word *yes* if they do or *no* if they don't.
2. **Summaries.** The grid can serve as a guide to help students write a summary or essay about the topic.
3. **Grid addition.** Students can add to the grid as they learn more about the topic.

Morphology

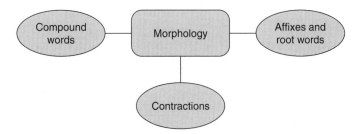

Description

Morphology . . . is the study of word formations that include compound words, contractions, prefixes, and suffixes. Knowledge of morphemes helps children expand their vocabulary beyond root words and aids in comprehension of printed materials.

Affix . . . a prefix, suffix, or inflectional ending that is added to a root word to change the function of the word or add to its meaning.

Compound word . . . a word that is formed by combining two or more words, such as *cowboy* and *mailbox.*

Contraction . . . formed by omitting one or more letters or sounds from an expression and replacing the omitted letter(s) with an apostrophe; example: *didn't* for *did not.*

Root word . . . the word that is left after you take away all affixes.

Compound Words

Description

Compound words usually do not create much difficulty because students already know each of the smaller words that make up the compound word. Students who have difficulty with compound words may not have recognized that the words are made by combining already known words. Attention should be drawn to the compound word's makeup.

Explicit Instruction

1. Select a story or poem that contains a compound word pattern (especially in its title). Write the title of the story on the board (e.g., Eric Carle's *The Grouchy Ladybug* or Suzanne Tate's *Billy Bluefish: A Tale of Big Blues*).
2. Read a story or poem to students.
3. After reading the story, underline the compound word in the title. Ask students if they notice anything special about this word.
4. Write examples of other compound words on the board.

   > *fire* + *fly* = *firefly*
   > *shoe* + *box* = *shoebox*
   > *mail* + *box* = *mailbox*
   > *butter* + *fly* = *butterfly*

5. Have students brainstorm other compound words. Write these on the board or word wall chart.
6. Show students copies of sentences in which a deleted word is a compound word. Have students write the compound words that correctly complete each sentence.

   > On the way to the beach we bought a beach_____. (*ball*)
   > We saw a beautiful blue_____ land on the fence. (*bird*)
   > The air_____ flew very fast. (*plane*)

7. Read the story to students and have them listen for compound words.
8. Encourage the wide reading of stories and poems that contain compound words.

Reinforcement Activities

1. **Fish and animal compounds.** Locate animal or fish names that are compound words (*redbird, jellyfish*).
2. **Weather compounds.** Locate compound words related to weather. The elements of *rain, sun,* and *snow* will provide many (*rainbow, sunset, snowplow*) (Cunningham 1995).
3. **Compound word location.** Locate compound words that begin with *air, any, back, ball, fire, some,* and *every.* Students can list as many compound words they can think of and then check them in the dictionary to see if they really are compound words.
4. **Song and book compounds.** Have students locate, or bring in, songs and books that use compound words in the titles.

5. **Matching words.** Give students lists of words. Each list contains one element of a compound word. Students should match or pair the words to form a compound word and write the new word to the right.

flower	man	flowerbox
mail	hand	_____
joy	box	_____
cow	fully	_____

6. **Matching illustrations.** Prepare index cards with pictures that represent each part of a compound word (such as a flower and a box). Students match the pictures and then pronounce the words.

7. **Newspaper compounds.** Locating compound words in newspaper articles offers an interesting alternative activity for your students.

8. **Scavenger hunt.** Students should go on a scavenger hunt around the classroom or the school and identify compound words, objects, or articles.

9. **Timed compounds.** Give students a specific amount of time in which to write down as many compound words as possible.

10. **Compound creation.** Students will enjoy creating and illustrating their own compound words.

11. **Listing words.** Students can identify as many compound words as possible that contain the word *over* (*overland, overheard, overcoat*).

12. **Cloze activity.** Provide students with sentences in which compound words are used to complete the blank.

The _____ ball is in my _____ room.

The *base*ball is in my *bed*room.

Books for Children

Ehlert, L. *Planting a Rainbow.* New York: Harcourt Brace & Company, 1992.

Numeroff, L. *If You Give a Pig a Pancake.* New York: HarperCollins, 1998.

Pfister, M. *Rainbow Fish.* New York: North-South Books, 1996.

Tate, S. *Billy Bluefish.* Nags Head, NC: Nags Head Art, 1988.

Contractions

Description

Contractions usually do not create problems because they maintain the same meaning and often have similar structures. Directing students' attention to the "lazy way of writing" is often sufficient during silent or oral reading.

Explicit Instruction

1. Read the story *I Can't Said the Ant* to students. Point out that the word *can't* is a very special word because of the way it is written.
2. Show students a list of words and contractions side-by-side.

cannot	*can't*
was not	*wasn't*
it is	*it's*
they have	*they've*
should not	*shouldn't*

3. Pronounce the words and contractions with students.
4. Have students state the difference between the pairs of words and contractions.
5. Give students multiple response cards with the contractions written on them.
6. Dictate sentences to students with the contraction left out. Have students hold up the card for the deleted contraction.
7. Show students sentences with the contraction omitted. Have students write the correct contraction into the sentence.
8. Read a story to students that contains contractions. Have students identify the contractions.
9. Make semantic maps using contractions. The center might be *n't*. Around the map would be many contractions with *n't*.

Reinforcement Activities

1. **Matching activities.** Students can match the contraction to the two words for which it stands. Matching can be done in a variety of ways: matching a baby lamb with its mother, placing a frog on a lily pad, matching a car with a gas pump, or simply drawing lines between the contraction and the words for which it stands.
2. **Sentence changing.** The teacher reads a sentence using two individual words instead of contractions. Students change the sentences by inserting the contraction in place of the individual words.

    He *did not* have a ride.
    He *didn't* have a ride.

3. **Contraction scavenger hunt.** Have students search newspaper and magazines for word combinations that can be changed into contractions

or contractions that can be changed into two separate words. Students can highlight or underline these words.

4. **Contraction listening.** Have students listen for the number of contractions you use during a half hour, an hour, or a day. As students hear you use a contraction they should write it down.

5. **Matching.** Give students contractions and pairs of words (*couldn't–could not; shouldn't–should not; can't–cannot*) mixed in an envelope. Students then match the compound word with its two individual words. This matching can be done on a flannel board if pieces of Velcro are attached to the back of the word pieces. The word pieces can be placed in pocket charts if they are made large enough, or they can be matched at the students' desk.

Selected Contractions

aren't	isn't	shouldn't	we're
can't	it's	that's	we've
couldn't	I'd	there's	what's
didn't	I'll	they'd	where's
doesn't	I'm	they'll	who'll
don't	I've	they're	won't
hadn't	let's	wasn't	wouldn't
haven't	she'd	weren't	you'll
he'd	she'll	we'd	you're
here's	she's	we'll	you've
he'll			

Books for Children

Comics provide many opportunities to read contractions.

Ashsworthy, A. *Guess What I'll Be.* Cambridge, MA: Candlewick Press, 1998.

Heller, R. *Chickens Aren't the Only Ones.* Los Angeles: Price Stern Sloan, 1993.

McGuire, R. *What's Wrong with This Book?* New York: Viking Childrens Books, 1997.

Milgrim, D. *Cows Can't Fly.* New York: Puffin, 2000.

Zamorano, A. *Let's Eat.* New York: Scholastic, 1999.

Explicit Instruction: Affixes

(Prefixes are used in this example.)

1. Provide students with a list of words that contain prefixes.

redo	*repaid*	*repack*
undo	*unpaid*	*unpack*

2. Have students read the words aloud and identify how these words are alike and different.
3. Ask students how the meanings have changed.
4. Have students write the words on movable cards (construction paper, oaktag).
5. Read sentences to students with the words omitted. Students should hold up the word that best completes the sentence.
6. Give students printed sentences with blank spaces for the words containing prefixes. Students complete the sentences with the correct word.
7. Read *The Napping House* to students and have them identify words that contain prefixes.
8. Encourage students to locate examples of prefixes taught in other printed materials.

Reinforcement Activities

1. **Prefix and suffix searches.** Prefix and suffix searches provide students with the challenge of searching through books and newspapers for examples of words containing the prefix or suffix learned. For each word found, students should write the sentence in which it is contained and write their own sentence using the word.
2. **Collage.** Students might create a collage using words containing prefixes and suffixes and sentences containing words that contain prefixes and suffixes.
3. **Completing sentences.** Write incomplete sentences with choices of words containing affixes. Students must select the correct form of the word.

   Helen was happy and felt _____. (loved, unloved)

4. **Changing sentence meaning.** Students can change the meaning of sentences by adding affixes to as many words as possible.

   unlocked
   Jack ~~locked~~ the door to his room.

5. **Affix race.** Divide the class into two teams. Print a selected prefix or suffix on the chalkboard. One by one, each student in the team comes to the board and writes a word that contains the affix. The team with the most words at the end of a specified time limit wins.

6. **Newspapers.** Encourage students to peruse newspapers or magazines for words that contain selected affixes.

7. **Concentration.** Print combinations of prefixes (or suffixes) and matching root words on index cards (3 by 5 in.). Turn all the cards face down and place them in mixed order in rows and columns. Each player turns over two cards at a time. The player keeps both cards if both the prefix and root word match and he or she can use the word correctly in a sentence. If this cannot be done, both cards are returned face down in the same place from which they were picked. Players take turns until all the cards are matched. The player with the most matches wins.

tri	angle
de	part
hydro	plane
in	come
bi	cycle
sub	marine

8. **Morphology jeopardy.** Using the format of the jeopardy game, give students a definition. They, in turn, must present the answer in the form of a question.

   a. Category (root word): *part.*
   b. Definition: to leave.
   c. Answer in the form of a question: What is *depart?*

Selected Prefixes

ab- (away from)	de- (away, down, reversing)	mono- (one)
a-, an- (not)		non- (not)
ante- (before)	dis- (apart from, not)	out- (beyond)
anti- (against)	en-, em- (in, to make or become)	post- (after)
auto- (self)		pre-, pro- (before, in front of)
be- (treat as)	ex- (out)	
bi- (two)	hemi- (half)	re- (back, again)
bene- (well)	hyper- (overly)	semi- (half)
co- (together, jointly)	il- (not)	sub- (under, below)
com-, con- (with, together)	in-, un- (not)	super- (over, above)
	mal- (bad)	trails- (across)
contra- (against)	mid- (middle)	un- (not, to do the opposite)
counter- (against)	mis- (wrong)	

Selected Suffixes

-able, -able (tending to, able to)

-al (pertaining to)

-en, -em (having the nature of, to make or become)

-ence, -ance (state of)

-er, (one who, that which, more [in comparisons])

-est (most [in comparisons])

-ful (full of)

-hood (state of)

-ic (pertaining to)

-ism (quality of)

-or (one who)

-ist (one who)

-ive (having the nature of quality of)

-ish (having the nature of)

-less (without)

-ly, y (in the manner of)

-man (one who)

-ment (resulting state)

-most (most [in comparisons])

-ness (quality of state of being)

-ous (having the quality of, state or condition)

-ship (office, profession, art or skill)

Books for Children

Allen, M. *The Rainy Day Band.* Huntington Beach, CA: Creative Teaching Press, 1999.

Tafuri, N. *Early Morning in the Barn.* New York: Puffin, 1986.

Wood, D., and A. Wood. *The Napping House.* New York: Red Wagon, 2000.

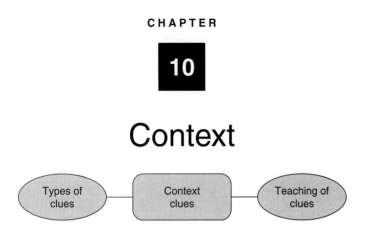

Context

Types of clues — Context clues — Teaching of clues

Description

Context . . . words that surround a particular word and help in identifying it.

If students are to use context clues, they must be given specific instruction in their use. Teachers must remember that they already know the meanings to the words students are trying to learn. Students, on the other hand, must be taught how to arrive at meanings that are unknown to them.

The method of teaching may influence whether students use context. Students taught through a strong decoding approach with heavy reliance on phonics may not use context. Students taught with a strong meaning approach, such as whole language, may tend to overuse context.

The students' view of what reading is will also influence their use of context. Better readers who view reading as "getting meaning" use context. Less able readers tend to view reading as "decoding" or pronouncing words. These readers are less inclined to use context because context is based on comprehension.

Also, the use of context is limited to a reader's experience because most context clues involve inference (Vacca and Vacca 2002).

Even though the use of context seems to be limited, Tompkins (2003) makes the following point: ". . . if students read 20,000 words a year, and they learn 1 of every 20 words from context, they would learn 1,000 words, or one-third of the average child's annual vocabulary growth" (p. 220).

Six types of context clues:

1. **Direct definitions and explanations.** Words such as *is* and *means* give clues that a definition or explanation will follow. "A *kalanchoe* is a type of flower."
2. **Explanation through example.** Sometimes writers use explanations to help the reader understand a word's meaning. "The car has *rust* spots; these are reddish brown spots that have decayed or worn away."

3. **Words in a series.** The reader can get an idea about a word's meaning if it is included among other words that belong to the same category. "We visited Hirosaki, *Toyota,* and Tokyo."
4. **Synonym or restatement.** Unknown words may be identified because different words with similar meanings are used in conjunction with it. "The *ingenuous,* or unsuspecting, man let the thief enter his home."
5. **Comparison or contrast.** Words are compared or contrasted with words that are known already. "Karl was a *malevolent* person, while his brother Ron was considerate and generous."
6. **Familiar expressions or figures of speech.** At times metaphors and similes may be used to convey meaning. "The dog *perambulated.* His movement was as slow as molasses."

Explicit Instruction: Teacher Modeling

1. Choose four or five difficult words from a selection students will read.
2. Write the words on the board.
3. Find the places in the text where the words occur.
4. Read the passages aloud to students.
5. Model (talk aloud) the thought process you use to determine their meanings.

Explicit Instruction: Student Modeling

1. Select five words from the text students will be reading.
2. Have students predict, before reading, the meanings of these words.
3. Show students two sentences in which the meaning of these words can be determined from context. (You probably will have to write these sentences.)
4. Students read these sentences and determine the meaning of the words.
5. Students explain how they arrived at the meanings of these words by using context.
6. Did the meanings after using context differ from their original predictions?
7. Students, using page numbers provided by the teacher, locate the word as it is used in the context they will be reading. What is the meaning of the word in this situation?

Reinforcement Activities

1. **Selecting pictures.** Orally present sentences to students, leaving out a word. Students must select a picture that correctly completes the sentence. Discuss why the specific picture was selected.

   Pictures: a ball, a broom, a car
   We swept the room with the _____.

2. **Selecting pictures to complete a series of sentences.** Write three sentences, each with a word missing, on the board and show students three different pictures to be used in completing the sentences. Read the sentences to the students, then have them select the picture that properly completes each sentence.

   Pictures: ice cream, a car, people playing baseball
   a. We played _____ at the picnic. (baseball)
   b. We ate _____ when we finished our chores. (ice cream)
   c. We washed the _____ because it was dirty. (car)

3. **Supplying missing words in sentences.** Have students read a sentence with a word missing. They should then enter words into the blank spaces.

   The house is _____.
   red
   big
   brick

4. **Supplying missing words that contain the same initial consonant.** Give students a sentence with a word missing. An initial consonant is supplied for the missing word. Students must supply an appropriate word that begins with that initial consonant.

   The dog b_____ at the gray cat.

5. **Selecting the appropriate word to complete a sentence.** Give students a sentence with a word missing. Provide two or three words from which the students may select.

   Did the dog (bark   bend) at the horse?

6. **Locating key words in text.** Locate key words in a text. Then challenge students to determine their meanings from the surrounding words. Be sure you select words whose meanings can be identified through context. Students should discuss how they arrived at the meanings.

7. **Homograph sentences.** Write pairs of sentences that contain homographs (words that are spelled the same but pronounced differently). Then encourage students to use context as they read the pairs of sentences while pronouncing the homographs correctly.

   The *wind* was blowing.
   I will have to *wind* my watch.
   Pat had the *lead* role.
   The pipe was made of *lead*.
   There were *tears* in his eyes.
   His jeans had *tears* in them.

8. **Student sentences.** Have students create their own sentences using pairs of homographs.
9. **Silent reading time.** Provide silent reading time so that students can practice reading words in context. Students may want to engage in buddy reading during this time.
10. **Motivating through reading materials.** Provide students with a large number of high-interest books to read.

Books for Children

Daly-Weir, C. *Knights.* New York: Crosset & Dunlap, 1998.

dePaola, T. *Strega Nona: Her Story.* New York: Aladdin Library, 1988.

Gordon, M. *Day and Night.* Florence, KY: Thomson Learning, 1995.

Martin, J. B. *Snowflake Bentley.* Boston: Houghton Mifflin, 1998.

Worth, B. *Oh Say Can You Seed: All About Flowering Plants.* New York: Random House, 2001.

Word Relationships

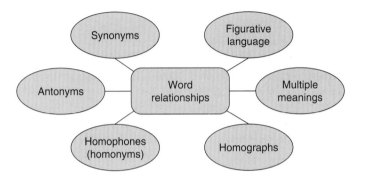

Description

Words have many different relationships to each other that students should be aware of in order to understand differences in meanings. Understanding these differences in meaning helps students use the dictionary and comprehend material they read (Crawley and Mountain 1995).

Antonyms . . . words that are opposite in meaning.

Figurative language . . . words that contain meanings that are different from their literal meanings. They have connotative rather than denotative meanings.

Homophones (homonyms) . . . words that have the same *(homo)* sound *(phone)* but are spelled differently and have different meanings. These are often confusing to students.

Homographs . . . words that have the same *(homo)* spelling *(graph)* but are pronounced differently.

Multiple meanings . . . the various meanings and shades of meaning words can have.

Synonyms . . . words that have the same meanings.

Synonyms

Explicit Instruction: Synonyms

(You can also use these techniques with antonyms but substitute opposite meanings.)

1. Present the following pairs of words to students:

big	large
sleep	nap
pull	drag
old	aged
happy	cheerful

2. Ask students if they notice anything special about these words.
3. Write the word *synonym* on the board. Tell students that words with similar meanings are called *synonyms.*
4. Ask students if they can think of other pairs of words that are synonyms.
5. Give students a paragraph from a story and ask them to substitute synonyms for words in the paragraph.

Reinforcement Activities

1. **Word wall.** Create a synonym or antonym word wall that students can add to. Be sure to talk about the words and meanings.
2. **Science and social studies synonyms.** Give students a list of words from a science or social studies lesson. Ask them to think of synonyms that could be used.
3. **Interesting synonyms.** Have students create a list of interesting words (synonyms) for overused words *(said, good, great, fun, neat).*
4. **Color synonyms.** Create a list of words that can be used instead of basic colors such as *red, blue, yellow, green* (such as *ruby* or *sapphire*).
5. **Overused words.** Give students a paragraph containing common, overused words, and have students rewrite it using interesting words. Have students rewrite the paragraph using antonyms and notice the difference in meaning.
6. **Advertisement switch.** Check advertisements in magazines and newspapers. Have students change the words that describe the products in positive terms to antonyms that would be the opposite.
7. **Antonyms.** Using an article from the newspaper, prompt students to change as many words as possible to their opposites. Then guide students in discussing how these substitutions have changed the article's meaning.
8. **Synonyms.** Using an article from the newspaper, challenge students to change as many words as possible to appropriate synonyms. Next, have students discuss how these substitutions have changed the article's meaning.

Homophones (Homonyms)

Explicit Instruction: Homophones (Homonyms)

1. Read one of Peggy Parish's Amelia Bedelia books (such as *Amelia Bedelia Helps Out*).
2. Have students help Amelia Bedelia so that she does the tasks correctly.
3. With your students, make a list of Amelia Bedelia's mistakes and ask students what she should have done.
4. Write the correct homophone next to the mistake Amelia made (for example, *stake–steak, sew–sow*).
5. Ask students if they notice a difference between the pairs of words. (Words are spelled differently but sound the same.) Note: Amelia Bedelia also mixes up words with multiple meanings *(dusted)*.

Reinforcement Activities

1. **Same-sound puzzles.** Students must identify two words that begin with the same sound and match the clues given. (Any letters may be used.)

   The two words that match these clues must begin with the letter *b.*

   Clue: a vegetable, or to spank

   Answer: *beet* and *beat*

   Clue: a branch, or to bend at the waist

   Answer: *bough* and *bow*

   Clue: an animal, or to be uncovered

   Answer: *bear* and *bare*

2. **Homophone searches.** Direct students to cut as many homophones from the newspaper and magazines as they can find. Students then paste the words on a sheet of paper and write their corresponding homophones. Next, direct students to compose a sentence using each homophone.

   Example:

   horse–hoarse

   The *horse* galloped quickly around the track.

   The announcer spoke with a *hoarse* voice.

Selected Homonyms (Homophones)

air, heir	blue, blew	dear, deer
basis, bases	bowl, bole	earn, urn
be, bee	brake, break	eight, ate
beach, beech	bury, berry	fair, fare
bear, bare	by, buy, bye	feet, feat, fete
beat, beet	days, daze	fur, fir

flower, flour	low, lo	right, write, rite
fourth, forth	maid, made	rode, road
great, grate	meat, meet	sea, see
grown, groan	need, knead	seem, seam
hale, hail	new, knew, gnu	sale, sail
hear, here	night, knight	sore, soar
hole, whole	not, knot	some, sum
I, eye	one, won	sun, son
in, inn	our, hour	so, sow, sew
its, it's	pail, pale	stake, steak
know, no	peel, peal	their, there, they're
knows, nose	plane, plain	wait, weight
led, lead	principle, principal	where, wear
lone, loan	raise, raze	wood, would

Books for Children

Homophones

Gwynne, F. *Chocolate Moose for Dinner.* New York: Aladdin Library, 1988.

Gwynne, F. *The King Who Rained.* New York: Aladdin Library, 1988.

O'Donnell, R. *Kids Are Punny.* New York: Warner Books, 1997.

Parish, Peggy. *Amelia Bedelia* books. New York: HarperColllins, 1992.

Homographs / Multiple Meanings / Figurative Language

Explicit Instruction: Homographs / Multiple Meanings / Figurative Language

1. Present examples of the words in context.

   I will *wind* my watch.
   The *wind* is blowing.
   She had a *tear* in her slacks.
   He had a *tear* in his eye.

2. Have students read the sentences and try to determine the word meanings.
3. Look the word up in the dictionary and identify which of the meanings best fits the use of the word in the sentence.

Reinforcement Activities

1. **Word wall.** Create a homograph, multiple meaning, or figurative language word wall.
2. **Figurative language map.** Create a semantic map to show types and examples of figurative language.
3. **Word detectives.** Encourage students to locate examples of homographs, multiple-meaning words, and figurative language in books, newspapers, or magazines they read.

Books for Children

Figurative Language

Arnold, T. *More Parts.* New York: Dial Books, 2001.

Christopher, M. *Baseball Jokes and Riddles.* Boston: Little, Brown, 1999.

Terban, M. *It Figures! Fun Figures of Speech.* New York: Clarion Books, 1993.

Extending an Interest in Vocabulary

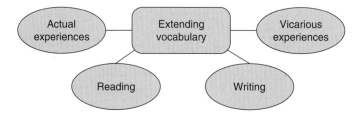

Vocabulary development is an ongoing activity, and many opportunities should be provided to encourage its expansion. Many of the activities listed here can be adapted to previously discussed topics or may stand alone as a means of expanding students' interest in words.

Reinforcement Activities

1. **Providing real experiences.** The more real or concrete the experiences you provide for your students, the better: cooking, painting, sewing, going on field trips, bringing objects from home, conducting experiments, or eating. It's not enough just to have these experiences with your students—you should ask them questions as they are engaged in the experience. Can they name the items and things they're seeing or doing? How do they feel? What are they thinking? Vocabulary expansion will take place through discussion.
2. **Providing vicarious experiences.** Provide your students with indirect experiences. Show films and videotapes. Let your students watch television. Bring pictures from books and magazines to class for discussion.
3. **Encouraging wide reading.** Students who have weak vocabularies are often those who do not read widely. Provide opportunities for reading during the day (sustained silent reading). Read to your students to interest them in books. See Chapter 25, "Developing Interests," for additional ideas.

4. **Word histories.** When possible, take time to tell students about the history of words—this often stimulates them to learn more about words. Where did our words come from? (Did you know that *good-bye* comes from "God be with ye"? Did you know that melba toast was named after a singer who was given overly cooked toast and liked it?)

Direct your students to some of the following books:

Arnold, O. *What's in a Name: Famous Brand Names.* New York: Julian Messner, 1979.

Ashton, C. *Words Can Tell: A Book About Our Language.* Simon and Schuster Trade, 1989.

Asimov, I. *Words from History.* Boston: Houghton Mifflin, 1968.

———. *Words from Myths.* Boston: Houghton Mifflin, 1961.

Brennan-Nelson, D. *My Teacher Likes to Say.* Chelsea, MI: Sleeping Bear Press, 2004.

Cleary, B. P. *Pitch and Throw, Grasp and Know: What Is a Synonym?* Minneapolis, MN: First Avenue Editions, 2007.

Cox, J. A. *Put Your Foot in Your Mouth and Other Silly Sayings.* New York: Random House, 1980.

Crane, C. *D Is for Dancing Dragon: A China Alphabet.* Chelsea, MI: Sleeping Bear Press, 2006.

———. *L Is for Lone Star: A Texas Alphabet.* Chelsea, MI: Sleeping Bear Press, 2002.

Dickson, P. *Dickson's Word Treasury: A Connoisseur's Collection of Old and New, Weird and Wonderful, Useful and Outlandish Words.* New York: Wiley, 1992.

Hazen, B. S. *Last, First, Middle and Nick: All About Names.* Englewood Cliffs, NJ: Prentice-Hall, 1979.

Herzog, B. *T Is for Touchdown: A Football Alphabet.* Chelsea, MI: Sleeping Bear Press, 2004.

Jack, A. *Red Herrings and White Elephants: The Origins of the Phrases We Use Every Day.* New York: HarperCollins, 2004.

Leedy, L., and P. Street. *There's a Frog in My Throat: 440 Animal Sayings a Little Bird Told Me.* New York: Holiday House, 2003.

Nevin, A. and D. *From the Horse's Mouth.* Englewood Cliffs, NJ: Prentice Hall, 1977.

Schwartzman, S. *Words of Mathematics.* Washington, DC: Mathematics Association of America, 1994.

Steckler, A. *101 Words and How They Began.* Garden City, New York: Doubleday, 1979.

Ulmer, M. *H Is for Horse: An Equestrian Alphabet.* Chelsea, MI: Sleeping Bear Press, 2004.

———. *J Is for Jump Shot: A Basketball Alphabet.* Chelsea, MI: Sleeping Bear Press, 2005

Weiler, S. K. *Mini-Myths and Maxi-Words.* Longman, 1986.

Weiss, A. E. *What's That You Said? How Words Change.* New York: Harcourt Brace Jovanovich, 1980.

5. **Developing classroom dictionaries.** Synonyms, antonyms, homonyms (words that are spelled differently but pronounced alike: *male–mail, horse–hoarse*), borrowed words, and idioms can be placed in class-developed dictionaries.

6. **Prefix–suffix searches.** After they learn a prefix or suffix, challenge students to search through books and newspapers for examples of words containing the prefix or suffix. For each word found, they should write the sentence in which it is contained and write their own sentences using the word.

7. **Interesting-word charts.** Make a chart of new or interesting words that students discover in their reading. You might categorize the words as describing words, action words, naming words, and so on.

8. **Word hunts.** Hunt for words and phrases that depict different moods. Find pictures that illustrate these moods. Make mood collages.

9. **Word races.** Form small classroom groups. Give each group a word such as *said.* See which group can come up with the most synonyms in a specified period of time.

10. **Listening walks.** Take your students on a listening walk. They should be very quiet and listen carefully as they walk. When they come back to the classroom they should describe the sounds they heard.

11. **Mystery box or bag activities.** Place an object inside a box or bag. Without looking, students should feel the object and then describe what they feel. Other students might try to guess what the object is from the description.

12. **Object description.** A student thinks of an object, describes it to the class without naming it, and has other students guess what object is being described.

13. **Vocabulary scavenger hunts.** Give your students a list of items and categories into which they might fall. Instruct students to guess the categories in which the items belong. Then put your students into groups. Each group member will select several of the items on the list and try to find pictures of them, make drawings of them, or bring the objects to class. The group that brings in and correctly categorizes the most items wins the scavenger hunt.

14. **Crossword puzzles.** Teach your students how to do crossword puzzles. Make crossword puzzles to reinforce vocabulary they are learning. Suggest that students locate words from the newspaper to complete the crossword puzzles.

15. **Writing descriptive poems.** Ask each student to write his or her name (or a noun given by the teacher) vertically on the paper. Each student

must then write an adjective for each letter in the noun. Each adjective must begin with a letter in the noun. Look at the word *Pam*.

Placid

Accordant

Mysterious

16. **Category selection.** Permit one student to select a category (such as farm animals or flight). Other students then call out as many words as they can that fit the category. When students have finished contributing the words, they should categorize them.

17. **Definition up.** Select words that the students are studying in science, math, social studies, or another area. Form two teams and give each team a packet of words. The teams take turns asking each other words and giving their accurate definitions. The team that gives the most definitions correctly wins.

18. **Acronyms.** Encourage students to find articles in newspapers or magazines that contain acronyms (words formed from the first or first few letters of several words). Paste the article(s) to a sheet of paper. Then list the acronyms and the words they represent.

19. **Vertical name.** Students should print their names vertically down the left side of the paper, leaving three spaces between each letter. They should then locate as many new words as they can find that begin with the letters in their names. When students have finished, they should select three words and learn their meanings.

Example:

K   kindle, kindred

I   inquisitive, inquisition

N   null, native

G   generous, gem

20. **Finishing sentences.** Provide students with incomplete sentences. Prompt them to search the newspaper or magazines to find words that can be used in completing the sentences. Students should cut the words out and paste them into the pattern space. (Present students with 10 samples of the same sentence pattern.)

Example 1:

The horse _____ is running _____ around the track.

The horse _____ trotted _____ around the track.

Example 2:

The horse won the race in a record-setting time.

The horse was sent out to pasture because he was too old to work.

Example 3:

I like ice cream, candy, pizza, apples, and carrots.

I like to lie on the beach and soak up sun during summer vacation.

21. **Things I like.** Instruct students to read the newspaper quickly to find words that tell what they like. Cut out these words. Then try to locate pictures to illustrate these words.

22. **Categorizing.** Encourage your students to read the newspaper quickly and find words and/or pictures that fit into specific categories. Then paste the words or pictures under the correct category.

Example:

Fruits	Vegetables	Dairy products	Cereals	Meats
_____	_____	_____	_____	_____
_____	_____	_____	_____	_____
_____	_____	_____	_____	_____
_____	_____	_____	_____	_____

23. **Same-sound puzzles.** Students must identify two words that begin with the same sound and match the clues given. (Any letters may be used.)

The two words that match these clues must begin with the letter *b*.

Clue: a vegetable, or to spank
Answer: *beet* and *beat*

Clue: a branch, or to bend at the waist
Answer: *bough* and *bow*

Clue: an animal, or to be uncovered
Answer: *bear* and *bare*

24. **Anagrams.** Students rearrange letters to spell pairs of words and then supply the meanings of the pairs of words.

Letters: *tsho*   Words: *shot, host*
Letters: *aref*   Words: *fear, fare*

25. **Vocabogram.** Students rearrange the letters of a given word to make a new word that matches a given definition.

Example 1:
Given word: *tore*
Definition: mechanical memory
New word: *rote*

Example 2:
Given word: *sure*
Definition: a trick
New word: *ruse*

26. **Palindrome word puzzles.** Words that are spelled the same way backward and forward are called *palindromes (mom, pop).*

Example 1:
Definition: midday
Palindrome: *noon*

Example 2:
Definition: observes
Palindrome: *sees*

27. **Palindrome sentence puzzles.** Some phrases or complete sentences have the "same backward and forward" characteristic.

    Example:
    Madam I'm Adam. Adam I'm Madam.

28. **Palindrome riddles.** Each of the following couplets defines two words, the first the reverse of the second in spelling but otherwise unrelated to it.

    Example:
    If I bore you by boasting and putting on airs,
    Turn me around, and I'm something one wears.
    Answers: *brag, garb*

29. **Tom Swifties.** These are sentences in which the final adverb has a catchy relationship with some of the other words in the sentence.

    Examples:
    "Our hot dogs are good," the cook said frankly.
    "I failed my exam," the student said testily.

30. **Hink-pinks.** These are rhyming riddles that teach synonyms and definitions. Ask your students for three synonyms of an adjective. Then ask for three nouns that rhyme with the adjectives. Have students compose the answer to some rhyming riddles using these synonyms and adjectives.

    Adjective: *wonderful*
    Three synonyms for *wonderful: great, super, terrific*
    Three nouns that rhyme with the adjectives: *bait, trooper, Pacific*
    Riddle: What do you call a wonderful police officer?
    Answer: *super trooper*
    Riddle: What do you call a wonderful ocean?
    Answer: *terrific Pacific*

31. **Association match.** Provide students with three or four words related to a topic. Students cross out the word that does not belong and explain the reason for their choice.

Examples:

triceps   biceps   lung

(*Lung* does not belong. It is an organ, not a muscle.)

treble   key   bass

(*Key* does not belong. Treble and bass are both clefs.)

32. **Picture books read-alouds.** Select appropriate picture books related to science, social studies, or math concepts being studied. Picture book read-alouds can be used to scaffold vocabulary important to the topic.

33. **Word sorts.** Provide 10 to 20 words from the word wall. These should be written on index cards or sticky notes for students (or depending upon age, students can write their own). Direct students to sort the words into different categories according to their characteristics. After giving their rationales for sorting, you may find that students sort the words into different categories.

34. **ABC or AlphaBoxes.** Students are given a chart with letters of the alphabet in individual boxes or letters written vertically down the paper. They may work individually or in pairs. The goal is to complete as many boxes as possible with words or phrases related to the topic. More than one word may be placed into a box.

     The ABC boxes can be used in a couple of ways. Before reading, students can work in pairs and brainstorm words or phrases related to the topic and complete as many boxes as possible. Remember, the topic should be broad enough to generate many words (e.g., environment, Civil War, famous people, a state). Or, as students read a passage, chapter, or story, they can write important or interesting vocabulary or phrases (three to four words long) that begin with each letter of the alphabet into the boxes. After completion of the reading, each group of students reports or shares the words placed into the boxes. These can be the beginning of a word wall for the topic. See example charts below.

Example 1:   ABC Boxes

Name(s): _____   **Topic:** _____

A *absolute*	B	C	D
E	F	G	H
I	J	K	L
M	N	O	P
Q	R	S	T
U	V	W	XYZ

Example 2:   ABC Boxes Variation.   Write the word or phrase on the line next to the letter.

A   *absolute*

B

C

D

Books for Children

Brennan-Nelson, D. *My Momma Likes to Say.* Chelsea, MI: Sleeping Bear Press, 2003.

———. *My Teacher Likes to Say.* Chelsea, MI: Sleeping Bear Press, 2004.

Cleary, B. P. *Dearly, Nearly, Insincerely: What Is an Adverb?* Minneapolis, MN: Lerner Publications, 2005.

———. *Hairy, Scary, Ordinary: What Is an Adjective?* Minneapolis, MN: Carolrhoda Books, 2000.

———. *Pitch and Throw, Grasp and Know: What Is a Synonym?* Minneapolis, MN: Carolrhoda Books, 2004.

———. *Stop and Go, Yes and No: What Is an Antonym?* Minneaplis, MN: Millbrook Press, 2006.

———. *To Root to Toot to Parachute: What Is a Verb?* Minneapolis, MN: Carolrhoda Books, 2001.

———. *How Much Can a Bare Bear Bear? What Are Homonyms and Homophones?* Minneapolis, MN: First Avenue Editions, 2007.

Gwynne, F. *The King Who Rained.* New York: Aladdin, 2006.

Heller, R. A. *Cache of Jewels and Other Collective Nouns.* New York: Putnam, 1998.

———. *Fantastic! Wow! And Unreal!: A Book About Interjections and Conjunctions.* New York: Putnam Juvenile, 2000.

———. *Kites Sail High: A Book About Verbs.* New York: Putnam Juvenile, 1998.

———. *Many Luscious Lollipops: A Book About Adjectives.* New York: Putnam Juvenile, 1998.

Hill, E. *Spot's Big Book of Words.* New York: Putnam, 1988.

Leedy, L., and P. Street. *There's a Frog in My Throat: 440 Animal Sayings a Little Bird Told Me.* New York: Holiday House, 2003.

Terban, M. *Eight Ate: A Feast of Homonym Riddles.* New York: Clarion Books, 1982.

———. *It Figures! Fun Figures of Speech.* New York: Clarion Books, 1993.

UNIT

IV

Fluency

Unit Introduction

Fluency . . . being able to decode words automatically, group them meaningfully, and read with expression. These components of fluency facilitate comprehension. Being fluent in reading allows students to focus on comprehension—interacting with text and attaching meaning to printed symbols. The following diagram presents the major categories of fluency discussed in this unit.

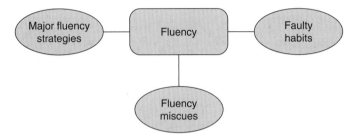

Oral reading . . . communicating an author's message by reading aloud to an individual or an audience.

When students read words automatically they have good accuracy, and speed is not interrupted by frequent attempts to decode words. Fluency instruction has been found to result in improved reading comprehension (Dowhower 1987). In a summary of numerous studies Blachman (2000) concluded that "without accuracy and fluent word recognition, there will always be constraints on comprehension" (p. 493). Less fluent readers tend to focus more on decoding words with little time left to pay attention to comprehension. More fluent readers are better able to make connections between their background knowledge and the printed page. Fluency also helps students develop more positive self-images of themselves as readers.

Often fluency is associated with oral reading because it is more easily observed; however, fluency in silent reading also is important. Carver (1989) identified the following silent reading rates for students who understood material at various grade levels:

Grade 1: 81 words/minute (WPM)
Grade 2: 82–108 WPM
Grade 3: 109–130 WPM
Grade 4: 131–147 WPM
Grade 5: 148–161 WPM
Grade 6: 162–174 WPM
Grade 7: 175–185 WPM
Grade 8: 186–197 WPM

Grade 9: 198–209 WPM
Grade 10: 210–224 WPM
Grade 11: 225–240 WPM
Grade 12: 241–255 WPM

Round robin oral reading instruction was once used as a method of fluency instruction. (It is still used in some classrooms today.) Round robin reading involves having students turning to a page in their textbooks and selecting a student to begin reading orally. While this student is reading the rest of the students are instructed to follow along. "EJ, begin reading at the top of page 34. Thank you. Tina, please continue reading."

Several problems are inherent in this method of instruction. Not all students are following along. Some students are reading ahead, thus discouraging the development of listening skills. The oral reading has no purpose except to please the teacher with good decoding. It takes away from the time spent on purposeful reading. It is of little value instructionally, and damages the self-esteem of poor readers.

Problems with fluency may stem from a variety of causes: inadequate sight vocabulary, poor decoding skills, an overdependence on word analysis skills, or inattention to punctuation. Students may view reading as pronouncing words quickly and accurately and not focus on comprehension. Students may not have been taught how to read in phrases, or they may be reading material that is too difficult.

The 5- and 10-finger rules are good guides to use in selecting, and helping students select, books at appropriate levels. Have a student count on his or her fingers each word not known in 100 words. If the student puts five fingers down, the book is too hard to read alone or independently. If the student puts 10 fingers down, the book is too hard to be used for instruction.

Nichols (2002, p. 83) summarizes the results of the *National Reading Panel* report:

- Repeated and monitored oral reading had a significant positive impact on word recognition, fluency, and comprehension.
- Fluency instruction was appropriate for children in grades 2 through high school, particularly for struggling readers.
- Fluency instruction was equally effective for good and poor readers.
- There was no evidence to support the effectiveness of encouraging independent and recreational reading, as for example in sustained silent reading programs.

This final conclusion should be tempered, however, because a close look at the *National Reading Panel* report indicates that the "panel was unable to determine if silent reading improves fluency, as research on this is insufficient. Studies do show that the best readers read silently more frequently than do poor readers, but this may simply be because they are better at it" (International Reading Association, 2002). Perhaps the topic was too obvious to investigate. Practice improves performance, as is also true for riding a bike, playing a musical instrument, singing opera, and learning to drive.

Major Fluency Strategies

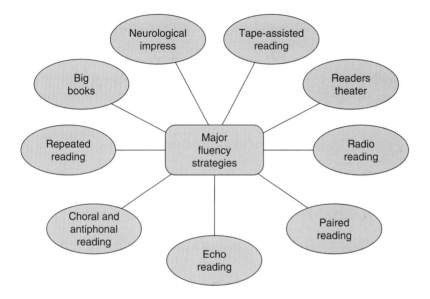

Description

Big books and the neurological impress method are discussed in Chapters 4 and 28, respectively, so they will not be discussed in this chapter. They are included in the "major fluency strategies" map as a reminder of their use in developing fluency.

The *National Reading Panel* report (2000) recommended methods such as the neurological impress method (Heckelman 1969), repeated readings (Samuels 1979), paired reading (Topping 1987a and 1987b), radio reading (Searfoss 1975), choral reading (Schreiber 1980), readers' theater (Young and Vaardell 1993), and tape-assisted reading (Blum et al. 1995).

> **Antiphonal reading** . . . groups of students are assigned to read parts of a selection or text in unison. This is similar to choral reading except the selection is divided into parts for different groups of students to read. For our purposes, this will be discussed under choral reading.
>
> **Choral reading** . . . students read text together or in unison. Less fluent students learn expression as they read along with other skilled readers.

Echo reading . . . fluency is modeled. Students immediately echo a phrase read by a skilled reader. Short phrases are increased in length to full sentences, and so on, as the students' skills increase.

Paired (partner) reading . . . a capable reader and a student who is having difficulty reading materials written at an instructional level are paired or partnered together. A parent, teacher, or more advanced student may serve as the partner.

Radio reading . . . students are asked to think back to the days when people sat around the living room (or other room in the house) in anticipation of stories being read on the radio. In radio reading one student is the announcer. This student reads a selection or part of a story aloud. Other students are the radio audience and do not have any books open. This promotes listening skills and audience reading.

Readers' theater . . . students practice reading their script parts. After practicing their parts, they present the script to an audience of parents or peers without memorizing a script, using full costumes, movement, and perhaps props.

Repeated readings . . . students practice reading a selection until it is read perfectly (zero miscues).

Tape-assisted reading . . . students read along in their books as they listen to an audiotaped recording of their book by a fluent reader. This has been called "talking books" (Carbo 1978).

Repeated Readings

Explicit Instruction

1. Select short passages or stories of about 50 to 225 words. Longer selections may be broken down into shorter passages and used over a period of days.
2. Ask the student to read the passage orally, and record his or her miscues and reading rate. (Reading rate in words per minute (WPM) equals the total number of words in the selection divided by the number of minutes it takes to read the selection.)
3. To ensure that the student is reading and attending to comprehension, ask the student a couple of questions about the selection.
4. Students might like to plot the number of miscues on a graph with one color, and the time in WPM with another color line. With practice, they should notice that as their speed increases, the number of miscues decreases.
5. Have students practice rereading the passage, trying to increase speed and reduce the number of miscues each time it is read.
6. Follow this procedure for 2 to 3 days. Students can practice at home, when they first come into the class in the morning or after lunch,

during sustained silent reading time, or when they have completed an assignment.

7. A motivation for doing the repeated readings might be to engage in radio reading or readers' theater. Or they might want to read a story to younger children or record the story so younger children can listen to the recording.

Choral Reading

Explicit Instruction

1. Determine the type of choral reading you will have your students engage in: unison, refrain, or dialogue.
2. Select text that is appropriate for choral reading. Predictable books, lyrics, and poems are good for choral reading.
3. Read the entire selection aloud to students, modeling fluent reading with expression.
4. Show students a copy of the selection and ask them how the lines should be read. What clues do they find to help them read the lines fluently?
5. Next, have students read along with you.
6. When students become comfortable reading along with you, you can divide the lines in the selection so that you read one part and students read other specified parts. For example, in *Goldilocks and the Three Bears,* you might serve as the narrator, and you might divide the class so that some students read the lines of Goldilocks, some read the lines of Mama Bear, some read the lines of Father Bear, and others read the lines of Baby Bear.
7. These same steps are followed for antiphonal reading.

Books for Children

Christelow, E. *Five Little Monkeys Jumping on the Bed.* Boston: Houghton Mifflin, 1998.

Martin, B. *Brown Bear, Brown Bear, What Do You See?* New York: Henry Holt, 1992.

————. *Polar Bear, Polar Bear, What Do You Hear?* New York: Henry Holt, 1997.

Mountain, L.; S. Crawley; and E. Fry. *The Gingerbread Man: Heritage Readers.* Provincetown, RI: Jamestown Publishers, 1991.

————. *Goldilocks and the Three Bears: Heritage Readers.* Provincetown, RI: Jamestown Publishers, 1991.

————. *The Little Red Hen: Heritage Readers.* Provincetown, RI: Jamestown Publishers, 1991.

Silverstein, S. *A Light in the Attic.* New York: HarperCollins Juvenile, 1981.

————. *Where the Sidewalk Ends.* New York: HarperCollins Juvenile, 1974.

Echo Reading

Explicit Instruction

1. This is one step in the neurological impress method.
2. Select materials that are easy for students to read. Begin with small segments (phrases) and gradually increase the length to sentences or longer.
3. The reader sits beside the student and reads a portion of text to the student using proper expression and speed. The student then echoes or repeats the phrase.
4. If the student correctly echoes the phrase, the reader holds the book in front of the student. Synchronizing voice and finger pointing, the reader points to the words s/he is reading out loud while the student looks at the words and repeats what is being read. Be sure to use expression.
5. If the student incorrectly echoes the phrase, reread the phrase immediately and have the student echo it. Then synchronizing voice and finger pointing, the reader points to the words s/he is reading out loud while the student looks at the words and repeats what is being read. Be sure to use expression.

Paired Reading

Explicit Instruction

1. Select material at the student's instructional level. Or allow the student to select material from a selection at his or her instructional level.
2. Pair a more fluent reader with the student.
3. The readers sit side-by-side.
4. First the reader and student discuss the book cover and title. They may predict what will happen.
5. The reader and student read chorally together.
6. When the student feels able to read alone, he/she signals the reader to continue alone.
7. If the student does not know a word, allow him/her several seconds to figure it out, then help with the word. If the reading becomes too difficult, begin choral reading again.
8. At times allow the student to select books at the independent level. When reading books at the independent level, the student will have more success in reading aloud without assistance. If the student begins having difficulty, pick up choral reading with the student.
9. Only 15–30 minutes, three days per week, are needed to produce positive results.

Radio Reading

Explicit Instruction

1. As a prelude to radio reading, have students sit and listen to a story on tape without any text in front of them. Ask them what happened in the story. Ask them how the reader kept their attention.
2. Explain that there is a type of reading called radio reading. In radio reading, you pretend that you are sitting in a room with a radio and listening to someone on the radio read a story.
3. Students are given part of a text to practice reading for the next day. The material may come from any source—science, social studies, basal reader, or a trade or chapter book. The student also develops one or two questions to ask the rest of the class when she/he has finished reading.
4. The radio announcer (student reader) reads his/her section of the text orally as an announcer (you might even have a microphone or karaoke machine for students to read into).
5. After reading, the questions are asked of the audience.

Readers' Theater

Explicit Instruction

1. As a prelude to readers' theater, have students sit and listen to a story on tape without any text in front of them. Ask them what happened in the story. Ask them how the reader kept their attention.
2. Tell students to pretend that they are going to audition or read for a part in a Broadway play. They and other actors are standing in front of the play's producers and reading the script as best they can, using good speed, phrasing, and expression.
3. Model a way the script could be read.
4. Ask students how they can tell, from the script, how the parts should be read.
5. Have students read scripts silently or with a buddy.
6. The next day, assign students the roles of various characters.
7. Students practice these roles and then present their readers' theater production to other classes and parents.

Books for Children

Bauer, C. F. *Presenting Reader's Theater: Plays and Poems to Read Aloud.* New York: H. W. Wilson, 1987.

Byars, B. *My Brother, Ant.* New York: Viking, 1996.

Eastman, P. D. *Are You My Mother?* New York: Random House, 1960.

Fleischman, P. *Seedfolks*. New York: Harper Trophy, 1999.

Frederick, A., and A. Stoner. *Frantic Frogs and Other Frankly Fractured Folktales for Readers Theatre*. Westport, CT: Teacher Ideas Press, 1993.

Glasscock, S. *10 American History Plays for the Classroom*. New York: Scholastic, 1999.

Kraus, R. *Whose Mouse Are You?* New York: Aladdin, 1986.

Noble, T. H. *The Day Jimmy's Boa Ate the Wash*. New York: Pearson Scott Foresman, 1992.

Tape-Assisted Reading

Explicit Instruction

1. Give the student an audiotape of a book at his or her independent reading level. (This book should be taped by a fluent reader.)
2. The tape should be made without sound effects or music in order to focus the student's attention on the print.
3. During the first reading the student follows along and points to each word as it is being read.
4. Next the student reads along orally with the tape.
5. The student should read along until she/he can read the selection without the assistance of the tape.

Reinforcement Activities

1. **Silent reading.** Give students a chance to read all material silently before oral reading. Silent reading gives students the opportunity to practice words they are unsure of, get acquainted with the author's style, and become familiar with the message the author is trying to communicate.
2. **Providing easy reading material.** Provide very easy (independent-level) reading material for students to reduce anxiety and improve fluency.
3. **Working with phrases.** Use phrase cards. As you rapidly flash the cards, challenge the student to identify the phrase seen. The fast presentation of phrases not only will increase eye span but will lessen the student's dependence on word-attack skills.
4. **Using mechanical devices.** Use mechanical devices such as computers, the Controlled Reader (Educational Developmental Laboratories), Tachomatic X500 (Psychotechnics), Reading Accelerator (Science Research Associates), and Flash-X (Educational Developmental Laboratories) to increase the rate at which students see words and phrases.
5. **Highlighting punctuation.** If your student does not pay attention to punctuation, you might highlight it to attract the student's attention.

6. **Reading along.** The content of books can be put on cassette tapes. Students can then read along as the story or content material is presented on tape. (Many commercial read-alongs are available for young children.) Students can also read aloud with computer programs.
7. **Singing songs.** Print and duplicate song lyrics so that students may follow them as they sing along. Singing along aids with fluency.
8. **Modeling.** A person who is a good oral reader should read one page as a model the student can follow. Then the student follows and reads the next page orally. Continue alternating oral reading with the student.
9. **Taping oral reading.** Tape-record your students' oral reading. Let the students listen to the tape recording and analyze how they performed. Did the students

   - Pronounce the words correctly?
   - Read in phrases or thought units?
   - Pay attention to punctuation?
   - Read slowly enough for people to follow?
   - Read loudly enough so that people could hear?
   - Convey the author's meaning to the audience?

10. **Neurological impress method.** Allow your student to select a favorite book. Sit next to this student and read directly into his/her ear. The student should read orally with you as you read. (See Chapter 28.)
11. **Dramatizing.** Use dramatization in conjunction with oral reading. The dramatizing creates a more natural setting in which to communicate an author's message.
12. **Establishing purposes.** Give students purposes for their audience reading.

   Examples:

   Read to prove an answer to a question.

   Read aloud the section of the story you thought was scariest, funniest, or saddest.

   Read aloud the part of the story that best describes (<u>name of the character</u>).

   Read a children's book to a much younger student.

Fluency Miscues

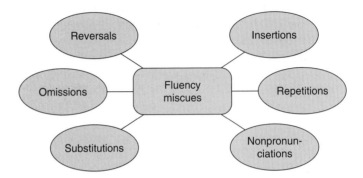

Miscues are oral reading responses that are different from the printed text. Fluency miscues are observable and provide one means of describing a student's oral reading behavior.

Miscue . . . oral reading responses that are different from the printed text.

Insertions . . . the addition of one or more words during the oral reading of printed material. Sometimes these are called *additions.*

Nonpronunciations . . . also known as teacher assistance, aid, or teacher pronunciations. The student does not pronounce the word. Instead, the student waits for the teacher to pronounce it.

Omissions . . . leaving out one or more words during the oral reading of printed materials. Students may skip or leave out a whole word, a group of words, or part of a word.

Repetitions . . . saying a word, phrase, or sentence two or more times during oral reading.

Reversal . . . misreading or miswriting letters, words, or numbers by changing their direction or rotation. *Static reversals* involve changes in rotation. (The *d* in *dog* is rotated and the word is read *bog.*) *Kinetic reversals* involve changes in direction. (The direction of the word *was* is changed and read *saw.*)

Substitutions . . . replacing one or more words with an incorrect word or words during the oral reading of printed materials. Substitutions often make sense in the context of the printed material but do not look like the printed word or words.

The major fluency strategies described in the previous chapter are excellent ways of reducing the number of fluency-related miscues during oral reading. Some students, however, need a little more concentrated help or focus. The following corrective activities are presented to provide specific focus.

Decreasing Reversals

Description

During the act of reading, students may confuse and change the directions of letters (b–d, b–p, b–q) or individual words (was–saw, no–on) or the order of words in sentences (The rabbit *quickly hopped* away. The rabbit *hopped quickly* away.) These direction changes are called *reversals.*

Reversals may be caused by immaturity, inconsistent left-to-right eye movements, carelessness or inattention to details, or lack of attention to meaning.

If the reversals are caused by immaturity, the student will "outgrow" them. This usually occurs by age seven. On the other hand, if the reversals are the result of the other causes mentioned, the following might help.

Sometimes a reversal of the order of words in a sentence does not change the meaning of the selection. If the meaning is not changed, the reversal should be ignored.

Corrective Activities

1. **Developing chart stories.** Encourage your students to dictate stories to you. As you are writing their stories, emphasize the left-to-right movement in writing. Then, to further emphasize the left-to-right direction of reading, use a pointer as you and your students orally read the story.
2. **Color coding desk edges.** The left or beginning side of the student's desk should contain a green strip of tape. The right or ending side should contain a red strip of tape.
3. **Color coding wrists.** Have your students wear wrist bands. The left wrist or starting side should have a green band on it. The right wrist or stopping side should have a red band on it.
4. **Underlining.** Underline the first letter of the word with green (go) and the last letter with red (stop).
5. **Arrow coding words.** Place an arrow under the confused word. The arrow should be placed in the direction the word should be read.

was
→

6. **Tracing.** Help the student trace the unknown word or write it in the sand. The student should say the confused word, then say each letter as it is traced. Repeat the word when tracing is complete.

7. **Using markers.** The marker should be moved from left to right so that one letter of the confused word is shown at a time. (A marker can be made by cutting a piece of tagboard into a narrow strip.)
8. **Converting the capital B.** If students confuse the lowercase *b* and *d*, tell them to picture the capital *B*. Then erase the top loop, and they will have a lowercase *b*.

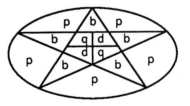

9. **Typing and computers.** Using typewriters and computers for writing can aid students with reversal problems.
10. **Providing letter-or-word exercises.** Provide letter-or-word exercises such as the following:

    Circle every *bad*.

    (bad) dad   dap (bad) pad   bab
    dad (bad) pap (bad) pad (bad)

11. **Providing designs of minimally contrasting letters.** Provide designs in which students color minimally contrasting letters different colors.

    Color the *b* spaces blue.
    Color the *d* spaces red.
    Color the *p* spaces yellow.
    Color the *q* spaces green.

12. **Reading lists of minimally contrasting letters.** Be sure to let students use a marker when this is being done.
    Read the following letters aloud:

    p b q d h d b g w d c b x

13. **Searching for letters.** Provide students with the opportunity to search for numbers and letters moving in a left-to-right direction.

Move from left to right. Circle the letters from *a* to *i* in order.

c (a) d g (b)(c) f g (d) h j
l (e) c (f) b e (g) i c f (h)(i)

14. **Sentence writing.** Students make displayed sentences by circling words in order from left to right.

Circle words to make the sentence you see. Move from left to right. Then circle the words in the order in which you see them. When you have finished, write the sentence.

Pat and Pap, the cats, sat on a mat.

Pam tap (Pat) an (and) pop pit pat (Pap)
(the) sat (cats) tap (sat) in son (on) tap (a)
nap tam (mat) tam pit pat Pap lap map

_____

- -

_____

Decreasing Omissions

Description

Omission miscues may be caused by nervousness, carelessness, trying to read too fast, reading materials that are too difficult, or simply because the student's eyes are ahead of his/her voice. This latter cause is apparent with students who are increasing their reading rate. Often the omission occurs because students do not know how to pronounce or decode the word, and they skip it. You can easily determine whether the cause is inadequate decoding skills by going back to the word after the student has finished reading the selection and asking the student to reread it.

Sometimes omissions do not change the meaning of a selection. If the omissions are infrequent and do not change the meaning, the omissions should be ignored.

Corrective Activities

1. **Tape-recording by teacher.** Let the student listen to a recording of omissions read by the teacher. Identify any omissions by circling them on a printed copy of the text being read.
2. **Choral reading.** Through choral reading, students do not feel singled out. They also have the fluency and accuracy of other students to help them along.

3. **Silent reading.** Allow students to study and read material silently before they are expected to read it aloud.
4. **Tape-recording.** Students can tape-record their oral reading. Then have them read a copy of the selection as they listen to the tape. They should circle each omitted word.
5. **Sentence writing.** Students re-create sentences by circling words in left-to-right order. Then the students write the sentences.

Directions:
Circle words to make the sentence you see. Move from left to right. Circle the words in order to make the sentence you see. Write the sentence you make.

The dog barked fiercely as it ran after the cat.
cat   box   the   dog   ran   baked   fire   barked   finely
fiercely   at   a   as   lin   it   nan   rat   ran   ate   after
a   the   tack   cat

_____

- -

_____

6. **Using markers.** Some students may need to use a marker in order to read along and not omit words.
7. **Questioning.** Ask students detail questions that require their careful attention to the written material.
8. **Repeated readings.** Permit students to read a short, meaningful passage several times until it is fluent and without miscues. You might want to pair your students for this activity, or the student might read to a classroom aide. (See "Major Fluency Strategies," Chapter 13.)
9. **Echo reading.** Read the selection to the student and let him/her follow along. Then have the student echo read a sentence or paragraph. The teacher or aide should read a sentence, and then the student immediately reads the same sentence. Next, the teacher and student choral read the entire selection. (See "Major Fluency Strategies," Chapter 13.)
10. **Speed.** Tell the student to slow down.

Decreasing Substitutions

Description

Essentially, substitutions fall into the following categories:

Similar configuration: similar meaning (*house* for *home*)
Dissimilar configuration: similar meaning (*house* for *cabin*)
Similar configuration: dissimilar meaning (*house* for *horse*)
Dissimilar configuration: dissimilar meaning (*house* for *ax*)

There are several reasons why students might substitute words with similar meanings. First, they may be putting printed words into their own spoken language, thus substituting words they would use daily. Second, students might be using their skills in prediction. Or students might visually recognize a word, know the word's meaning from appearance and context, but be unable to pronounce it.

Since substitution errors are common, attention should understandably concentrate on errors that change the meaning in the passage being read. The *house-*for*-horse* error indicates overreliance on configuration and breakdown of meaning in the sentence. The *house-*for*-ax* error shows little attention to either word analysis or contextual clues.

Corrective Activities

1. **Nonattention to substitution.** Do not draw attention to substitutions in which meaning is maintained.
2. **Discouraging interruption.** If a selection is to be read orally for whatever reason (and there should be a good reason), discourage any interruption by other pupils when mild substitutions occur. This will minimize breaking the train of thought. You might use the *shh* (index finger to the lip) sign to indicate that students should not interrupt the person who is reading.
3. **Tape-recording.** Use a tape recorder, perhaps set up in a learning center format. Have the student record the selection for playback. This will develop student awareness of errors that change the meaning of a passage.
4. **Rereading.** You may have to tell students to reread a sentence or paragraph if the substitution does not maintain meaning.
5. **Sentence completion.** Provide close-type sentences that students must complete with words that maintain meaning (such as "I ran rapidly across the _____ ").
6. **Listening for substitutions.** Direct students to listen for substitutions that do not make sense in sentences that you read aloud.
7. **Easier materials.** Since meaning is critical, consider adjusting instructional materials to an easier readability level, or at least a level in which the vocabulary (especially content area) won't be a problem.
8. **Neurological impress method.** Try a variation of the neurological impress method for students with pronounced tendencies to make meaning-related substitutions. Simply let your student read a selection aloud with you, but be sure that she/he can keep up with you. Adjust your pace. (See Chapter 28.)
9. **Reducing oral reading.** For circumstances in which meaning is not sacrificed, reduce the frequency of oral instructional reading. Eye movements precede the voice and may lead to saying equivalent or similar-meaning words.

10. **Read-along stories.** Try teacher-made or commercially prepared silent read-along stories. This is a great center-type activity involving a tape recorder, storybooks, and headsets.

11. **Emphasizing meaning.** In any case, encourage your students to read for meaning. Emphasize that reading is an active and not a passive process. Ask students questions such as "Does that make sense?" "Does what you just read mean something to us?"

12. **Using goal-oriented materials.** Since many students, especially boys, prefer goal-oriented selections, include reading selections calling for accurate interpretation of words. For example, instructions for the construction of a model or other articles of interest require step-by-step assembly.

13. **Choral reading.** Try some choral reading. This is especially popular with third graders.

14. **Checking sight word capability.** Check for adequate basic sight word capability. For example, you might want to administer the Fry's Instant Word List. (See Chapter 4 for word lists.)

15. **Word analysis testing.** Constant oral miscues with different meanings may indicate problems in word analysis. The student may not have the ability to attack words from either a phonic or structural analysis standpoint.

Decreasing Nonpronunciations

Description

Repeated requests for pronunciations may indicate an inadequate sight vocabulary, lack of appropriate instruction in word analysis, fear of taking a chance at decoding unknown words, or a teacher who tells students unknown words too quickly.

Corrective Activities

1. **Wait time.** If you tend to tell students unknown words immediately or very quickly, increase your wait time to five or more seconds. This will give students time to think about an unknown word and attempt to use their decoding skills.

2. **Reading the entire sentence.** Sometimes students stop at an unknown word. They do not look at the rest of the sentence and attempt to use context clues. Encourage students to read the entire sentence and identify words beginning with the same sound that would make sense.

3. **Rereading the previous sentence.** If finishing the sentence does not help, students can reread the previous sentence and the entire sentence in which the unknown word is found.

4. **Sandwiching sentences.** Suggest that students read the sentences occurring before and after the sentence containing the unknown word.

5. **Encouragement.** Some students are reluctant even to attempt any form of word attack because they lack confidence in their own decoding ability. If this appears to be a problem, encourage them by asking, "What word makes sense?"

6. **Using context to aid metacognition.**

   - Try identifying the initial sound before identifying the word. Then have students use this initial sound to identify a word that might fit the sentence.
   - Give students practice with cloze activities. Start by leaving one word out of a sentence and having students identify the missing word.

   Example: We patted the s____ into a round, cold ball.
   Next, give students short paragraphs with omitted words. Then have them discuss which words belong in the blanks. Be certain you discuss the reasons why the specific words fit each blank.

7. **Successful experiences.** Be certain to give students much easy (independent-level) material so they will be able to read without worrying about unknown words.

8. **Partner reading.** An adult or older student might read one page aloud as the student follows along. This will provide an opportunity for the student to identify unknown words ahead of time. Then let the student take a turn reading the following page or paragraph. (Remember, the student should have read this selection silently prior to oral reading.)

9. **Identifying familiar word parts.** Your students can identify familiar word parts, thus moving from the known to the unknown in the word. For example, in a polysyllabic word students might identify already known prefixes, suffixes, and root words.

10. **Phonograms.** Encourage recognition of phonograms generally consistent in pronunciation between word parts. These combinations of letters can be used to build words. (See Appendix C.)

    Examples:

    ed is a phonogram. Have students identify words they can make from this phonogram *(bed, red, fed).*

    it is a phonogram. What words can students make from this phonogram? *(sit, fit, hit).*

11. **Card file or word bank.** Have students keep a card file of words they have unlocked.

Decreasing Repetitions

Description

Repetitions are common phenomena in reading and serve as a time during which readers develop understandings or try to decode a word or thought. Students may be using repetitions as a way to aid or increase their comprehension. Repetitions may also be a delay tactic as students try to decode the following word. Nervousness and tension may cause an increase in the frequency of repetitions, and an increase in repetitions may be noticed as the difficulty of reading passages is increased.

Repetitions are desirable if students recognize their lack of comprehension and reread or repeat words or sentences to increase understanding. If the material is too difficult, or students do not have adequate decoding skills, adjustments in reading material and remediation are appropriate.

Corrective Activities

1. **Visual defects.** Check for the possibility of visual defects.
2. **Creating awareness.** The student may not be aware of these repetitions. Awareness can be created by having the student read into a tape recorder for playback.
3. **Graphing.** Encourage students to practice reading silently until they think they can read the selection without error or repetitions. Then graph the number of repetitions that were made. The students' goal is to have the number of repetitions decrease to zero.
4. **Developing a good sight vocabulary.** Language-experience stories are an excellent format for developing sight vocabulary. See Chapter 30 for specifics on language experience.
5. **Follow-alongs.** Let students follow along as you read a selection orally to them.
6. **Read-along materials.** Select popular trade read-along materials (see Appendix H) that use cassette recorders and headsets. Students read along with the tapes. They can finger point to verify eye contact with each spoken word on the tape.
7. **Providing easy material.** Check to be sure that the reading material is not too difficult. Give the student easy (independent level) material to provide more success in fluency. The number of repetitions should decrease if the student knows the words and understands the material.
8. **Choral reading.** Reading along with other students or the teacher helps eliminate repetitions.
9. **Marking phrasing.** Mark the correct phrasing of sentences and paragraphs that have been written on cards. Have the student read these materials using the marked phrasing.
10. **Machines.** Machines such as computers and the Controlled Reader can be used to emphasize left-to-right directionality and prevent the student from looking back.
11. **Markers.** Sometimes students have trouble reading words above and below the line in addition to repeating words. If this happens, give the student an index card (3 by 5 in.) with a center window cut to the size of one word. Then increase the size of the window to a phrase and then an

entire line. Move on to a straight-line card, having the student move from top to bottom on the page. Finally, progress to no card.

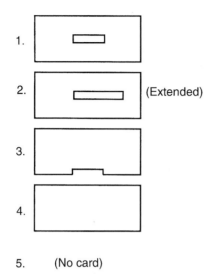

1.

2. (Extended)

3.

4.

5.   (No card)

12. **Silent reading before oral.** Remember to let students read everything silently before orally.

Decreasing Insertions

Description

Insertions or additions may be caused by the reader attempting to embellish the passage being read. (Sometimes this embellishment actually improves the author's story!) The student may be anticipating what comes next. Again, as with other miscues, focus attention on insertions that change the selection's meaning. Sometimes these occur at the end of words, changing the tense or number. Insertions may also appear when the reader is trying to correct another error. Usually insertions are minor miscues.

Corrective Activities

1. **Bringing insertion to attention.** Since we are attempting to get the student to focus on what she/he is saying, bring the insertion to the student's attention by saying, "Now, does that (word) make sense to you?" Do this only if the insertion changes the meaning.
2. **Easier material.** Give your students easier material to read.

3. **Silent reading or rehearsal.** Provide opportunities for students to read the selection silently before any oral reading is done.
4. **Finger pointing.** If the student makes many insertions, pointing to each word may help to reduce the insertions.
5. **Teaching basic sight words.** Are the insertions common sight words, such as those on the Fry Instant Word List? You may need to begin teaching these so-called glue words that hold sentences together.
6. **Modified cloze.** Cover or omit key words in a given selection and have students supply the missing words or closures.
7. **Following directions.** Give written directions for students to follow and carry out.
8. **Neurological impress method.** Ask the student to read along with you.
9. **Decreasing oral reading.** Decrease the frequency of oral reading. Encourage careful silent reading. You can't drive 65 mph in a 15-mph zone. There are different rates for different types of reading.
10. **Reviewing punctuation.** With insertions involving "new" punctuation, emphasize that the sentence's meaning is influenced by punctuation. You may want to review common punctuation marks and their meaning with your students.
11. **Decreasing speed.** Encourage your students to read with care or slow down when insertions begin occurring frequently.

Decreasing Faulty Habits

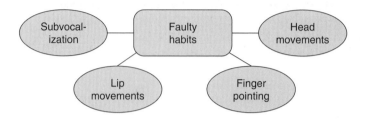

Description

Faulty habits are symptoms of reading problems that may interfere with fluency, reading rate, and comprehension.

> **Faulty habits** . . . symptoms of reading problems that may interfere with reading rate and comprehension.
>
> **Finger pointing** . . . use of a finger (usually the index finger) to keep place while reading either silently or orally. Pointing serves as a bond between the eye and the printed word(s).
>
> **Head movements** . . . unnecessary side-to-side movement of the head for students with no physical problems in using both eyes.
>
> **Subvocalization and lip movements** . . . whispering or mumbling of words. The physical movement of the lips may or may not be apparent during subvocalization.

Subvocalization and Lip Movements

Description

Subvocalization tends to be very common during the early stages of reading in grades one through three. It is often the result of students trying to decode words through the use of phonics. Sometimes subvocalization is used as a means of attending to meaning. Reading material that is too difficult also is another cause of subvocalization. If comprehension and decoding skills are good but speed is slow, subvocalization should be corrected. If, however, the subvocalization serves as an aid to comprehension, it should not be corrected immediately.

Corrective Activities

1. **Using a pencil.** Students can hold a pencil between their lips as a reminder not to subvocalize or move their lips. If students move their lips, the pencil will fall out.
2. **Gum chewing.** If students chew gum while their mouths are closed, subvocalization and lip movements become difficult. Be sure to set up rules for the gum chewing if you use this technique.
3. **Finger on lips.** Urge students to place their index fingers on their lips; it will remind them to keep from subvocalizing. This is similar to what teachers do when they want their students to be quiet.
4. **Index card.** An index card may be held lightly against the lips in the same way the index finger is used. It again reminds students of the quiet sound.
5. **Buddy system.** Students may be paired with each other for the purpose of reminding each other if they are subvocalizing during silent reading.
6. **Easy materials.** Give students a lot of easy-to-read books at their independent levels. If stories are easy to read, there will be less need to subvocalize.
7. **Phrase cards.** Encourage students to read in phrases rather than reading individual words. This can be done by using phrase cards.
8. **Marked phrases.** Mark passages in such a way that students know what groups of words to read together. This can be done by color coding or by using slashes (//) between phrases.
9. **Mechanical devices.** Mechanical devices (e.g., computers and Controlled Reader) can be used that force students to move their eyes ahead quickly. Time for subvocalization can thus be decreased.
10. **Tape recorder.** You might place a tape recorder near the student to pick up subvocalizing. This can then be played back to the student to create an awareness of the subvocalizing.
11. **Sight vocabulary development.** Provide many opportunities for the development of a large sight vocabulary. The more words are known by sight, the less the need for subvocalization. See Unit III on vocabulary.

Finger Pointing

Description

Finger pointing is normal for a beginning reader. Discouraging finger pointing can be more harmful than helpful, especially for a beginner. Finger pointing is actually recommended in speed-reading courses. Before remediation of pointing, determine if there is a present need for it. This need may be to prevent repetitions or reversals or simply to keep place when the type is small and the space is narrow between the lines on the page. If the student has difficulty with the return sweep to the next line, you may actually suggest the use of finger pointing as a temporary aid. Finger pointing also may be the symptom of a visual problem. It is a good idea to check vision carefully.

Corrective Activities

1. **Continuous hand movements.** If you have determined that pointing is needed, encourage students to use a continual hand movement from left to right, avoiding the stop–start–stop pointing that may occur. Consistent movement in this manner should also help correct reversal problems and repetitions. Remember, this is a temporary technique that should be discarded when no longer necessary.
2. **Line marker.** Use of a line marker may be of benefit. Move the marker from the top of the page down, thus covering up what has already been read.
3. **Transparent marker.** Cut out a marker (2 by 4 in.) from a transparency. Using a fine-point, permanent magic marker, draw a line across the middle of the long part. Students can now see the lines above and below, but they have the security of a line placement.

Head Movements

Corrective Activities

1. **Cupping hands.** Students can rest their chin in a V formed by their hands, with their elbows being used as a support. This V can be used as a vise to keep the head from moving.
2. **Videotaping.** Students may be unaware of these head movements. Videotaping can create an awareness.
3. **Easy materials.** Consider moving students to easier, independent-level reading materials.
4. **Telling the student.** Sometimes students are unaware of their head movements. Sometimes just telling the student about the movement is enough to make him/her aware.

Text Comprehension

Unit Introduction

Comprehension . . . comes from interacting with the text and constructing or attaching meaning to the printed symbols. The main purpose of reading is to understand or comprehend the communication between the author and the author's audience. Fluency in reading is one major step that allows students to focus on comprehension. Fluency, however, does not ensure comprehension. Students may verbalize the words but not understand the author's message. The following map presents the major categories of comprehension teaching discussed in this unit.

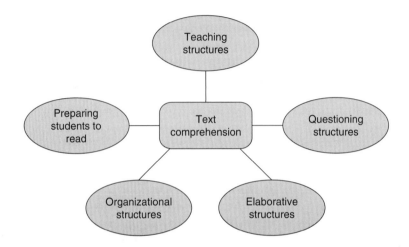

The lack of comprehension may be the result of many factors. The reading material may be too difficult (too many long words, sentences that are too complex, sentences that may be too long, too many concepts outside the students' background of experiences). It may be dull or uninteresting. Students often have difficulty reading informational texts because of the high density of concepts and abstract ideas presented, "ideas, facts, and principles related to the physical, biological, or social world" (Fountas & Pinnell, 2005, p. 399).

Poor comprehension may also be the result of the students not having the necessary background or schema for reading a selection. Students may over rely on decoding skills and view reading as a word-calling process. Students may have had an instructional emphasis on oral reading during which they concentrated on decoding and not meaning. Students may read too slowly and therefore be unable to chunk enough information together at a time to create meaning. The students may not know or understand that comprehension is the major purpose for reading and therefore may read without a purpose. Students may not concentrate on or attend to the reading task. Previous instruction may have concentrated on getting facts and not on higher levels of comprehension. Or students may not be interested in reading or the subject they are reading about.

We wish to make several recommendations before you use any comprehension strategy or activity with your students. First, explain to your students the skill that you are going to practice. Second, we recommend that you work with oral activities before proceeding to written activities. Third, be sure you relay your thought processes to your students. By this we mean that you should explain why you have answered a question in a specific manner. By doing this you are modeling thought processes. Fourth, be certain to have students explain the reasoning behind their answers. Sometimes students can understand each other's explanations better than an adult's. Finally, resist merely using paper-and-pencil activities that will do little more than test. When using paper-and-pencil activities, give students the opportunity to explain the reasons behind their answers.

The *National Reading Panel Report* (2000) highlights a concern about reading instruction in classrooms. Rather than engaging in explicit instruction, teachers seem to "mention" skills to students and "assign" practice exercises. The panel further reports that comprehension monitoring, cooperative learning, graphic organizers, story structure (who, what, when, where, why, how), question answering, question generating, summarization, and other combination strategies are effective in teaching comprehension. These strategies that were highlighted can be incorporated into the teaching of organizational structures (main idea, sequence, and so on) and used in writing narrative and expository text.

After an extensive summary of research on comprehension, Pressley (2000) wrote that comprehension is not isolated; it is multidimensional. Pressley recommends teaching decoding skills, developing sight words, teaching the use of semantic context cues, teaching vocabulary, encouraging extensive reading, encouraging students to ask themselves "why" questions about the text, and teaching students to use comprehension strategies.

In another extensive review of research on comprehension, Duke and Pearson (2002) wrote that approaches to teaching informational text structure are quite varied and range from the use of graphic organizers (such as concept maps, charts, and graphs) to summaries. The researchers concluded "almost any approach to teaching the structure of informational text improves both comprehension and recall of key text information" (p. 217). They also concluded that research supports the use of comprehension strategies that teach readers to make predictions, activate prior knowledge, think aloud, use text structure, use visual displays of text (e.g., diagrams, flow charts, semantic maps), summarize, and generate and respond to questions.

Preparing Students to Read

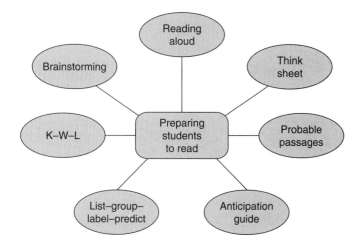

Preparational Strategies

Description

As Tompkins (2003) writes, the reading process begins before a student picks up a book. Readers, or teachers guiding readers, help them activate prior knowledge, set purposes for reading, preview, and predict. Learning is more effective if students already know something about the topic. Linking new information to prior knowledge is a means of helping students develop a purpose and activate curiosity and interest in a topic.

These preparational strategies are used in various teaching structures:

1. **Activating prior knowledge.** Connections are made to the actual or vicarious experiences of students prior to reading. The teacher might bring in realia, show a video or CD on the topic, read a section on the topic aloud, or have students brainstorm what they know and place it into a semantic or concept map. Students who are interested in a topic will have more in-depth knowledge than those who do not have an interest.

2. **Setting purposes.** The two main purposes of reading are to read efferently (to obtain information) and aesthetically (for pleasure or enjoyment). Purpose setting can be directed by the teacher or students. Gradually, students set their own purposes for reading. Will students be reading to create a semantic feature analysis map, a story map, or a Venn diagram? Or to confirm or reject their predictions?
3. **Previewing.** Students look at the title, pictures, section headings, and subheadings. They may read an introduction to get an overview of the selection. During previewing students gain insight into what the selection is about.
4. **Predicting.** Predicting helps students establish a purpose for reading. This begins in the very early emergent literacy stage by having students look at pictures and guess what is going to happen. As students predict, write their predictions on the board. Survey the number of students who agree with each prediction. After reading, identify which predictions are correct.

Students with reading difficulties often just want to "read and get it over with." They don't take time to think about what they already know and how it relates to reading assignments. Strategies that prepare students for reading help them activate prior knowledge and set purposes for reading.

Read alouds are an appropriate prereading activity because they can help activate prior knowledge, scaffold learning, build background, create interest, increase vocabulary, help students gain information about a wide variety of subjects, and help develop listening and comprehension skills.

The following strategies are appropriate to use during the preparational stage:

Anticipation guide . . . this strategy was used and described by Herber (1978). It involves presenting students with a list of four to ten short statements related to a topic. Students agree or disagree with the statements, then read to determine the author's position on the statements. Students activate prior knowledge and make predictions.

Brainstorming . . . goes back to Osborn in the late 1930s, more recently Osborn (1953). It is a group technique (but can be used individually) to generate a large number of ideas. Students can recognize that they already know information by brainstorming what they know about a topic and by calling out associations or ideas they think are connected with the topic.

K–W–L . . . before reading, students list what they already think they know about a topic (K), then list what they would like to know (W) about the topic, and after reading list what they have learned (L) about the topic (Ogle 1986). The K stage helps students activate prior knowledge, the W stage helps students establish a purpose or purposes for reading, and in the L stage students compare what they thought they knew with the information they gained from their reading, listening, and viewing.

Text Comprehension

List–group–label–predict . . . list–group–label was developed by Taba (1967) and is a basis for a follow-up of the K–W–L strategy. Students think about words related to a topic or major concept and discuss the possible relationships that exist between the words and topic. The "predict" step is added to help students establish a purpose for reading.

Probable passages . . . Beers (2003) uses probable passages to activate prior knowledge. The teacher chooses seven to fifteen terms from the selection students will read. Students categorize these words and then create a "probable" statement or statements that predict what the selection is about.

Read alouds . . . planned oral reading providing a listening experience related to narrative or expository text in which the listener hears fluent reading, gains information, listens for enjoyment, and develops background knowledge.

Think sheet . . . a strategy developed by Clewell and Heldemos (1983) to help students identify the author's organizational pattern and to predict content.

Explicit Instruction: Brainstorming

1. Identify or set the problem for students. For example, what do we already know about Benjamin Franklin?
2. Ask the student(s) to generate (brainstorm) as many ideas as they can (e.g. about Franklin).
3. Focus on the quantity of ideas being generated. Do not criticize. Welcome unusual ideas.
4. If no ideas come forth from the student or group, suggest an idea or two to get people thinking.
5. Encourage the student(s) to elaborate on the idea. (Benjamin Franklin was an inventor. Elaborate: What did he invent? What personality characteristics do you think Franklin had to be an inventor?)
6. When the time is up, categorize ideas. If working individually or in small groups, ideas can be placed on sticky notes and moved around for organization.
7. Put the ideas on a categorized word wall.
8. These ideas serve to activate background knowledge and can be used to set a purpose for reading.

Explicit Instruction: K–W–L

The K–W–L strategy was designed to overcome some of the shortcomings of the DRA and allow students to work more independently with expository text. Students identify what they *know* (K), what they *want* to learn (W), and what they *learned* (L). Three columns are used to structure this activity.

(K) Know	(W) Want to Learn	(L) Learned

1. Identify what students *know* (K). During this stage students brainstorm what they know about a topic. Keep a visible list of information students generate. Using this list, categorize and label the information with students. (Encourage students to identify their own categories and labels.) Identify which information students know is correct and which information they are unsure about or may disagree over.
2. Assist students in deciding what they *want* to learn (W). Guide students in formulating questions to which they would like to know the answers based on gaps in knowledge or uncertainties in step one. Direct students toward important questions that may not have come up through discussion. Use these questions to set purposes for reading.
3. Determine what students have *learned* (L). After reading, discuss the answers to the questions generated in step two. Then have students write what they have learned into the columns. Unanswered questions or new questions that arise after reading can be used as a basis for further reading or research.

Explicit Instruction: List–Group–Label–Predict

List–group–label–predict is related to brainstorming.

1. Identify a topic, word, or experience (film, CD, experiment, and so on) and present it to your students.
2. Brainstorm by asking your students what words are related to the topic. Write students' responses on the board (or have students write their responses on sticky notes). Try to limit this to about twenty-five to thirty words.
3. Read through the list of words with students.
4. Ask students if any of the words or items belong together. Have students identify their basis for categorizing words.
5. Encourage students to identify and verbalize their reasons for selecting these categories.
6. Let students discuss and rationalize their groupings and reasoning with the rest of the class.
7. Have students make predictions by writing several questions they think the selection will answer.

Explicit Instruction: Anticipation Guide

1. Select a text or reading selection.
2. Write four to ten statements based upon the selection. Some statements should be supported with evidence from the text. A couple should *not* be supported by the text. At least one statement should be answered without reading the text.
3. Before reading the text, give the student(s) a copy of the anticipation guide. Have students complete the guide prior to reading the text. Have students do this individually and then with a partner or in a small group.
4. Have students discuss their answers to questions on the anticipation guides prior to reading the selection. They should give reasons for their answers.
5. Have students read the text. During this step they should write down ideas that support or refute their first reactions to the statements.
6. Have a class discussion after reading. Refer back to the statements—did students agree or disagree with them? Did the author agree or disagree with them? Have their positions changed?

Anticipation Guide: What Do You Know About Hummingbirds?

Directions: Before reading and studying about hummingbirds, read the statements below. Put a + in the "Before I read" column if you agree with the statement or think it is true. Put a 0 in the column if you disagree with the statement or think it is false. Be prepared to give reasons for your answers. You will answer these again after you have read the lesson.

Before I read	Do you agree or disagree with the statement?	After I read
	1. People do not wish to attract hummingbirds.	
	2. Hummingbirds flap their wings slowly.	
	3. Some hummingbirds weigh less than two dimes.	
	4. Hummingbirds drink gallons of water.	
	5. Banding hummingbirds should be stopped.	
	6. Hummingbirds fly in groups of 100 at a time.	
	7. It is impossible for hummingbirds to fly 500 miles non-stop.	
	8. The Ruby-throated hummingbird is the only known species of hummingbird.	
	9. The smallest hummingbird is 3½ inches long.	
	10. A good title for a book would be, *H is for Hummingbird.*	

After reading: Answer the "After I read" column of your anticipation guide. Use the section of the guide below. Identify information that supports or refutes your before reading reaction. What did the author write that supports or was different from what you thought? Where did you find this information?

Question number	Page on which I read the information	Information I read that supports or refutes my reaction
1.		
2.		
3.		
4.		
5.		
6.		
7.		
8.		
9.		
10.		

Explicit Instruction: Probable Passages

1. Identify words and phrases. After reading the selection, identify seven to fifteen key words and phrases from the selection.
2. Create a list of these words and phrases for students and distribute it to students.
3. Review the words with the students. Pronounce them and discuss their meanings.
4. Have students categorize words (e.g. characters, settings, actions; characters, setting, problem, outcomes; who, what, when, where, why).
5. After students have categorized the words, have them make a prediction about the narrative or expository text.
6. After reading the selection with students, have them compare their prediction with the selection read. Have students rewrite their prediction to make it an accurate statement.

Probable Passage

Directions: In the box below, you will find words from *Because of Winn-Dixie*. First, write the words into the categories in which they belong. Then, using the words you categorized, write your prediction of the story.

lonely	Winn-Dixie	grocery store	Opal
Naomi, FL	errand	father	preacher
friends	Otis	lost	dog
Miss Fanny	run away	Gloria Dump	

Characters   **_Setting_**   **_Actions_**

Problem   **_Outcome_**

My prediction of the story: _____

_____

_____

Explicit Instruction: Think Sheet

1. Identify a chapter or other reading selection.
2. Organize headings and subheadings. List the headings and subheadings in boldface print. Leave space between each heading or subheading for student writing.
3. Have students predict what information might be included under each subheading. Have students write this information in the spaces provided.
4. Read and confirm. Students read the chapter and determine which predictions were supported by information in the chapter.
5. Students revise their original predictions.

Guidelines for Read Alouds

1. Select a book related to the theme, concept, or information you are teaching.
2. Locate the part of the book or selection that is appropriate for reading aloud. Picture books are excellent sources for read alouds.
3. Mark points to stop and ask questions.
4. Practice reading the book or selection aloud.

5. Identify the title, author, and illustrator. If there is a picture on the front cover, look at the picture.
6. Predict what the book might be about. Ask students what they think might happen or what they might find out in the story.
7. Read the selection or book aloud to students using expression.
8. Show the pictures to students as you are reading the book.
9. Questions should be asked at selected parts of the story to keep students involved.
10. Use wait time. After you have read the selection, wait a few minutes before you begin discussion. Were students' predictions correct? What did they learn? What did they think of the book?

Picture Books for Read Alouds

Alphabet with Content

Cassie, B., and J. Pallotta. *The Butterfly Alphabet Book.* Charlesbridge, 1995.

Herzog, B. *T Is for Touchdown: A Football Alphabet Book.* Chelsea, MI: Sleeping Bear Press, 2004.

Pallotta, J. *The Underwater Alphabet Book.* Charlesbridge, 1991.

Scillian D., and D. Scillian. *A Is for America: An American Alphabet Book.* Chelsea, MI: Sleeping Bear Press, 2001.

Ulmer, M. *H Is for Horse: An Equestrian Alphabet.* Chelsea, MI: Sleeping Bear Press, 2004.

———. *J Is for Jumpshot: A Basketball Alphabet.* Chelsea, MI: Sleeping Bear Press, 2005.

Biographies & Journals

Burleigh, R. *Flight.* Putnam Juvenile, 1991.

Coles, R. *The Story of Ruby Bridges.* Scholastic, 2004.

Ehrlich, A. *Rachel: The Story of Rachel Carson.* Harcourt Trade, 2003.

Monroe, M. A. *Turtle Summer: A Journal for My Daughter.* Sylvan Dell, 2007.

Stanley, D. *Bard of Avon: The Story of William Shakespeare.* HarperTrophy, 1997.

———. *Cleopatra.* HarperTrophy, 1997.

Social Studies

Bunting, E. *A Day's Work.* Clarion Books, 1997.

———. *A Smokey Night.* Clarion Books, 1994.

———. *The Wall.* Clarion Books, 1992.

Say, A. *Grandfather's Journey.* Hougton Mifflin/Walter Lorraine, 1993.

Schotter, R. *Nothing Ever Happens on 90th Street.* Scholastic, 1999.

Thomson, S. *Stars and Stripes: The Story of the American Flag.* Harper-Collins, 2003.

Mathematics

Burns, M., and S. Hoff. *The Greedy Triangle.* Scholastic Press, 1995.

Crane, C. *Round Up: A Texas Number Book.* Sleeping Bear Press, 2003.

Neuschwander, C. *Sir Cumference and the Great King of Angleland.* Charlesbridge, 2001.

Pappas, T. *Fractals, Googols, and Other Mathematical Tales.* Wide World Publishing, 1993.

Scieszka, J. *Math Curse.* Viking Juvenile, 2007.

Tang, G. *Math Fables: Lessons That Count.* Scholastic Press, 2004.

Williams, R. L. *The Coin Counting Book.* Charlesbridge, 2001.

Science

Arnosky, J. *Following the Coast.* HarperCollins, 2004.

Cole, H. *On the Way to the Beach.* Greenwillow, 2003.

Collard, S. B. *Beaks.* Cambridge Publishing, 2002.

———. *Deep-Sea Floor.* Cambridge Publishing, 2003.

Davies, N. *Ice Bear: In the Steps of the Polar Bear.* Candlewick, 2005.

Dewey, J. O. *Paisano, the Roadrunner.* Millbrook, 2002.

DuQuette, K. *They Call Me Woolly: What Animal Names Can Tell Us.* G. P. Putnam's Sons, 2002.

Gibbons, G. *Giant Pandas.* Holiday House, 2002.

Micucci, C. *Life and Times of the Ant.* Hougton Mifflin, 2006.

Miller, D. S. *Arctic Lights, Arctic Nights.* Walker and Company, 2003.

Reed-Jones, C. *Salmon Stream.* Dawn Publications, 2002.

Organizational Structures

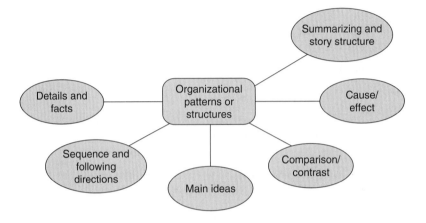

Description

Organizational structure provides the framework of skills used to comprehend narrative and expository texts. Researchers have identified that students' awareness of text structure or organizational structure positively affects comprehension. Geva (1983) found that instruction in identifying text structure improved the comprehension of less skilled readers. The use of organizational patterns of text aids in recall (Meyer, Brandt, and Bluth 1980). These structures should be expanded from use with narrative to expository or informational texts.

Comparison/contrast . . . the identification of likenesses and differences among objects, plots or events, characters or people, and settings or places. Words that cue comparison include *as well as, but, but also, by contrast, conversely, even though, in spite of,* and *on the other hand.*

Cause/effect . . . the interrelationships among different events, reasons, motives, feelings, or actions; anything that creates a result voluntarily or involuntarily.

Details or facts . . . the small or specific parts of a selection.

Listing . . . a random organization of facts. The order is not important.

Main idea . . . the central thought or meaning of a passage or selection; the major topic of a passage or selection.

Sequence and following directions . . . a connection, stated or implied, of successive ordered sets of ideas or events. Order is important.

Shared reading . . . developed by Holdaway (1982), this is like a read-aloud except that the students see a copy of the selection that is being read aloud by the teacher. Students follow along as the teacher or reader engages in oral reading.

Summarizing and story structure . . . describing a happening or event, or retelling a story in a succinct manner.

Guidelines for Shared Reading

Shared reading is a strategy that can be utilized to encourage the integration of comprehension and organizational skills with expository or narrative text. Shared reading helps scaffold learning, and is a springboard to discussing and identifying different organizational patterns in printed materials.

1. Select a book related to the theme, concept and organizational skill you are teaching.
2. Locate the part of the book or selection that is appropriate for reading aloud and is an example of the organizational patterns we are teaching. This may only be a passage but could also be a picture book.
3. Mark points to stop and ask questions.
4. Practice reading the book or selection aloud.
5. Identify the title, author, and illustrator. If there is a picture on the front cover, look at the picture.
6. Predict what the book or selection might be about. Ask students what they think might happen or what they might find out in the story or expository writing.
7. Read the entire selection or book aloud to students using expression. Do not stop often and interrupt the content. Go back and ask questions after you have read the selection.
8. Students follow along as you are reading. They may follow along with their own text copies (or electronic versions could be shown with computer technology).
9. Show the questions to the students using an overhead projector or having them written on paper.
10. Ask questions which require students to identify the organizational pattern (or use other comprehension skills) and make connections to the literature.
11. Reread parts that answer these questions.
12. Use wait time. After you have read the selection, wait a few minutes before you begin discussion. What organizational patterns did we identify? What did we learn?

Details and Listing

Explicit Instruction: Using a Picture to View and Remember

1. Locate a picture from your picture file or one from a children's book. Make sure that the picture has good details.
2. Tell students that you are going to show them a picture and you would like them to look at it very carefully and try to remember everything they can about the picture. They are going to look for details.
3. Show students the picture for a couple of minutes.
4. When the time is up, have students brainstorm everything they remembered about the picture. List their remembrances on the board or chart paper.
5. Stop and allow time to reiterate why the details are important. ("Big, brown, white, and fast are good details because they tell us about Nag the dog." "Calm, serene, blue, and warm are good details about the ocean.")
6. Congratulate students on all the details they remember about the picture.
7. You might use a semantic map and group the details under different categories.

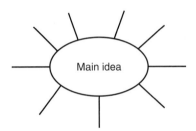

8. Have students write a sentence or two including details from the picture.
9. Once students understand locating details in pictures, have them move on to remembering details in short paragraphs, chapters, and then books.

Explicit Instruction: Using an Easy Book to Listen and Remember

1. Select a children's book (such as Stickland's *Ten Terrible Dinosaurs*).
2. Tell students that they are going to be looking for details.
3. Have students look at the cover after reading the title to them.
4. After looking at the cover, ask students what details they think they will find in the book. (Remind students what details are.)
5. Tell students to listen to the story to remember as many details as possible.
6. Read the story aloud to students.
7. After reading the story, have students recall as many details as they can. Ask students to tell you everything they remember about the story.

8. Make a list of students' remembrances on the board.
9. Comment on all the details they remember about the story.
10. Group or categorize their remembrances (about characters, about setting, about events, etc.) This can be done using a semantic map or just by listing items under appropriate category headings.
11. Have students write a sentence or two including details from the story.
12. Encourage students to read additional books and identify details.

Explicit Instruction: Read and Remember

1. Select a children's book (such as Eve Bunting's *Fly Away Home,* a book about a boy and his dad who live at the airport).
2. Tell students that they are going to be reading for details.
3. Read the title, author, and illustrator to the students.
4. Have students look at the cover. Ask them what details they think they will find in the book. (Remind students what details are.) Make a list of their predictions on the board.
5. Have the students read the story silently to remember everything they can.
6. Without looking back at the book, have students individually make a list of their remembrances on the "Things I Remembered" organizer.

Things I Remembered

Name: _____   Book: _____

Details I Remembered:

_____

_____

_____

_____

_____

My sentences that include details about the story:

_____

_____

_____

7. Have students share their remembrances.
8. Make a list of students' remembrances on the board.
9. Comment on all the details they remembered about the story.
10. Group or categorize their remembrances (about characters, setting, events, etc.).
11. Have students write several sentences that include details about the story.

Explicit Instruction: Five-step Procedure (Herber and Nelson 1975)

1. Tell students that you are going to have them locate facts or details in a selection. (Move from a sentence to a paragraph and on to short selections.)
2. Ask students a question. Tell them the answer. Tell them on what page the answer is located. Then have the students locate the answer.
3. Ask students a question. Do not tell them the answer. Tell them on what page the answer can be found. Then have students locate the answer.
4. Ask students a question. Do not tell them the answer. Do not tell them the location of the answer. Have them locate the answer.
5. Ask students a question. Students must find the answers on their own.

Reinforcement Activities

1. **Oral picture description.** Select a picture containing details students will be able to identify. Explain to students that you are going to have them look at the picture and tell you as many things as possible about it. Guide students in looking at a picture and describing the details they see. Be certain to inform students that they should focus on telling you the details.
2. **Scene drawing.** Tell students that you are going to have them listen to some details and then draw a picture of what you have described. Using details, describe a scene or picture to the students. Allow your students to draw pictures of the scene you described.
3. **Categorizing.** Inform your students that you are going to show them a topic. (Write the topic in capital letters on the board or a transparency.) Then urge students to tell you what they know about the topic. Tell students that you are listing the details or facts they are telling you. Then ask students specific factual questions about the details they gave you.

   Example:
   BEES
   > Live and work in groups
   > Have one queen bee
   > Live in homes called hives
   > Workers search for food
   > How many bees are in a colony?
   > What are bees' homes called?
   > What job do workers do?

   Other possible topics might include fire drills, pets, fruits, or baseball. Be sure to use topics familiar to your students.
4. **Matching details to the main topic.** Provide a main topic and list details below it. The students must identify the details that are essential to develop the main idea or topic.

Example:

GOING ON A LONG TRIP
    Using a map
    Determining mileage
    Having a safety check of the car
    Reserving a motel room

5. **Reading selection and answering questions.** Direct the students to read a selection; then ask a specific question that requires a specific answer. Be sure to discuss how the students arrived at these answers.

Example:

John took out his shopping list. He went down aisle 1 and picked up lettuce, tomatoes, and cucumbers. While going down aisle 4, he put paper towels, aluminum foil, and facial tissues into the cart. While going down aisle 5, he put cans of beans, peas, corn, and soup into his cart.

- List the items John picked up from aisle 4.
- List all the items that John can eat.

6. **Sentences and the 5 Ws.** Lead students to read sentences in which they must answer *who, what, when, where,* and *why* questions. Remember, these *W*s must be specifically stated.

Example:

Mary threw the ball across the field.

- Who threw the ball?
- Where was the ball thrown?

7. **Using the newspaper.** Using newspaper articles, guide students to identify the five *W*s *(who, what, when, where, why)* and *H (how).*
8. **Five Ws and H chart.** Tell students to read sentences or articles and complete the five *W*s and *H* chart.

	Who	What	When	Where	Why	How
1.						
2.						
3.						
4.						
5.						

9. **Sports articles.** Try having students read a baseball article and cut and paste words to complete the following sentences:

_____ pitched for the home team.

_____ pitched for the visiting team.

_____ was the manager for the winning team.

_____ (name of player) had the most hits.

_____ was the losing pitcher.

_____ was the winning pitcher.

The final score was _____.

10. **Sports charts.** Using sports stories, keep a chart of football games.

Team Names	Date	Final Score	Yards Rushed	Yards Passed	Winning Quarterback	Losing Quarterback
Home						
Visiting						
Home						
Visiting						

11. **Watching the weather.** Using weather information, complete the following charts.

Example 1:

High–Low Temperature of Cities

Date		City	Temperature
Sept.12	High	Thermal, CA	117
	Low	Pinedale, WY	25
	High		
	Low		

Example 2:

Our City's High–Low Temperatures

Date	High Temperature	Low Temperature

12. **Story mapping.** Develop student-made maps that identify the characters, setting, and story plot. A map is a series of geometric shapes connected to a central shape by spokes. Details emanate from the geometric shapes.

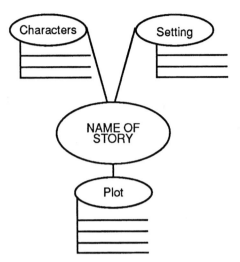

13. **Feature-analysis chart.** A feature-analysis chart is a means by which students may check off the characteristics or properties of specified elements. Place a plus sign (+) if the feature is present and a minus sign (−) if the feature is absent.

Families of the Orchestra
Features

Elements	String	Woodwinds	Percussion	Brass	Keyboard
Chimes	−	−	+	−	−
Viola	+	−	−	−	−
Flute	−	+	−	−	−
French horn	−	−	−	+	−
Harpsichord	−	−	−	−	+
Castanets	−	−	+	−	−
Organ	−	−	−	−	+
Piano	?	−	−	−	+
Guiro	?	?	?	?	?
Double bass	?	?	?	?	?

14. **Detail spinner.** Provide a game board on which students may move pieces around; a spinner with *Who, What, When, Where;* and a series of

story cards containing questions about stories they have read. (Example: Who found Goldilocks?) Students select the story card, twirl the spinner to find out which *W* question they will answer, and move around the board if the question is answered correctly.

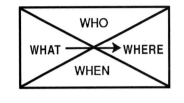 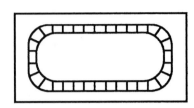

15. **Reading and drawing.** Give students a description of a scene and have them read it. Then direct students to draw a picture of the scene with as many details as they can remember.

16. **Using reference books.** Reference books give many specific details. Provide students with articles from reference books such as the encyclopedia, then have them answer factual questions distributed to them.

17. **Making up questions.** After reading a selection, give students the answers to detail questions, then have them make up their own questions.

18. **Newspaper comparisons.** Collect several different newspapers for the same day. Then compare the front-page lead stories.

Example:

	Paper 1	**Paper 2**	**Paper 3**
About whom is the article written?			
Where does the story take place?			
When did the event happen?			
What was the event?			

19. **Paragraph construction.** Provide your students with a topic sentence and supporting details. Then have them construct paragraphs incorporating this information.

Example:

Topic sentence: Florida is a vacationer's state.

Details:

Disney World

Sea World

Atlantic Ocean and Gulf of Mexico

Beaches

Many golf courses

Warm weather and sunshine

20. **Questions to ask.** Ask questions that direct the students' attention to details, such as the following:

- Who?
- What did _____
- What texture, color, or size?
- How many (much) _____
- When did it take place (happen)?
- How did it happen?
- Who said _____?
- How long _____?
- What city _____?
- What are the names of the characters?

Books for Children

Brenner, B. *Annie's Pet.* New York: Bantam/Bank Street, 1989.

Galdone, P. *The Gingerbread Boy.* New York: Clarion Books, 1975.

Morris, A. *Houses and Homes.* New York: Mulberry Books, 1995.

Trimble, P. *What Day Is It?* New York: Harcourt, 2000.

Ziefert, H. *The Magic Porridge Pot.* New York: Puffin, 1997.

Zolotow, C. *I Know a Lady.* New York: Mulberry Books, 1992.

Sequence and Following Directions

Description

Sequence involves noting the order in which events take place. Following directions requires students to use or apply a specific sequence in carrying out or explaining an activity. Some students need to physically work through steps and activities before they are ready to read a paragraph and recognize the sequence. Examples of words that identify sequence are *first, second, then, next, last, finally, after, previously,* and *meanwhile.*

Explicit Instruction: Using Activity

1. Tell students that they are going to watch a video or DVD on the TV.
2. Holding the video or DVD in your hand (do not turn the TV on), sit down and quietly look at the TV. Ask students why you can't see the video or DVD.
3. Put the video or DVD into the player without the TV on. Again, sit down and quietly look at the TV. Again, ask students why you can't see the video or DVD.
4. Emphasize to students that you have to do things in a sequence or order to watch the movie.
5. This time follow a correct sequence and let students see the movie. The movies *Brown Bear, Brown Bear* by Eric Carle and *Rainbow Fish* (more complicated) by Marcus Pfiser are good possibilities.
6. After the movie, ask students what happened first, second, and so on to emphasize the sequencing.

Explicit Instruction: Using Text

1. During Halloween, two good sequencing books to use are *Halloween Night* by A. Druce and *Big Pumpkin* by E. Silverman. Eric Carle's and Bill Martin's books are also easy to use for introducing students to sequencing.
2. Tell students to listen to the order, or sequence, in which things happen in the story.
3. After reading the book, give students pictures of events in the story and ask them to put them into the correct sequence (or order) in which things happened in the story.
4. The same procedure can be followed with books on history or science. Words can be written on cards instead of using pictures. Students place the cards into the correct sequence. These cards can be strung together to make a time line. This information may be transferred to a listing time line.

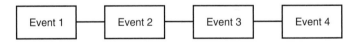

5. Have students write a paragraph to a visitor from another planet explaining what happened.
6. Next, have students identify sequence in pictureless paragraphs. Show them how to underline words depicting sequence (*first, second, next, last*).
7. When students can sequence simple narrative or fictional stories, and pictureless paragraphs, move to sequencing simple social studies books (biographies are good) or science books (water cycle, growth of a plant).

Reinforcement Activities

1. **Making popcorn.** Make popcorn (or something else of your choice) with your students. As you are making the popcorn, be sure to emphasize the order (sequence) in which you are performing the steps, saying, "First I'm going to . . . ," "The second thing I'm going to do . . . ," and "Finally, or last, we get to eat." When you have finished and students have enjoyed the final product, make a chart of the order in which these things were done. Have students dictate the steps as you write them.

2. **Performing.** Prompt students to perform a sequence of activities. (Stand up. Go to the chalkboard. Pick up the ruler. Bring the ruler to me. Hop on one foot. Jump off both feet. Skip to the back of the room.) Then ask questions such as, What did you do first? What did you do second? What did you do after . . . ? What was the last thing you did?

3. **Story-picture sequence.** Prepare a sequence of pictures that depict a story (inexpensive trade books may be cut apart). Read the story to your students; then have them arrange the pictures and retell the story in the proper sequence.

4. **Picture sequence.** Prepare pictures that depict a sequence of events. The middle event should be missing. Next, have students arrange the pictures in a sequence and draw a picture of the missing event.

5. **Comic-strip sequence.** Cut cartoons from newspapers. Mount each cartoon frame on a separate piece of tagboard. The student must rearrange the cards so that they tell a story.

6. **Paragraph sequence.** Cut paragraphs from a selected short story. Mount each paragraph on a piece of tagboard. Instruct students to rearrange the mounted paragraphs so that they tell a story.

7. **Paragraph questions.** Give your students a paragraph to read. When they have finished reading the paragraph, ask questions that involve noting the sequence in which events occurred.

   Example:

   Mary hit a single. Next at bat came John. He also hit a single. Another single was hit during Paul's time at bat. The bases were loaded. Jane hit a grand slam home run! The Eagles won the game by four runs!

   1. Who was first at bat?
   2. Who was second at bat?
   3. What did the last person at bat do?

8. **Sentence rearranging.** Instruct students to read a selection that requires noting sequence. Then give them a list of statements pertaining to the selection. Lead students in cutting the statements apart and physically rearranging them in the order in which the events occurred in the selection. (Note: Physically rearranging statements is easier than numbering statements in the correct sequence.)

    Using the passage in activity 7, the following statements might be written:

    The bases were loaded after Paul's turn at bat.
    Mary hit a single.
    After Paul, Jane hit a home run.
    John was second at bat.

9. **Numbering sequence statements.** Present your students with a paragraph to read that involves sequence. Give them a list of events or happenings that are arranged out of order. After reading the paragraph, the students must number the events in the order in which they occurred. Using the passage in number 7, direct students to number the following statements from 1 to 4. Number 1 is the first thing that happened; number 4 is the last.

    _3_ The bases were loaded after Paul's turn at bat.
    _4_ After Paul, Jane hit a home run.
    _1_ Mary hit a single.
    _2_ John was second at bat.

10. **Index-card time lines.** Distribute to each student six index cards (5 by 7 in.) and a piece of yarn (about 5 ft. long). Students should think of six significant events in their lives. Each index card will represent one of those events. Next, instruct students to illustrate one event on each card. When the index cards have been completed, they can be attached in proper sequence to the yarn. Thus students have a time line of the important events in their lives. This later can be expanded to time lines of events in stories and social studies.

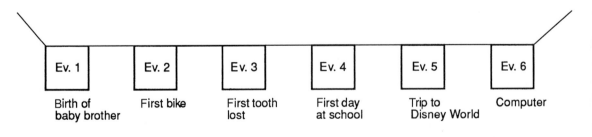

11. **Direction writing 1.** Let students demonstrate how to perform an activity they do well (curling hair with a curling iron, tying a knot). After they have demonstrated the activity, students should write the directions on how to do it.

12. **Direction writing 2.** Suggest that students select their favorite food or game. Then have each student write directions on how to cook the food or play the game.

13. **Directions for the day.** If you are working with groups of students (such as during reading), write directions on the chalkboard for the other reading groups to follow. These directions will involve a list of the things they should do while you are working with other groups.

14. **Prepare direction charts.** Prepare charts for students that contain directions on what to do during a fire drill, how to get ready for lunch, or what to do during indoor recess.

15. **Paper folding.** Provide opportunities for your students to read paper-folding directions and make various objects.

16. **Questions to ask.**

- What happened first (last)?
- What was done before (after)?
- What happened before (after)?
- Who was first (second, last)?

Books for Children

Brown, M. *Stone Soup*. New York: Simon and Schuster Children's Division, 1975.

de Brunhoff, J. *The Story of Babar*. New York: Random House, 2002.

Carle, E. *The Very Hungry Caterpillar*. New York: Philomel Books, 1983.

Eastman, P. D. *Are You My Mother?* New York: Random House, 1960.

Hogrogian, N. *One Fine Day*. New York: Aladdin Library, 1986.

Jackson, A. *I Know an Old Lady Who Swallowed a Pie*. New York: Dutton Books, 1997.

Mosel, A. *Tikki Tikki Tembo*. New York: Henry Holt & Company, 1989.

Silverstein, S. *The Giving Tree*. New York: HarperCollins, 1986.

Main Ideas

Description

A main idea may be expressed or implied. If main ideas are directly stated, they are at the literal level of comprehension. Other times the main idea is not directly stated and must be inferred.

Explicit Instruction: With Pictures

1. Show students a picture (e.g., related to a holiday, sports, travel).
2. Ask students to look at the picture and tell you what it is about in a few words or one sentence. Tell students that this is the main idea of the picture. The main idea tells what a picture, paragraph, or story is about in a few words.
3. Now ask students about the details in the picture. What details let us know that this is about (topic chosen)?
4. Have students write one sentence that tells the main idea of the picture.

Explicit Instruction: With Text

1. After students have identified the main idea or central thought of a picture, move on to paragraphs. Remember to tell students that they are studying the main idea. Read several paragraphs with well-stated ideas to students.
2. Have students identify the main ideas in these paragraphs. Encourage students to identify the statements that support the main ideas. A good idea for this is to create a spider map (semantic map used for comprehension). The main idea is in the center; the supporting details go out from the center. You might also like to write the sentences on cards and have students align the cards. The top card is the main idea; the cards with details are lined up under the main idea card. The advantage of this is that students can physically manipulate the cards until they have the main idea and supporting details in correct order.

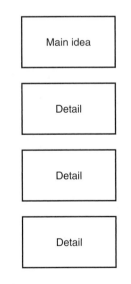

3. Have students write a paragraph containing the main idea and supporting details.
4. Students should progress to reading a short text and identifying the main ideas. (Cards and graphic organizers such as the herringbone technique and pyramid-building techniques can be used. These are described under reinforcement activities.)

Reinforcement Activities

1. **Classifying activities.** Provide students with main categories or topics (fruits, vegetables, meats, mountains, rivers, forests). Guide students in identifying or classifying items that would go under each category. Students might brainstorm ideas, or you could give them a list of specific items to classify individually.
2. **Titles to movies.** Show students a movie, but don't show them the title. When they have finished viewing the movie, ask them to furnish a good title for it.
3. **Pictures and captions.** Provide students with pictures and separate cards with captions for these pictures. Students should match the pictures and captions.
4. **Easy selections to identify.** Begin with selections in which the main idea is easy to identify. The main idea should be clearly stated when students are beginning to learn this skill.
5. **Main ideas in simple sentences.** Give students simple sentences and tell them to underline the main ideas. Usually this will be the subject and verb.
6. **Using headlines.** Use articles cut from the newspaper. Cut the headlines from the main article. Mount these headlines on tagboard. Mount the remaining articles on separate pieces of tagboard. Students must then match each article with its appropriate headline.
7. **Title matching.** Print short stories on paper. Follow each story with several possible titles. Students should select the best title for the story.
8. **Writing titles.** Writing titles for paragraphs or articles cut from the newspaper highlights the concept of main idea.
9. **Building pyramids.** Print the details and main ideas from a passage on strips of paper that have been cut apart. Students should physically move these strips until they form an outline. Then, if these have been taken from specific paragraphs, have students read the paragraphs.

Going to the circus is fun and interesting.
Clowns make me laugh.
People do tricks with animals.
People perform trapeze acts far
above the ground.

10. **Herringbone technique.** This activity is recommended by Tierney, Readence, and Dishner (1980). Students supply the information in the form given here. To supply this information, students answer the six questions. They then write one sentence that specifies the main idea. The questions include the following:

- Who was involved?
- What was done?
- When was it done?
- Where did it take place?
- How was the act or event accomplished?
- Why did it happen?

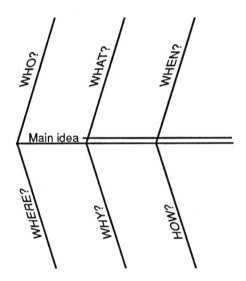

11. **Describing a character.** After reading a story, have students select one word to describe each character.
12. **Writing main ideas.** Give students (or have them locate) articles from the newspaper. Then have them write or underline the main ideas.
13. **Selling.** Allow students to locate a picture, an object, or an item in a newspaper or magazine. Students should then write an ad to sell the item.
14. **Writing summaries.** Instruct students to write a one-sentence summary of a paragraph.
15. **Questions.** Use questions such as the following to direct the students' attention to main ideas.

   Tell me what the story is about.
   What do you think the best title for this story is?

16. **Paragraph starters.** The following examples will help students structure their writing to meet a specific purpose related to the story they read.

Literature charts and Venn diagrams are helpful when completing these paragraph starters.

Example 1: Character trait

___(name of character)___ is the central, or most important, character in the story. S/he is important because _____. At the end of the story ___(name of character)___ ____(does what)____.

Example 2: Character trait

_____ is a character in the story. S/he is likeable (imaginative, self-reliant, lonely, rude, honest, intelligent, etc.). I know this because _____.

Example 3: Setting

____(name of story)____ takes place _____(where)_____, _____(when)_____. The author reveals this to me by _____.

Books for Children

Aesop's Fables (any of the collections). Example: Pinkney, Jerry, ill. *Aesop's Fables.* New York: SeaStar Books, 2000.

McCully, E. A. *Mirette on the High Wire.* New York: Putnam, 1992.

McGrath, B. B. *More M&M's Math.* Watertown, MA: Charlesbridge Publishing, 1998.

Meddaugh, S. *Martha Speaks.* New York: Houghton Mifflin, 1995.

Pfister, M. *Rainbow Fish and Friends: Lost at Sea.* New York: Night Sky Books, 2001.

Piper, W. *The Little Engine That Could.* New York: Grosset & Dunlap, 1978.

Silverstein, S. *The Giving Tree.* New York: HarperCollins, 1986.

Comparison/Contrast

Explicit Instruction: With Pictures

1. Tell students that you are going to show them two pictures; you would like them to be good detectives and figure out what is the same and different between the two pictures. (With computer graphics you can generate two identical pictures of children playing with a dog, cat, and flowers around them. On the second picture you can leave out items or change the color of other items.)

2. Show students the first picture. Tell them to look at it and try to remember everything they can about it. Give them a couple of minutes to look at the picture.

3. Give students a chance to brainstorm everything they can remember about the picture.
4. Next, show students the second picture. Tell them it is similar to the first picture, but some things have been changed. Tell them to be good detectives and look very closely and try to remember everything that is different from the first picture.
5. Have students brainstorm everything that was different.
6. Make a list of their remembrances on the board.
7. From this list, have students dictate sentences (while you write) indicating similarities and differences.

Explicit Instruction: With Text

1. Tell students that you are going to read a story (such as *City Mouse and Country Mouse*) to them. While you are reading it, tell them to be good listeners and try to find out how City Mouse and Country Mouse were alike and different. They are going to compare and contrast City Mouse and Country Mouse.
2. Read the story of *City Mouse and Country Mouse* to them.
3. When you have finished, prepare a Venn diagram with students showing how City Mouse and Country Mouse were alike and different.

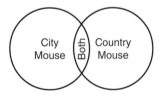

4. Have students discuss the differences.
5. Students can now write descriptive sentences explaining how City Mouse and Country Mouse were alike and different.
6. A comparison/contrast chart can be substituted for a Venn diagram.

Reinforcement Activities

1. **Objects.** Show students objects or pictures of objects (pans, socks, plants, cars, houses). Have students identify how these objects are alike or different.
2. **Friends.** Have students identify how they are like their friends and different from them.
3. **Video or DVD.** Show students two video or DVD versions of the same movie. Students can identify how they are alike and different.

4. **Different story accounts.** Read two different story accounts of a situation or happening (e.g., *The Three Little Pigs* and *The True Story of the Three Little Pigs*). Students can identify how the versions are alike and different.
5. **Different story versions.** Read two different versions of the same story (e.g., *Three Billy Goats Gruff*). Compare how each version is alike and different.
6. **Newspaper accounts.** Read newspapers from different communities and compare their versions of a high school or college sports event. How differently does each community describe the game?
7. **Biographies.** Read two biographies of the same person or a biography and autobiography of that person. Describe how they are alike and different.
8. **Historic events.** Read two different accounts of the same historic event. How are the accounts alike and different?

Books for Children

Angelou, M. *Kofi and His Magic.* New York: Knopf, 2003.

Asch, F. *Ziggy Piggy and the Three Little Pigs.* Toronto: Kids Can Press, 1998.

Gray, N. *A Country Far Away.* New York: Orchard Books, 1991.

Louie, A.-L. *Yeh-Shen: A Cinderella Story from China.* New York: Putnam, 1982.

Thayer, E. L., and C. Bing, ill. *Casey at the Bat: A Ballad of the Republic Sung in the Year 1888.* New York: Handprint Books, 2000.

Cause/Effect

Description

Cause–effect relationships may be directly stated or implied. Students predict or identify reasons why one event or happening may lead to another event or happening. Several signal words for cause–effect patterns include *as a result of, because, consequently, if . . . then, nevertheless, since, therefore,* and *this led to.*

Explicit Instruction: Demonstration

1. When beginning cause/effect, start with simple examples that can be demonstrated. For example, blow up a balloon. Then break it with a needle (you might prefer to sit on the balloon).
2. Ask students what caused the balloon to break. (A word of caution: If you are going to conduct an activity that has a loud popping noise, alert other teachers and administrators in the school so they will not be frightened.) Emphasize that they are identifying cause and effect.

3. Ask students other questions: If I don't water the plant in the room, what will happen? (What will the effect be?) If we don't clean our desks, what will happen?
4. Have students brainstorm other causes and effects (for example, the sun comes out, and it gets warm).

Explicit Instruction: With Text

1. Read a story such as *I Know a Lady* by Charlotte Zolotow. Before reading the story, have students look at the front cover and predict what the story is about.
2. Tell students to listen carefully and find out what caused the little girl to love the elderly lady.
3. After reading the story, ask students what caused the little girl to love the elderly lady. Make a list on the board.

   Effect: _____
   Cause 1: _____
   Cause 2: _____
   Cause 3: _____

4. Students can write several sentences about why the little girl liked the elderly lady.
5. Encourage wide reading of cause–effect books. As you are reading, have students identify examples of causes and effects.

Reinforcement Activities

1. **Videotapes.** Show students videotapes. Have them identify causes and effects of events in the story.
2. **Newspaper pictures.** Show students pictures from the newspaper. Urge them to identify possible feelings of the people pictured, what may have caused the situation, or why the photographer may have selected this picture.
3. **Newspaper headlines.** Give students newspaper headlines or the first sentence of an article to read. Have them predict the cause of this event or happening.
4. **Reading an article.** Read an article to your students, then have them predict the event that will happen next. Ask, "What caused you to predict this effect?"
5. **Identifying what could happen.** Select an article from the newspaper. Highlight the first sentence. Then think of 5 to 10 possible effects or outcomes.
6. **Comic strip endings.** Select a comic strip. Cut off the last picture. Ask students to tell what could happen. What was the effect of everything that happened in the cartoon?

7. **Newspaper hunts.** Using newspaper articles, have students underline or highlight as many causes and effects as they can find.

8. **Mood or tone.** Using the newspaper, identify causes of the mood or tone depicted in editorials or sports articles.

9. **Newspaper detective.** Locate a sentence containing the cause–effect pattern. Find the clue word and underline it. Then try substituting the word *because* for the clue word.

10. **Writing *Why* questions.** Select an article, comic strip, picture, or editorial from the newspaper. Have students write a *why* question about the article, then write their answer to the *why* question.

Books for Children

Greenfield, E. *Grandpa's Face.* New York: Philomel, 1988.

Numeroff, L. J. *If You Give a Moose a Muffin.* New York: HarperCollins, 1994.

———. *If You Give a Mouse a Cookie.* New York: HarperCollins, 1985.

———. *If You Give a Pig a Pancake.* New York: HarperCollins, 1998.

Potter, J., and C. Claytor. *African Americans Who Were First.* New York: Cobblehill Books, 1997.

Rathmann, P. *Officer Buckle and Gloria.* New York: Putnam, 1995.

White, E. B. *Charlotte's Web.* New York: HarperTrophy, 1999.

Summarizing and Story Structure

Description

Summarizing is one of the important and most useful skills to learn. Good summarizing requires students to be able to identify main ideas and details. It takes many years to develop.

Explicit Instruction: Oral Summarizing or Retelling

1. Tell students that they are going to learn how to summarize, or retell a story in a short way.
2. Begin by using oral activities for modeling the process.
3. Show students a DVD or movie of a short story. (Move from the movie or DVD to a short narrative story, then to longer selections and expository texts.)
4. Use leading questions to help students summarize. Who were the main characters or most important people in the story? Where did the story take place? What main thing happened to the characters? (What did the characters do? Can you tell me what happened in a short way?) How did the story end? (Can you tell me how it ended in a short way?)

5. Present the information in a story map.

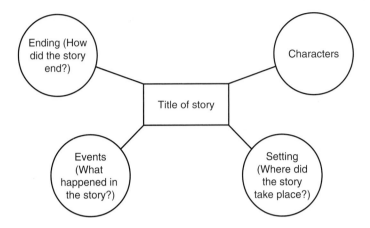

6. Have students retell the story in a short way using the map.
7. Note: For young children, use pictures and words in the story map.

Explicit Instruction: Summary Writing

1. Move from narrative to expository text.
2. Provide students with short text and gradually increase the length.
3. After reading the selection, Bean and Steenwyk (1984) suggest directing students to follow six rules:
   • Delete material that is not important.
   • Delete material that is repeated.
   • Substitute or use a higher-order term or concept for a list of terms.
   • Substitute or use a higher-order term or concept for components of an action or process.
   • Identify and incorporate topic sentences.
   • Where there are no topic sentences, write them.
4. Put this information into a graphic organizer. The organizer will depend on the type of material read.
5. Using the graphic organizer, have students write a one-sentence or paragraph summary of the material.

Reinforcement Activities

1. **Events of the day.** Summarize events of the day or what you did as a class.
2. **Pictures.** Show students pictures from magazines or books and have them tell about each picture in a sentence or two.
3. **Subtitles.** Guide students to use subtitles to help them summarize.

4. **Paragraph frames** (Nichols 2002). Students are given summary paragraphs of information contained in the text. These paragraphs have words deleted. Students must fill these deleted spaces with information from the text. After reading the fable of *City Mouse and Country Mouse,* the following paragraph frames could be completed:

   The City Mouse and Country Mouse were quite different. City Mouse liked _____. Country Mouse liked _____.

   Even though they were quite different, they also were alike. Both mice _____.

5. **Newspaper articles.** Summarize newspaper articles.
6. **Magazine articles.** Summarize magazine articles.
7. **Literature charts.** Literature charts provide a way of identifying, summarizing, and comparing character traits. They provide a means to summarize appearances, actions, and feelings. Literature charts also can be used to compare plots and characters in different stories.

Little Red Riding Hood

Appearance	*Actions*	*Feelings*
Small	Walked in the woods	Lonely
Wore a red hood	Carried a basket	Frightened
Alone	Talked to a wolf	

Books for Children

Beaton, C., and S. Blackstone. *How Big Is a Pig?* Cambridge, MA: Barefoot Books, 2003.

Burton, V. L. *Mike Mulligan and His Steam Shovel.* New York: Houghton Mifflin, 1939.

Grindley, S. *Where Are My Chicks?* New York: Phyllis Fogelman Books, 2002.

Hopkins, L. B., ed. *Surprises.* New York: HarperTrophy, 1986.

Johnson, C. *Harold and the Purple Crayon.* New York: HarperCollins, 1977.

18

Elaborative Structures

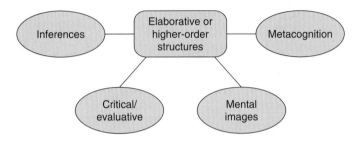

Description

Elaborative or higher-order structures provide the framework for expanded responses. Connections are made between students' schemata and integrated into the schemata of the text. Elaborative structures provide a framework for extended thinking and reaction. Students' thinking involves reorganizing information, personalizing connections between their schemata and the text, and reacting affectively. Literal comprehension forms the basis for elaborative comprehension structures.

> **Critical / evaluative reading** . . . the process of making evaluations or judgments when reading.
>
> **Inference** . . . the process of reaching a conclusion based on facts and premises.
>
> **Mental imagery** . . . creating visual, auditory, tactile, or olfactory images in one's mind.
>
> **Metacognition** . . . knowing whether you are understanding or comprehending what you are reading and knowing how to improve your comprehension.

Inferences

Students become active readers when they engage in inferential comprehension. During inferential comprehension students must make hypotheses by combining what the author has written in the text with their own schemata or backgrounds of information. Students predict or identify reasons why an author used the words she/he used. They hypothesize about the nature or personality of characters. Students identify details that support a main idea. They can also identify main ideas that are not explicitly stated in a selection, then draw their conclusions.

Explicit Instruction: Without Text

1. Show students a picture of a child with an umbrella, raincoat, and wet shoes. Ask them what kind of day it is. Students will respond with "rainy." Next, ask them why they think it is a rainy day (umbrella, raincoat, wet shoes).
2. Tell students that they are being detectives and using information from the pictures to answer your question. They are inferring what happened because they can't see the rain.
3. Show students several other pictures and have them infer what happened.
4. Have students be detectives using the book jackets from several picture books. Ask them to look carefully at the book jackets and find evidence that might tell something about the stories.

Explicit Instruction: With Text

Question–answer relationships (QAR) (Raphael 1982, 1984, 1986) provide an excellent vehicle for teaching inferential comprehension. Students first make a distinction between information located in the book and information that comes from their heads. They then make further distinctions between "in the book" and "in my head." These further distinctions are "right there," "think and search," "author and you (me)," and "on my own."

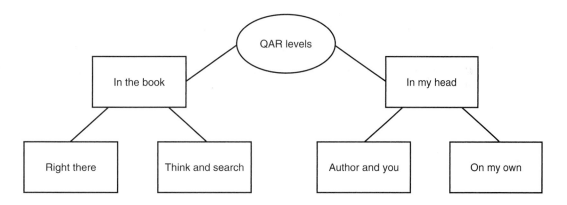

1. "Right there" means the answer can easily be found. Both the word in the question and the words needed to answer the question are in the same sentence.
2. "Think and search" questions require information from different parts of the story. Words from the question and answer are not found in the same sentence.
3. "Author and you (me)" answers are not in the story. You think about what you already know and what the author tells you.

4. "On my own" answers are not in the story. You can answer the question without reading the story. You use your own experiences (Crawley and Mountain 1995).

Begin by teaching students the two major sources of information: "in the book" and "in my head." Spend several days on each step below. First the teacher models. Then students work in small groups. Finally students work independently.

1. Show students a paragraph and read it together.
2. Then give students several factual ("in the book") questions and several inferential ("in my head") questions. Have students read and answer the questions individually, then come back as a group and discuss their answers. Have students identify whether they obtained the answers "in the book" or "in my head." Discuss how each answer was arrived at.
3. Next, teach students to distinguish between "right there" and "think and search." Show students another passage. Read the passage with them. Then show them several questions at the "right there" and "think and search" levels.
4. Students should search the passage and their heads to answer these questions. Encourage students to discuss (model) how they arrived at the answers and whether the question's answer was "right there" or they had to "think and search" for it.
5. When students can identify "right there" and "think and search" questions, introduce them to "author and me" and "on my own." Again, read a passage with your students, and prepare several questions at each level for them to answer. After students have finished answering the questions, have them identify what type of question each is and how they arrived at the answer. Initially use easy books, and then increase the difficulty and use content or subject area books.

Reinforcement Activities

1. **Concentrated work.** Provide concentrated work on inferences. Rather than asking different types and/or levels of comprehension questions, have students spend two or three weeks answering only inferential types of questions.
2. **Videotapes or films.** Show students a videotape or film of a children's story. Stop at the climax or an interesting point, then have students predict the next event or outcome.
3. **Pictures.** Show students pictures of the story they are going to read (or photos taken in a country they are going to study). Have the students predict the topic of the story, how the people feel, the character of the people, or causes for the situation pictured.
4. **Newspaper pictures.** Show students pictures from the newspaper. Urge them to identify possible feelings of the people pictured, what may have

caused the situation, or why the photographer may have selected this picture.

5. **Picture sequence.** Show students a sequence of pictures. One of the middle pictures should be missing. Students should then infer sequence by identifying what happened between the pictures.

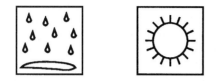

6. **Reading stories.** Read stories aloud to students. While reading the story, stop at the climax or an interesting point, then have students predict what will happen next. While reading aloud, stop and ask students to identify why the author may have chosen the words used, and how the students felt as they listened to the selection.

7. **Newspaper headlines.** Give students newspaper headlines or the first sentence of an article to read. Then tell them to predict the subject of the article. As a variation, have students make as many predictions as they can and then compare predictions.

8. **Reading an article.** Read an article to your students, then have them predict what will happen next. Compare students' predictions.

9. **Inferential listening.** Read short selections to your students (initially one paragraph in length, then increase the length). Make up several literal statements and several inferential statements for each selection. Have students read the statements appearing in a random order, then determine whether they actually heard the statement or had to hypothesize or figure out the statement. If the statement is inferential, they must tell you what helped them figure it out.

10. **Inferential reading.** This is similar to number 6, except that you should direct students to read the selection and determine whether the information is directly stated (found on the page) or they have to figure it out.

11. **Pictures and facts.** Direct students to select a picture from the newspaper or magazine. Examine the picture, then make a list of facts about it. Finally, create a list of inferences you can make from these facts.

12. **Articles and facts.** Select an article. Make a list of facts in the article. Then make a list of inferences that can be drawn from the facts.

13. **Mood-and-tone words.** Select an article (e.g., sports story or news story). Have students underline the mood or tone words. Next, have them write a sentence that tells the mood or tone of the story.

14. **Substitute mood-and-tone words.** Students might select an article (sports story, news story) and underline the mood or tone words. Write a

sentence describing the mood or tone. Then have them substitute words to change the mood or tone.

15. **Topic-continuous file.** Guide students into making a continuous file of articles on one subject for three or four days. They should then read the articles and predict what will happen later.

16. **Comic strips.** Using a comic strip, clip the words from the ending balloons. Instruct students to read the cartoon and predict what will happen in the empty balloon.

17. **Friends from another planet.** Students can pretend that they have made friends with someone from another world. They should use the sports, ads, comics, movie, or news section of the newspaper. Then identify the conclusions this friend would probably draw about life in the United States. Direct students to write the conclusion they think this friend would reach. (How do people look? What do they eat? How do they travel? What do they wear?)

18. **Interviews.** Students can pretend that they are reporters and must interview a government official, sports hero, movie star, musician, etc. Allow them to compose a list of 5 to 10 questions they might ask, then add the answers they think this person would give.

19. **Social classes, age, or gender.** For variety, students can develop a game in which they must identify the social classes, age, or gender toward which ads are directed.

20. **Questions to ask.** Use questions such as the following to direct your students' attention to inferences:

- What evidence can you find that makes us think that (<u>character</u>) was a _____ person? List the evidence.
- Which character was _____ (happy, depressed, mysterious, greedy)? Explain why you can conclude this.
- What do you feel when you read (or listen to) the following passage? (<u>Read the passage aloud to students.</u>)
- What time of year do you think it was?
- Where could this story have taken place? Where else could this story have taken place? Why do you feel this story could have taken place there?
- Why do you think the author wrote this story? What was the author's purpose in writing the story?
- Find a part that makes us feel (<u>specify a mood</u>).
- Discuss how you think the author felt about (<u>specify a character, place, event</u>).
- Compare and contrast how (<u>character, place, period of time</u>) and _____ are alike (or different).
- How did (<u>character</u>) react when _____? Why do you think the character acted this way?

Books for Children

dePaola, T. *Pancakes for Breakfast.* New York: Harcourt, 1990.

Peddle, D. *Snow Day.* New York: Doubleday, 2000.

Mystery books are good for making inferences or drawing conclusions:

Levy, E. *The Schoolyard Mystery.* New York: Scholastic Inc., 1994.

Sobol, D. J. *Encyclopedia Brown Saves the Day.* New York: Bantam Books, 1982.

Critical/Evaluative Literacy

Critical literacy, or evaluating, is the process of making evaluations or judgments when experiencing "print, nonprint, image-based, and verbal" (Alvermann and Phelps 2002) communication. Critical literacy is the highest level of comprehension. It involves analysis, synthesis, and evaluation.

During critical reading, readers may be asked to determine the author's purpose or competence, the authenticity of sources, or facts and opinions. They may be asked to judge whether events, incidents, or characters are real or fictitious; or evaluate the suitability of a character's actions or identify favorite parts of the story.

Explicit Instruction Guidelines

1. Explain the skill to your students.
2. Provide examples or statements representative of the skill to your students.
3. Discuss the words or images used in the examples.
4. Allow opportunities for students to offer and explain their opinions.
5. Encourage rereading or viewing to become more critical consumers of print and other media.
6. Provide opportunities for practice.

Reinforcement Activities

Author's purpose and competence: activities 3, 6–8, 10, 13–18, 21–23

Authenticity of sources: 10, 12

Fact and opinion: 2, 5–12, 14, 17–21

Real or fictitious: 12–13

Character's actions: 1, 4

1. **Squirms.** Provide students with uncomfortable or controversial situations. Guide them in developing possible solutions to the uncomfortable situations (squirms).

Examples:

- Your father (or mother) told you not to climb trees because you might fall and get hurt. Your friend's kite gets caught in a tree. Although the limb isn't too high, it's higher than anyone can reach. You are the only person who knows how to climb the tree to get it out. What should you do?
- Your father (or mother) told you not to drive your six friends home from school. When you get out of school, your six friends jump into the car with you. What should you do? You don't want to risk losing their friendship.

2. **Fictitious quotations.** Develop quotations that characters might have said (but really didn't) based on their traits. Instruct students to match the fictitious quotations with the appropriate character and explain their matchings. Students can later develop their own fictitious quotations.
3. **Writer's competence.** Present students with a list of topics and possible writers on the topic. Students then select the writer who should be most competent to write about the topic.

Example:
Which writer do you think would have the most helpful information about how to swing golf irons?
   a. A man who has been a sports writer for eight years.
   b. A golf pro.
(Have students tell which writers they chose and why.)

4. **Acting.** Prompt students to act out or pantomime the part of the story they like best, then explain why they chose that part.
5. **Fact–opinion statements.** Give your students a list of statements—some fact, some opinion. Lead them into identifying which are fact and which are opinion.
6. **Editorials.** Tell students to bring to class an editorial and a news article on the same topic. Examine how the styles differ. Students next identify statements of fact and opinion.
7. **Differing opinions.** Find commentary columns that contain different opinions on the same subject. Compare how the columnists present their opinions. Have students identify statements of fact and opinion. Are there any fallacies in the columnists' reasoning? What was the purpose of each writer?
8. **Political speeches.** Listen to the political speeches of different politicians. Identify statements of fact and opinion. Identify what the politician says to sway the voters' opinion. How does the politician say this? Are there any fallacies in the politician's reasoning?
9. **News articles.** Compare news stories as they appear in various newspapers. If you can, have people from different states send their

newspapers to you. What factual statements were included in the accounts? What statements of opinion were included in the accounts?

10. **Editorial findings.** Students can locate editorials (or articles) in which the author is trying to persuade the reader. Your students should discuss how the author is trying to persuade the reader. What words were used? What statements of fact and opinion were used?

11. **Editorial writing.** After studying an issue and reading news accounts, students can write editorials expressing their opinions.

12. **Biographies.** Encourage students to read and compare two different biographies about the same person. Students should then identify how the opinions of the authors differ. Were the writers qualified?

13. **Author's purpose.** After reading a selection such as a news story, book, or poem, have students determine why the author may have written it.

14. **Commercials and videotapes.** Bring videotapes of commercials to class. Lead students in determining how the advertiser tried to sway or influence people to purchase the product. (With younger students, show tapes of toys and breakfast cereals. Talk about what advertisers did to influence them to buy the product. Then have the students bring the actual toys and cereals to class. What differences can they note between the commercial and the actual product?)

15. **Newspaper and magazine ads.** Analyze newspaper and magazine ads. What is included (or not included) in the ads to encourage people to want the product?

16. **Collage.** Using ads from magazines and newspapers, make a collage depicting one primary propaganda technique.

17. **Emotions and sympathy.** Direct students to identify words in an article that arouse emotions such as sympathy, hatred, fear, peacefulness, or love.

18. **Humorous ads.** Have students select humorous ads from the newspaper and identify the product. They should then identify what the advertiser did to encourage people to purchase the product. (The same can be done with romantic ads, ads for strength, and so on).

19. **Emotive sports articles.** Provide the opportunity for students to examine sports articles and identify figurative or emotional words that sports writers use. What conclusions are they trying to have the reader make by using these words?

20. **Comparative sports articles.** Select a sports article. Make a list of facts and a list of opinions in the article. If you can, compare the local papers of the home team and visiting team. How do these articles differ?

21. **Graphing.** Over a period of several weeks, develop a graph that illustrates the number and types of propaganda techniques used. You might make different graphs for various sections of the paper (sports, editorials, advertisements, etc.).

22. **Chamber of commerce.** Students can pretend that they work for a local chamber of commerce. Using information from the newspaper, their assignment is to develop a booklet to attract people to your community.

23. **Propaganda game.** Challenge students to develop a game (similar to "Old Maid") in which the player matches a propaganda technique to an example found in the newspaper.

24. **Questions to ask.** Use questions such as the following to direct your students' attention to reading critically:

- Is the author qualified?
- Are the things that happened in the story really true? How can you tell?
- Do you think _____ was correct? Why or why not?
- If you could give some advice, what would you tell _____?
- Do you think the solution was a good one? Why or why not?
- Is _____ always true? Why or why not?
- Is there any reason to believe that the writer has (or does not have) accurate information? Is the information up to date?
- Is there any reason to believe the writer may be biased? Why or why not?
- To what kind of person was the ad (editorial) appealing? Explain.
- Did the ad (editorial) tell anything specific about the product (issue)? Explain.
- Why were the words (insert words) used?
- What adjectives or adverbs does the writer use? Why were these words selected?
- In the selection you just read, which words are opinion and which are stated as facts? Explain.
- Does the writer support his/her opinions with facts? Give examples.
- Has the author left out anything important? Explain.

Forming Mental Images

Picturing events, scenes, people, and happenings is an important skill in reading. Students who are good readers state that they try to picture things in their minds as they read. Poor readers, on the other hand, concentrate their efforts on decoding or pronouncing the words.

Explicit Instruction: Exploring Mental Imagery

1. Have students get comfortable. (Take a couple of slow deep breaths [inhaling through the nose, exhaling through the mouth] . . . Let go of any tension as you are inhaling and exhaling . . .)

2. Ask students to imagine a variety of things and to notice what happens. "Imagine a square . . . notice what it looks like . . . imagine a large movie screen in front of you with this square on it. . . ."

3. Now clear the screen . . . now imagine a circle . . . let the circle get larger . . . let it get smaller . . . let the circle be the color of a red apple . . . let it become yellow like a lemon . . . now let it become green like grass . . . imagine this circle turning into a ball . . . let the ball roll . . . pick the ball up . . . toss the ball in the air . . . catch it . . . let someone join you for play . . . notice what this person looks like . . . toss the ball to this person . . . have this person toss the ball back to you . . . begin playing ball with this person . . . notice where you are playing ball . . . notice what the place looks like . . . notice the season . . . notice what you are wearing . . . now let the image fade . . . very gradually begin to bring your breath back to normal . . . rub your hands together . . . cover your eyes with your warm hands . . . gradually open your eyes into your hands. . . ."

4. Have students share their experiences. You will gain insight into students' skills of visualization. Use additional visualizations with your students (walking through a forest, swimming at the beach, skiing, having a birthday, playing a game, or the like).

Explicit Instruction: Simple Text

1. Explain to students that being able to form images of a story in their minds helps them understand the story and makes the story more interesting.

2. Before reading *Snowy Day* by Ezra Jack Keats (or another book), ask students what snow would feel and look like. What happens if it gets warm? (For students who have never seen or experienced snow, make a variation of snow with crushed ice. Let them see, feel, taste, and watch the "snow.")

3. Then read *Snowy Day* to students (without showing the pictures). Have students create mental pictures of what is happening.

4. Ask students what their imaginary TV screens looked like as you read the story.

5. After discussing the story, show them Keats's illustrations. Discuss similarities and differences between their images and those of Keats.

Reinforcement Activities

1. **Remembering pictures.** Show students a picture. Have them look carefully at the picture, then close their eyes and try to visualize it.

2. **Reading to students.** Read aloud a short selection to students. Have them close their eyes as you are reading it and try to visualize what is happening. Students can then share what they have visualized.

3. **Pantomime.** Pantomime elements of a story as you are reading it to students.

4. **Drawing pictures.** Students might draw pictures of settings in selections they have read.
5. **Discussing images.** Ask students to describe what they are visualizing or what comes to mind as they are reading a selection.
6. **Questions to ask.** Use questions such as the following to direct your students' attention to visualization:

- What did the scene (character, object) look like?
- What did you see in your mind as you read the paragraph (story)?
- What kind of picture could you draw of the events in the story?
- What kind of picture do you think the author might draw to illustrate the story?
- What would (<u>name character</u>)'s face look like as s/he (<u>name action</u>—fell, jumped, was frightened, succeeded)?
- If you changed the setting of the story, what would it look like?

Metacognition

You may have students in your class who will do the reading assignment, yet not know what they've read when finished. These students probably are not aware of their lack of comprehension during reading. It's not until you ask them questions after reading that their lack of comprehension become apparent. These students have not developed metacognition.

The term *cognition* means understanding or knowing. *Meta* means viewing from the outside. *Metacognition* means having a knowledge or understanding of our thought processes. It means being able to identify our purposes for reading and being able to monitor or check our understanding while reading. A *metareader,* therefore, is one who identifies the task or purpose, identifies a plan for attacking the problem, and self-checks comprehension while reading. Students monitor their reading.

There are a number of reasons why students may not be metareaders. Students' prior knowledge may not be activated. They may not know the difference between what they know and don't know. These students may not know how to ask questions. They may have difficulty building mental images as they read. They may have difficulty organizing text information. There may be a perception that the text controls the students; students may not feel they have any control over what ideas or information they get from the text. Students may know how to use metacognitive processes but not know why they are using them.

Explicit Instruction

To develop students' awareness of the metacognitive process by helping them formulate questions to guide their reading, the teacher guides students through a discussion of the process starting with developing a plan and ending with evaluation.

Developing My Plan for Reading (before Reading)

What do I know about this topic?

What should I do first?

What is my purpose for reading?

How much time do I have to complete the assignment?

Monitoring My Plan of Action (during Reading)

What should I do first?

Do I understand what I am reading?

What is important?

What can I do if I do not understand what I'm reading?

Evaluating How I Did (after Reading)

What do I remember?

Do I have to do anything else to help me remember?

What can I do to help me remember?

What do I think about what I read?

Reinforcement Activities: Developing a Plan

1. See Chapter 20, "Teaching Structures."
2. **Brainstorming.** Brainstorm a topic and list students' contributions.
3. **Semantic mapping.** Before reading a selection, have students identify what they already know about a topic or concept. Place the major concept in a geometric shape at the center of the board. Then ask students what they think of when they hear the term (such as *pollution*). For *pollution* they might say *invisible, dirty, unhealthy, cars, dumping, chemicals, disease, cancer, death, expensive, downtown,* or *in the house.* Next, ask

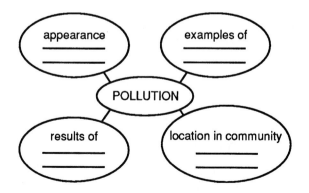

your students to categorize their associations and label these categories (for example, *appearance, examples of, results of, location*). These can be placed in a figure in which the center circle is joined by spokes to smaller circles on the outside.

4. **Predicting content.** Provide students with a chapter outline. This outline should contain the chapter's headings and subheadings. Leave space for writing between the subheadings. Students fill in these spaces with information they already know and anticipate what the authors will include in the selection.

5. **Anticipating questions.** Give your students an outline of the text that includes major topics and subtopics. Leave space between each of the topics. Then instruct your students to list the questions they predict the author will answer within these sections.

6. **Questioning the teacher.** This is similar to the game "20 Questions." Students try to find out what information is contained in a selection by asking the teacher questions. Within a certain time limit students are encouraged to question you all they can about the topic. Following the questioning step, give the students a "test" covering the information you consider important. All questions you consider important should be asked on the "test," even if their answers were not brought out in the previous discussion of students' questions.

7. **Reciprocal questioning (ReQuest).** ReQuest is a strategy developed by Manzo (1979a, 1979b) that encourages students to ask questions independently and set their own purposes for reading. (See Chapter 19.)

8. **Giving reasons.** Encourage your students to state why they are learning new strategies.

Reinforcement Activities: Monitoring

1. **Journal or learning log.** Students keep notes about their thinking and how they reacted to or dealt with any problems.

2. **Forming images.** Direct students to stop at selected places in the text and describe what they see in their minds. Then have them predict what will come next in the selection.

3. **Meaning of unknown words.** Stress the importance of students identifying the meaning of unknown words as they read.

Reinforcement Activities: Evaluating

4. **Organizing.** Help students organize the text material through mapping techniques or outlines.

5. **Peer discussions.** After reading a selection, have students work in pairs and explain the material to each other.

6. **Question–answer relationships (QARs).** Raphael (1986) identified four types of information found in reading selections. The two primary sources of information are "in the book" and "in my head." After students understand these classifications, "in the book" is further refined to include "right there" and "think and search." "In my head" is further refined to include "author and you" and "on my own."

Combination Activities: Planning, Monitoring, Evaluating

1. **K–W–L (know–want to know–have learned).** Ogle (1986) developed this strategy. Students list "what they know" and "what they want to know" before reading. After reading, they list "what I learned." Initially, this should be done as a class. As students gain skill, they can work in pairs or independently. (See Chapter 20.)

What I know about (topic)	What I want to know about (topic)	What I learned about (topic)

2. **Using study strategies.** Teach your students to use a study strategy such as SQ3R (survey, question, read, recite, review) as they read. During the survey phase, students look at the organization of the chapter's headings and subheadings, look at the pictures and illustrations, and read the introductory passages and the concluding passages. Next, going through the text subtopic by subtopic, they turn the subheadings into questions that they will try to answer as they read. The students read, then recite the answers to the questions they developed. Finally, students review what they have learned. This review should occur immediately after reading and then at frequent intervals after reading.

19

Questioning Structures

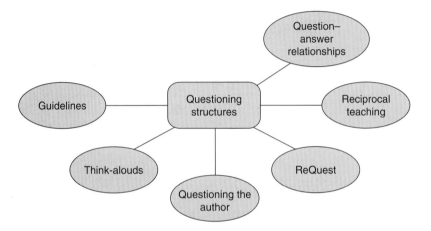

Description

Questioning structures are guidelines and strategies that help students generate questions, form connections between existing background experience and text, and increase the quality of interactions with text.

Inquiry charts . . . were developed by James V. Hoffman (1992) to help students connect what they already know or think about a topic with information gained from other sources.

Question–answer relationships . . . is a vehicle for teaching students how to analyze and understand questions. Initially, students make distinctions between "In the Book" and "In My Head." They then refine these distinctions to include: "Right There" and "Think and Search," and "Author and Me" and "On My Own."

Questioning the author . . . helps students identify that the contents of a textbook are ideas written down by the author. Students engage in initiating and following up queries (Beck, McKeown, Hamilton, and Kucan 1997).

Reciprocal teaching . . . is similar to ReQuest. It involves teacher modeling to help students learn predicting, question generating, clarifying, and summarizing

(Palinscar and Brown 1986). Then students form cooperative groups and model the steps with each other.

ReQuest (reciprocal questioning) . . . encourages students to ask questions independently and to set their own purposes for reading (Manzo 1979a, 1979b).

Think-alouds . . . the teacher thinks aloud while reading text orally and models questioning and comprehension skills so students can become aware of the reading process (Davey 1983).

Guidelines for Asking Questions

At times teachers find that students have difficulty answering their questions. Sometimes students' answers are incomplete; sometimes students may look perplexed. Students may not be able to set their own purposes for reading. They may not have skills to monitor their own comprehension. There may be students who never volunteer to answer questions. Using some of the following guidelines and teaching structures will improve comprehension, increase the number of students volunteering to answer questions, and improve the quality of their answers.

1. Use questions only to develop purposeful learning. Never use them as a means of punishment. As punishment, do not require students to write answers to questions at the chapter's end. Do not require students to stay in during recess or after school and orally answer your questions.
2. Increase your wait time before calling on a student. Pause, then increase your wait time to several seconds before calling on a student to answer the question. This gives slower students time to formulate an answer. It also improves the quality of students' answers and increases the number of responses by various students.
3. Ask only one question at a time, not a series of different questions. This way students have only one question on which to focus their attention. They do not have to think about several different answers at the same time.
4. If, after allowing appropriate wait time, students cannot answer your question, try rephrasing it.
5. If, after rephrasing your question, students still cannot answer it, try modeling the answer. Begin answering the question, and give your reasons for the answer. (For example: "I think it probably was winter because there was frost on the window. Do you remember the author wrote that cars were sliding on the streets?") Students usually are able to continue with the answer.
6. If students' answers are incomplete, prompt and encourage them to expand their answers by asking probing questions, such as "Can you explain that in more detail? Can you tell us more about your idea?"

7. Before calling on a student to answer your question, ask the question, pause, then call on a student. The attention level of students will be higher because the students will have to listen to the complete question. If students know a specified student will be answering the question, they don't have to pay attention.

8. If a particular student never volunteers because of fear, write a question on a card, and give it to him/her the day before class. Ask the student the question toward the beginning of the next class.

9. Ask questions in which divergent or evaluative answers can be given.

10. Do not respond to the answer of the first student. Wait and call on other students so students will continue thinking.

11. Use specific praise at spaced intervals several times during a lesson. *Specific praise* means telling students that they gave a good answer and why their answer is good. For example: "That's a good answer. Walking has an 'ing' at the end of it." "Good. If we add 3 to 6, our answer is 9."

12. Develop semantic maps as students contribute answers to questions.

13. Have students generate their own questions before reading, such as "What questions do you think the author will answer in the story or chapter?"

14. Give students the answers to questions about the selection, then have students think up questions that can be asked to arrive at these answers.

15. Use reciprocal questioning with students. Let students in the class ask you questions about a selection they just read. You answer their questions. If their questions are higher-order questions (questions involving thinking), respond with a statement such as, "That's a good question." Then answer their question. When students are finished asking you questions, ask them higher-order questions about the same material.

16. Pair students so they can ask each other questions. You might develop a sheet of questions and answers. Students can then work in pairs and ask each other those questions.

Questions	Answers
_____	_____
_____	_____
_____	_____
_____	_____

17. If students have difficulty formulating questions, have them play the game of "20 Questions."

Think-Alouds

Explicit Instruction

1. Explain think-alouds to your students. Tell them that you are going to demonstrate what you think about as you read a text.

2. Select a passage that might contain unfamiliar vocabulary, a part that is difficult to understand.
3. Read the passage aloud while students read it silently. Describe what you are thinking to students as you read.

> *First, I try to predict what the author is going to tell me. I wonder what the Inca Empire was like.*
>
> The Inca Empire was a large and great civilization in South America. *(Where is South America? I can look at a globe or map to find out. Here, I found it on the map.)* The government decided what work the people would do. It decided what crops farmers would plant and what buildings and roads would be built. The emperor's rule was law. *(I wonder what an emperor is. The sentence says that the emperor's rule was law. The emperor must rule the country.)* Several royal families helped him rule. The emperor owned all the land. It was each person's duty to serve the state. The emperor in return was responsible for the welfare of his subjects. *(I wonder what the word subjects means. I know it doesn't mean the courses we take in school. If I look back at the second sentence, it says that the government decided what work the people would do. Subjects must mean people.)*

The Wisconsin Literacy Education and Reading Network Source (WILEARNS) identifies prompts that will help focus think-alouds for different purposes. These include:

- Prior knowledge prompts
  I know all about . . .
  This reminds me of . . .
- Inferential prompts
  I am inferring that . . .
  I have this picture in my head . . .
- Summary prompt
  This is what has happened so far . . .
- Questioning/monitoring comprehension prompt
  I don't understand . . .
- Narrative prompts
  I think this word means _____ because . . .
  I predict this will happen when . . .
  I wonder if . . .
- Organizational prompt
  The author is using this expository pattern because . . .
- Main idea prompts
  This is important because . . .
  This is part of all stories because . . .
  The author wrote this because . . .
- Prove it prompt
  I think this because . . .

Questioning the Author

Explicit Instruction

1. Divide the text into logical segments to stop and discuss the text.
2. Develop questions to model how to make connections with the text and make the text clear.
3. Examples of *initiating queries* to help students understand concepts and main ideas include

    What is the author trying to say here?

    What is the author talking about? (Beck et al. 1997)

    What did the author tell us?

4. Examples of *follow-up queries* to help students make connections between the text and ideas include

    How do things look for the character?

    Given what the author has already told us about this character, what do you think the author is up to?

    How has the author let you know that something has changed?

    How has the author settled this for us? (Beck et al. 1997)

5. Introduce the selection to students. Have students read the selection one or two paragraphs at a time.
6. After reading each section, ask *integrating* and *follow-up questions.* If students have difficulty answering the questions, model an answer for them. "I came up with this answer. This is why I think . . ."
7. At the end of the selection have students, with your help, summarize the selection.

ReQuest

Explicit Instruction

1. Tell students that the purpose of the lesson is to help them improve their comprehension (understanding) of what they read. Tell them that they will read one sentence or paragraph at a time. Then you will each take turns asking each other questions. The students will ask you questions first; then you will ask them questions about the same sentence or paragraph.
2. Answer all questions they ask you fully, but do not elaborate if they are factual questions.
3. If students cannot answer a question, ask them to explain why they cannot.

4. As you and your students answer questions, be sure to justify your answers and have students justify their answers by referring to specific information in the text.
5. If students ask higher-level questions, respond by saying, "That's a good question. I have to think before I answer it." If students' questions are low-level, merely answer the question.
6. You and your students should continue through a paragraph until they have developed a purpose for reading the selection. You may have to continue through two or three paragraphs until a purpose is established. (You should model higher-level questions.)

Reciprocal Teaching

Explicit Instruction

1. After the teacher has modeled this strategy and students understand it, students work in cooperative groups to read a selection.
2. **Predict.** Have students read the title and/or subtitles and predict what they will learn from the text. Make a list of the students' predictions. You may add some of your own to the list.
3. **Read.** Read sections of the text aloud one part at a time.
4. **Question.** After each part is read, ask questions about the important content. Students may contribute additional questions.
5. **Clarify.** Tell students that it is important to be sure they understand important words and ideas in the selection. Have them clarify important vocabulary, figures of speech, or concepts. Identify sentences in which they occur. Discuss their meanings.
6. **Summarize.** Have students summarize what was read. Remind them that they should concentrate on important ideas in their summary. Students should explain how they arrived at the summaries.

Inquiry Charts

1. Identify several key questions related to the topic about which students will be learning. Place those questions across the top of the I-chart. (Or, students might identify several questions they would like to answer related to the topic.)
2. Ask students what they think they already know about the questions. Have them write this information in the box under each question.
3. Tell students that they will be reading several different sources of information and should write answers they have located in the boxes next to their references.
4. Finally, in the last row, write a summary of the information they found.

5. Creating a large I-chart on the wall will provide an opportunity for students to add the information they locate and make it prominent for everyone to see.

Inquiry Chart

	Question 1	Question 2	Question 3	Question 4
My own thoughts				
What I learned from reference 1				
What I learned from reference 2				
What I learned from reference 3				
What I learned from reference 4				
Summary of what I learned				

Explicit Instruction: QAR

Question–answer relationships (QAR) (Raphael 1982, 1984, 1986) provide an excellent vehicle for teaching inferential comprehension. Students first make a distinction between information located in the book and information that comes from their heads. They then make further distinctions between "in the book" and "in my head." These further distinctions are "right there," "think and search," "author and you (me)," and "on my own."

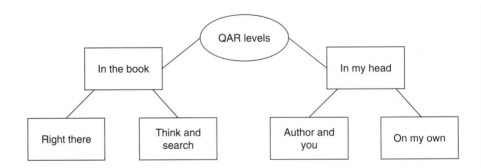

1. "Right there" means the answer can easily be found. Both the word in the question and the words needed to answer the question are in the same sentence.

2. "Think and search" questions require information from different parts of the story. Words from the question and answer are not found in the same sentence.
3. "Author and you (me)" answers are not in the story. You think about what you already know and what the author tells you.
4. "On my own" answers are not in the story. You can answer the question without reading the story. You use your own experiences (Crawley and Mountain 1995).

Begin by teaching students the two major sources of information: "in the book" and "in my head." Spend several days on each step below. First the teacher models. Then students work in small groups. Finally students work independently.

1. Show students a paragraph and read it together.
2. Then give students several factual ("in the book") questions and several inferential ("in my head") questions. Have students read and answer the questions individually, then come back as a group and discuss their answers. Have students identify whether they obtained the answers "in the book" or "in my head." Discuss how each answer was arrived at.
3. Next, teach students to distinguish between "right there" and "think and search." Show students another passage. Read the passage with them. Then show them several questions at the "right there" and "think and search" levels.
4. Students should search the passage and their heads to answer these questions. Encourage students to discuss (model) how they arrived at the answers and whether the question's answer was "right there" or they had to "think and search" for it.
5. When students can identify "right there" and "think and search" questions, introduce them to "author and me" and "on my own." Again, read a passage with your students, and prepare several questions at each level for them to answer. After students have finished answering the questions, have them identify what type of question each is and how they arrived at the answer. Initially use easy books, and then increase the difficulty and use content or subject area books.

Teaching Structures

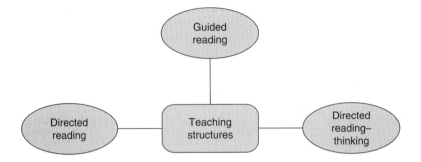

Description

Teaching strategies are organizational structures or plans for teaching reading. They provide specific steps to help students activate prior knowledge, establish background, engage in purposeful silent or oral reading, and extend learning.

> **Teaching structures** . . . organizational structures or plans for teaching reading.
>
> **Directed reading activity (DRA)** . . . a five-step framework or plan originally used in basal readers. The DRA was developed by Betts in 1946.
>
> **Directed reading–thinking activity (DRTA)** . . . a five-step framework or plan similar to the DRA. Students, however, use prediction and formulate their own purposes for reading. The DRTA was described by Stauffer in 1970.
>
> **Guided reading procedure** . . . a framework or plan in which the teacher closely monitors a student's reading and supplies assistance when needed. This was developed and described by Clay (1991) and also described by Fountas and Pinnell (1996).

Guided Reading Procedures

The purpose of guided reading is to have students become independent readers. Children are grouped according to their needs into early emergent, emergent, early fluency or fluency, levels. Books are selected at the students' instructional level or where they can decode 90–95 percent of the words accurately. Teachers assist students in their reading and use of reading strategies. Students progress from predicting, using picture clues, and establishing directionality and a one-to-one correspondence between the spoken and written word at the early emergent level to examining genre, style, imagery, and use of dialogue at the fluency level. Students move from finger pointing and oral reading at the early emergent level to silent reading at the fluency level.

The steps at the early emergent and emergent levels are similar:

1. **Picture talk.** Look at the cover and pictures in the book and talk about what might be happening. The teacher guides children to use words they will encounter in the text.
2. **Reading aloud to children.** As the teacher reads aloud, students point to the words in the text.
3. **Language play.** Students talk about punctuation and letters and their sounds. For example, find the letter that makes the /m/. Find a word that starts with the /m/. What kind of punctuation mark is at the end of this sentence?
4. **Rereading together.** The students reread the story together. As students are reading aloud, they point to the words and the teacher observes them.
5. **Retelling.** Students discuss the story.
6. **Follow-up.** Students partner-read to each other and take books home to read with parents or other siblings. They engage in science, art, or writing activities connected to the topic.

At the fluency level students become more independent. Students are taught to read with their minds and their eyes rather than their fingers and voices.

1. **Introduction.** Students discuss the cover and look at and discuss the title page.
2. **Picture talk.** Students look through the book and discuss the pictures.
3. **Read 2–3 pages silently.** Focus questions or a purpose for reading are given.
4. **Rereading.** Students locate the answers to questions asked by the teacher and read the answers aloud. (Find the place where it tells . . .)
5. **Retelling and discussion.** Students recall the entire story.
6. **Follow-up.**
7. **Language play.** Students answer questions related to phoneme–grapheme relationships, syntax, or semantics.

Directed Reading Activity (DRA)

The DRA is the structure that most basal readers follow. McKenna and Robinson (2002, p. 64) state that it is highly teacher directed; purposes and questions are determined by the teacher. DRAs are useful with all materials and also with unfamiliar materials. There are five basic steps whether fiction or nonfiction literature is read:

1. **Preparation and background.** The teacher introduces new vocabulary. She/he might tell students about the geographic location or period of history in which the story takes place. Students will be asked questions about the story title or pictures. Then the teacher gives students a broad

question (Find out what kind of person Abraham Lincoln was) to answer as they read the story rather than a question that requires students to know only one or two details (Find out where Abraham Lincoln lived).

2. **Silent reading.** Students read the selection silently (section by section or in its entirety) using the purposes given.
3. **Discussion and rereading.** The discussion after silent reading starts by determining whether the prediction was correct and citing evidence in the story to support or refute it. The teacher asks additional questions, and students locate and read information to support or prove their answers. Teachers should be careful that students find the answer to the question and don't just read everything in sight.
4. **Skills development and practice.** There is direct instruction in specific reading skills—grapho–phonic, semantic, or syntactic. Students learn new skills or work on weaknesses identified during oral reading, written work, or other content area subjects.
5. **Follow-up and enrichment.** Students engage in drama, writing, discussions, experiments, or art or music activities. Follow-up activities should be selected carefully and should not be used with every selection read.

Directed Reading–Thinking Activity (DRTA)

In the DRTA students begin to take responsibility for their own reading success. Students predict and then read to confirm or reject their predictions. Students set their own purposes for reading. This framework tends to be more appropriate for use with narrative materials, more limited to discussing students' predictions, and most useful with familiar topics (McKenna and Robinson 2002).

1. **Preparation and background.** To assist students in developing their own purposes, direct them to look at the title, pictures, heading, and subheadings. Then ask them to make predictions by asking guiding questions: What do you think the picture is about? What do you think the picture tells us about the chapter (story)? Write students' responses on the board. It is important not to forget to build the necessary background students will need to read the story. This can be done as students are making predictions or looking at illustrations.
2. **Silent reading.** Students read silently to confirm or reject their predictions. Students may read a few pages or an entire selection at a time. As students read, they should change their predictions.
3. **Discussion and rereading.** This is the same as the DRA. Students talk about their predictions and discuss why they were confirmed or rejected. Students read the evidence that supports or refutes their predictions.
4. **Skills development and practice.** The teacher discusses and models grapho–phonic, semantic, or syntactic skills used by the author.
5. **Follow-up.** The same as for the DRA.

Study Skills

Adjusting Reading Rate

Memory and Study Aids

Listening

Unit Introduction

Effective study skills help students become more proficient learners.

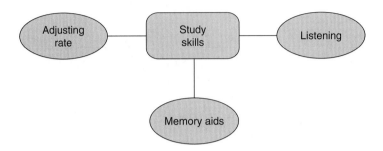

Study skills . . . skills and aids that help students learn more efficiently and understand or comprehend the material they are reading, viewing, accessing, or listening to.

From this definition you can see that many of the strategies described in the chapters on vocabulary and comprehension are appropriate to assist students in study. When learning from text, students activate prior knowledge, organize information during and after reading, talk and write about what they have read (synthesize information), and learn new vocabulary and concepts. They may also produce or create something new from their studying (Ruddell 2002). We are limiting our discussions here to the following:

Listening . . . the process of paying close and thoughtful attention to spoken or transmitted language and constructing meaning or comprehending.

Memory aids . . . strategies or skills that help students remember or memorize material.

Reading rate . . . the speed at which a person reads or locates information.

Adjusting Reading Rate

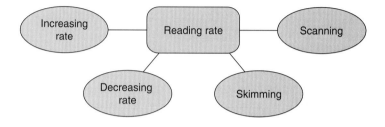

Description

Reading rate . . . the speed at which a person reads. It is one aspect of fluency. (See Unit IV.)

Scanning . . . reading or examining something very quickly to find a specific piece of information, such as the answer to a specific question. Students should not have to read every word on the page to locate an answer.

Skimming . . . reading rapidly and selectively, but purposefully, rather than carefully, to get an overview of what the material is about. During skimming, students identify main ideas and a few of the supporting details.

As a teacher you will find students who have two basic types of rate problems. The most common problem is reading too slowly; this student needs to increase reading rate. The second type of problem is reading too rapidly. The student with this type of problem needs to decrease reading rate.

Slow reading rates may be caused by a variety of factors, including word-by-word reading, finger pointing, lip movements, subvocalization, overanalyzing words, slowness in recognizing words by sight, many regressive eye movements (similar to repetitions made in oral reading), the amount of material that can be seen when the eyes pause (fixation), difficulty going from the end of one line to the beginning of the next (return sweep), and eye problems that have not been diagnosed properly. Additional causes of a slow reading rate are overuse of phonics, weak word recognition skills, inability to adjust rate for different purposes, poor comprehension, or expecting perfection.

Reading too fast is probably caused by trying to read rapidly to get through the material, viewing reading as rapidly pronouncing words, or not knowing how to adjust reading rate to fit the purpose.

Increasing Rate

Description

You may have noticed that some of your students plod along and read all, or almost all, material at a very slow speed. These students need to work on increasing the speed, or rate, at which they read.

Reinforcement Activities

1. **Using easy material.** Give your students large amounts of easy-to-read material. Encourage wide reading of this easy material.
2. **Rereading.** Encourage your students to reread their favorite stories as many times as they wish. They will be able to anticipate what's coming next and move their eyes along more rapidly.
3. **Timed reading 1.** Using easy, independent-level material, have students read for a specified amount of time (say 5 to 10 minutes). At the end of the period, they should write down everything they can remember about the selection (comprehension check). They should graph the number of pages read.

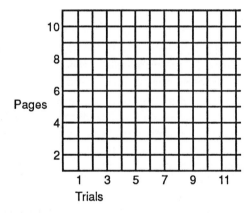

Students should be encouraged to force themselves to read more pages each time.

4. **Timed reading 2.** Commercial materials containing timed exercises can be used. These usually contain short selections that are followed by comprehension questions. Have students keep track of their reading rate and comprehension. Science Research Associates (SRA) and Contemporary are two companies that publish these materials.

5. **Page reading.** Using easy, independent-level material, have students read a specified number of pages (perhaps 5 to 10) and calculate the amount of time it took to read the pages. Have students write down the beginning and ending times to determine the amount of time they spent reading the pages. Next, direct them to jot down everything they can remember about the selection as a comprehension check. Finally, have them graph the amount of time it took to read the pages.

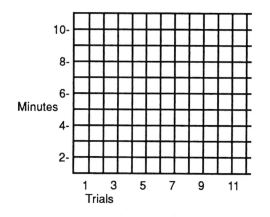

Students should be encouraged to decrease the amount of time spent reading with each trial.

6. **Finger moving.** Using easy, independent-level material, have students move their dominant-hand index finger under the lines of print. The index finger will serve as a guide to eye movements. Students should read a specified number of pages at their normal rate and jot down all ideas remembered. During the next trial, students should read the same amount of material but in half the original time. After students become comfortable at this rate, the time should be decreased again and again. After each reading, students should jot down the ideas they remembered.

7. **Word-and-phrase cards.** Print words and phrases on cards and flash them at the student. The student should tell you what he/she saw. Flash the cards faster and faster.

8. **Mechanical devices.** Use mechanical devices such as computers, the Controlled Reader (Educational Developmental Laboratories), Tachomatic X500 (Psychotechnics), Reading Accelerator (Science Research Associates), Harvard University Reading Films (Harvard University Press), and Flash-X (Educational Developmental Laboratories). It should be noted, however, that results from the use of mechanical devices are no better than results from the use of nonmechanical techniques.

Decreasing Rate

Description

On occasion you may have a student who believes that fast reading is good reading. The student generally works for speed but pays little or no attention to comprehension. Or the student may be unable to communicate the author's message during oral reading because of the emphasis on speed. This student needs to decrease his/her reading rate.

Reinforcement Activities

1. **Stressing the need to slow down.** Stress that fast reading is not always the best kind of reading. It is better to slow down and understand what is written.
2. **Graphing timed exercises.** Using short, commercially prepared reading exercises, have students read the selections, check their time, and answer comprehension questions. Each student should then graph the time it took to read the selection and check his/her comprehension. The goal of this student should be to decrease speed until comprehension improves.
3. **Purpose setting.** Provide the students with purpose-setting questions before reading. Immediately upon completing the reading assignment, the students should answer the comprehension questions.
4. **Students setting purposes.** Encourage the students to ask their own purpose-setting questions before reading. Again, immediately upon completing the assignment, students should try to answer the questions.
5. **Choral reading.** During choral reading the student will be required to slow down to the speed of other students who are conveying the author's message.
6. **Tape-recording.** Let the student tape-record his/her reading, then listen to the recording. Possibly the student is unaware that the rapid speed interferes with communicating the author's ideas.
7. **Oral reading to taped selections.** Tape-record a selection and have the student read along with the tape. By following the speed of the person reading on the tape, the student will slow down. Then have the student retell on tape the contents of the story.

Skimming

Description

Skimming is done when you want to quickly get an overview of a book or chapter. You might skim the introduction and conclusion to a chapter or book. You might skim the chapters in a textbook by looking at the headings and subheadings. You might skim a book jacket to decide if you want to read the book.

Explicit Instruction

1. Tell students that they are going to skim material to find out the main topic or message in the selection and some details.
2. Tell students to read the introduction and summary.
3. Starting at the beginning of the chapter, read the headings and subheadings.
4. Make an outline (list the headings and subheadings in outline form) or form an image of how the sections are related.
5. Read the topic sentences in each section.
6. Read the questions at the end of the chapter.
7. Read each section of the chapter carefully.

Reinforcement Activities

1. **Content skimming.** Request that students look through printed materials to determine if they contain the information desired. (Example: Does it contain information on the investment policies of major financial corporations in the United States?)
2. **Idea of chapter.** Before studying, tell students to look over the chapter and get a general idea of what it contains. Students then write down their ideas. When they have completed the chapter, students should determine whether their original ideas were correct.
3. **News articles.** Direct students to skim a news article to find out what happened during a recent headline event.
4. **Sports articles.** Have students skim a sports article to find out why their favorite team won or lost.
5. **Book sampling.** Before selecting a book, suggest that students skim a few pages to determine if they really would like to read it.
6. **Understanding.** Give students samples of difficult-to-read material and easy-to-read material. Have them skim the material to see if they can understand it.
7. **Story matching.** Give students envelopes in which short stories have been divided or cut in half. Students must rapidly read the story parts and match them. (Teams can be set up for competition when doing this.)

Scanning

Description

Scanning is done when you know the question you are trying to answer. You look only for the specific piece of information you desire. In locating facts or specific pieces of information, you might scan dictionaries, indexes, encyclopedias, telephone books, statistical tables and charts, the index of catalogs from which you wish to order, or the *TV Guide* when trying to locate a program you wish to watch.

Time students as they use the following activities to improve their scanning abilities. You can make the activities into races to enhance student interest.

Explicit Instruction

1. Tell students that they are going to scan material to find specific ideas or information.
2. Tell students to identify the question they want to answer.
3. Look back into the text to find the main word, concept, or idea in the question.

Reinforcement Activities

1. **Selection questions.** Before reading a selection, give students a list of questions they must answer by scanning.
2. **Using the encyclopedia.** Direct students to locate specific information in the encyclopedia. (Example: What is the state flower, bird, and nickname of Connecticut? What are the leading exports of Peru?)
3. **Names in the telephone directory.** Have students quickly locate the names and numbers of people in the telephone directory. (Example: What is the phone number of Peter Longstockings?)
4. **Businesses in the telephone directory.** Give students the task of locating the names and numbers of specific types of businesses. (Example: Locate the names of two businesses that sell aluminum storm windows and doors.)
5. **Telephone directory scavenger hunt.** Give students a list of names, types of businesses, and government offices. Students must locate their numbers in the fastest possible time.
6. **Newspaper classified section.** Students might scan the classified section to find specific telephone numbers. (Example: Locate the telephone numbers of three people who are selling computers.)
7. **Theaters.** Using the newspaper, locate the name of a theater where (name of movie) is playing.
8. **Newspaper scavenger hunt.** Give students a list of items that they must rapidly find in the newspaper.
9. **Textbook scavenger hunt.** Give students a list of questions that they must answer by rapidly finding information throughout the entire book.
10. **Mail-order catalogs.** Challenge students to rapidly locate specific information in mail-order catalogs.
11. **Statistical tables.** Students can scan statistical tables to locate specific information.
12. **Dictionary.** Time students in rapidly locating words in the dictionary.

Memory and Study Aids

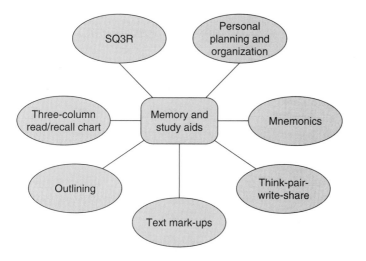

Description

Many people say they cannot remember what they read. Students not only must remember what they read—they must also remember bits and pieces of information learned in various content areas. Memory aids provide structures for helping students remember.

Memory aids . . . strategies or skills that help students remember.

Mnemonics . . . techniques for improving memory by using certain systems or formulas.

Outlining . . . an organizational structure for condensing content and placing it into a structured format by listing information under main points.

SQ3R . . . a general study strategy for independent silent reading. *SQ3R* stands for *survey, question, read, recite,* and *review.*

Text mark-ups . . . this is a strategy that encourages students to "mark up the text." Students are encouraged to circle unknown words, and make prediction, main idea, discovery, or connection notes in the margins.

Think-pair-write-share . . . is an open-ended discussion strategy developed by Frank Lyman (1981). Students individually think about an open-ended question, talk in pairs, write down their answers, and the pairs share their discussions with the class.

Three-column read/recall chart . . . this chart provides a framework for students to reread a reading selection to recall details and take notes. This is a good combination with the SQ3R Method.

SQ3R

Explicit Instruction

1. Tell students they are going to learn a strategy that will help them read and study content materials. It is called *SQ3R* (Pauk 1984). *S* stands for *survey. Q* stands for *question. 3R* stands for *read, recite, and review.*
2. **Survey.** Look at the headings and subheadings to get an overview of the chapter. Read the introduction and summary. Look at pictures and other illustrations.
3. **Question.** Turn each heading and subheading into a question that you will answer while reading the subsection.
4. **Read.** Read each subsection.
5. **Recite.** After reading the subsection, answer the question you developed.
6. **Review.** Review the chapter immediately. Review often after your initial learning. The most forgetting occurs 24 hours after you have learned something.

Three-Column Read/Recall Chart

Explicit Instruction

1. Select a short article related to a topic being studied. The article might be on "bats."
2. Have students make predictions about what they might learn from the article.
3. Give each student a copy of the three-column read/recall chart or have them draw one in their notebooks.

Three-Column Read/Recall Chart

Name: _____   Topic: _____
Name of Article or Chapter: _____

First Reading Recall	Second Reading Recall	Third Reading Recall

4. After previewing the text, have students write the information they recall under the first column (First Reading Recall).
5. After previewing the text, have students read the selection a second time to remember details to place under the second column.
6. Have students read the selection a third time, recall information, and write the information under the third column.
7. Share the ideas and details students recalled.
8. You can also use this strategy by giving students specific purposes for reading. Examples of questions might include: How many and what kinds of bats are there? Where do bats live? What do bats eat? In what ways are bats helpful or harmful?

Outlining

Explicit Instruction

Hofler (1983) identified a four-step strategy for teaching students how to outline, as follows:

1. List concrete items: California, Southeastern states, Florida, Oregon, Georgia, North Carolina, Washington, South Carolina, Western states.
2. First classification: Categorizing

Western States	*Southeastern States*
California	Florida
Oregon	Georgia
Washington	North Carolina
	South Carolina

3. Second classification: Initial Outline Format

   Western States
   California
   Oregon
   Washington
   Southeastern States
   Florida
   Georgia
   North Carolina
   South Carolina

4. Third classification
   Western and Southeastern States
   I. Western States
      A. California
      B. Oregon
      C. Washington

II. Southeastern States
    A. Florida
    B. Georgia
    C. North Carolina
    D. South Carolina

Text Mark-Ups

Explicit Instruction

1. First model this strategy using overhead transparencies of a nonfiction or expository selection.
2. Do a think-aloud and model how you might mark up the selection.
3. You might start out by making a prediction about what the selection will be about. You can indicate this with P =.
4. As you read along you might locate an interesting or important vocabulary word. You might circle the word and in the margin write V and a couple of key words that help define the word.
5. M might be used to indicate the main idea that you identified, or in a margin write M and the main idea you derived from the selection.
6. As you read on you might come across a section to which you can make a personal connection. Write PC in the column with a note that reminds you of this connection.
7. If specific questions were assigned to be answered, the notation Q1, Q2, Q3 could be used to indicate the answers to question 1, question 2, and so on.
8. If students cannot write on the text, sticky notes can be used.
9. As you model this activity for students, avoid making too many notes.

Think-Pair-Write-Share

This is an extension of think-pair-share that encourages students to engage in writing.

Explicit Instruction

1. **Think.** Present students with an open-ended question. Give them a few minutes to think about the question.
2. **Pair.** Pair students up with a partner (selecting different colored Tootsie Roll Pops, colored popsicle sticks, nearest neighbor, etc.). They discuss their answers to the question.
3. **Write.** Have students compare their answers and select the answers that they think are the most powerful or unique. These answers are written down for use during sharing.
4. **Share.** During sharing have each pair of students relate (share) the answers they wrote down.
5. The written answers can then be placed on a sharing wall (as compared with a word wall).

Mnemonics

Explicit Instruction

1. Demonstrate the techniques listed under reinforcement activities to your students as the opportunity arises.
2. When students understand the techniques, ask them to develop their own mnemonic aids as they encounter materials to be memorized. Do this as a class at first. Then students can develop their own mnemonic devices.
3. Have students explain how the aids will help them remember the material.

Reinforcement Activities: Mnemonics

1. **Putting information into alphabetical order.**
2. **Putting information into numerical order.**
3. **Creating acronyms** (such as *HOMES* for the Great Lakes).
4. **Creating sentences** ("Every good boy does fine" for the scale).
5. **Creating associations** (associating the name of a country with the name of a friend: Francis = France).
6. **Clustering or grouping similar items together.**
7. **Creating graphic organizers or maps.**

Personal Planning and Organization

1. **Taking notes.** When taking notes in class, use the two-column system (Palmatier 1971; Aaronson 1975; Pauk 1974, 1984). Students divide their paper in half vertically. On the left side of the page they take notes in class using one color ink. On the right side of the page, they add to their notes by reading the textbook. Make the notes on the right side of the paper a different color from those taken in class. A third color might be used to underline main ideas or write questions they have after studying.
2. **Well-organized material.** Well-organized material is easier to remember than disorganized material. Use of graphic organizers, outlines, or welltaken notes assists with organization.
3. **More than one reading.** A single reading usually is not enough. Review is necessary.
4. **Flash cards.** Write terms or concepts on one side of the cards and definitions or explanations on the other. Write possible test questions on one side and possible answers on the other.
5. **Reference file.** Keep a folder with old tests, quizzes, and study sheets to use as study aids.
6. **Selective recall.** Encourage students to be selective. They cannot memorize material verbatim from the book or class notes. They need to identify key ideas and words.

7. **Sticky notes.** Sticky notes can be used to pose questions that arise during reading, identify important vocabulary, jot down main ideas, and so on.
8. **Summary writing.** Writing summaries of materials studied aids in recall and in selecting important ideas.
9. **Rehearsal.** Repeat or say the material to be learned over and over again.
10. **Assignment notebook.** Encourage students to keep a calendar with dates assignments are due. In this way it is easier to better organize and schedule time.
11. **Distributed and massed practice time.** It is better to study a little each day over a longer period and review than to study large amounts at one time.
12. **Time management.** Have students prepare a schedule to encompass time in class, time for studying, and time for rewarding themselves after studying.

Books for Children

Butler, K. T. *Rip's Secret Spot.* New York: Harcourt, 2000.

Gibbie, M. *Small Brown Dog's Bad Remembering Day.* New York: Puffin Books, 2002.

Hartman, G. *As the Roadrunner Runs: A First Book of Maps.* New York: Maxwell Macmillan International, 1994.

Lee, B. B. *Little Lemon: Activities for Developing Motivation and Memory Skills.* Learning Abilities Books, 1997.

Lucas, J. *States and Capitals and the Presidents.* Templeton, CA: Lucas Educational Systems, 2000.

Saltzberg, B. *Phoebe and the Spelling Bee.* New York: Hyperion Books for Children, 1997.

23

Listening

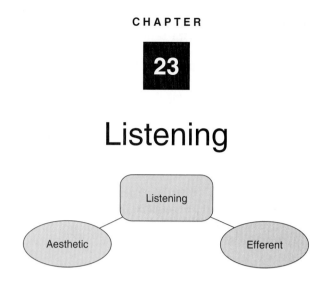

Description

Listening . . . the process of paying close or thoughtful attention to spoken language and constructing meaning or comprehending. This differs from auditory acuity or hearing, which is the ability to take in sounds of different frequencies. On the Informal Reading Inventory the listening comprehension level is defined as the highest level at which the student answers 75 percent of the comprehension questions correctly.

Aesthetic listening . . . listening for enjoyment.

Efferent listening . . . listening for information.

A poor listener in your class often will request to have directions repeated or will incorrectly follow directions. Students may exhibit poor listening skills for a variety of reasons. They may have a physical hearing problem that causes them to be distracted. Students may lack motivation and not identify learning as being of value. Too much noise or other distractions may contribute to poor listening. Teachers may talk for periods that are too long for students to be attentive. And not knowing the purpose for listening may contribute to an inappropriate focus during the time a student is expected to listen. Another reason for poor listening is that listening often is not taught in schools or encouraged at home.

Many of the activities identified in other chapters (especially in Units IV and V) can be used or adapted to improve listening skills. In addition to these activities, the following will be helpful.

Explicit Instruction: Guided Listening Procedure
(Cunningham and Cunningham 1976)

1. Tell students that they are going to listen to remember everything they can.
2. Tell students that you are going to play a recording. Direct them to listen and try to remember everything they can.
3. Play a prerecorded selection (lecture or reading material).
4. When the recording is finished, ask students to tell you everything they can remember. Students' responses are written on the board, even if inaccurate.
5. After students have finished adding information, have them listen to the recording again. This time they listen to find out any additions, omissions, or errors in the material on the board.
6. Make changes on the board.
7. Ask students which ideas on the board seem to be the main ideas. Categorize the information on the board.
8. Erase the board and give a short-term memory test on the material just discussed.

Explicit Instruction: Planned Inferential
(Cunningham, Cunningham, and Arthur 1981)

1. Tell students they are going to be listening to answer literal "right there") and inferential ("think and search") questions.
2. Listen to a selection that will be used during class.
3. Plan a series of literal and inferential statements based on the selection.
4. Students listen to the selection.
5. Students then answer the prepared questions.
6. Students must support their answers with actual statements they heard.

Reinforcement Activities: Aesthetic Listening

1. **Drawing to music.** Students listen to a musical selection. They then draw a picture of what they visualized, or pictured, in their minds as they listened.
2. **Orally describing music.** This is similar to drawing to music. Students, however, orally describe what came to mind as they listened to the music.
3. **Drawing a picture.** Students can listen to a story read aloud. They then draw a picture of what they visualized as the story was being read.
4. **Book panel.** A discussion panel can be formed by students who have read the same book or books on a similar topic. Students can then discuss their reactions to the books. Other students in the class can listen to the discussion and provide feedback.

5. **Conferences.** Hold individual conferences with students to get their reactions to a book or topic.
6. **Radio or advertisement.** Have students create a radio or television advertisement to "sell" a book to other students.
7. **Puppets.** Students can give a book presentation using puppets. The presentation can highlight the main points of the book or reactions to the book.

Reinforcement Activities: Efferent Listening

1. **Listening walk.** Take students on a silent listening walk through the school or outside the school. When you come back to the room, have students identify the different sounds they heard. A listening walk list can then be created.
2. **Series repetition.** On a tape, dictate a series of numbers, letters, or randomly selected words (1, 14, 9 or *n, z, e, x*). Dictate the elements in the series, allowing one second between elements of the series. Students must then write down on a piece of paper, or repeat aloud, the series that was dictated on the tape. (The advantage of using the tape is that it prevents students from asking you to repeat the sequence.) The number of elements dictated may increase in length as students become skilled with this activity.
3. **I'm going on a trip.** You pretend that the class is going on a trip. Each student must identify an item to take on the trip. To make it more of a listening activity, each student must repeat what the other student(s) contributed to the trip. (You might make it more challenging by requiring all items to begin with the same letter.) "I'm going on a trip to Canada. On this trip I will bring a clock. I'm going on a trip to Canada. On this trip I will bring a clock and a cloak. I'm going on a trip to Canada and on this trip I will bring a clock, a cloak, and a . . ."
4. **Sound bingo.** Students discriminate and listen for the details of various sounds. Make a bingo card. Place pictures of objects that represent the individual sounds in the cells of each bingo card. Call out a word and have students mark the picture that begins or ends with the sound of the word you called out.
5. **Treasure hunt.** Students can play "Treasure Hunt" by listening to oral directions. A student is blindfolded or steps into the hallway while a second students hides an object. (This object becomes the treasure that student one must find.) Once the treasure is hidden, the blindfold is removed (for safety reasons) and student one must try to find the treasure. As student one begins the search, a third student must provide directions to help student one locate the treasure.
6. **Following movement directions.** Have students listen to, and follow, a sequence of directions. "Listen to the things I am going to ask you to do.

When I have finished giving the directions, do what you were directed to do. (Go to the chalkboard. Pick up an eraser. Put the eraser on my desk.)" The complexity of the directions will increase as students become more skilled.

7. **Drawing a picture.** Have students follow a series of directions to draw a picture. The drawing directions should be repeated one step at a time.
8. **Propaganda techniques in advertising.** Acquaint students with propaganda techniques. Have students listen to the radio or television and identify propaganda techniques that are used. What is the advertiser saying to get you to buy the product?
9. **Book comparisons.** If students have seen the movie and read the book, they can make comparisons between the book and movie.
10. **Summarizing.** At the end of class, students can orally (or in writing) summarize what was taught during the class.
11. **Listening guides.** Provide students with an outline of a topic you will discuss during the class. Some of the information you will present during class will be included in the outline. Leave spaces for students to fill in additional information as they listen during class.

Books for Children

Axelrod, A. *Pigs in the Pantry: Fun with Math and Cooking.* New York: Simon & Schuster, 1997.

Cobb, I. G. *The Way We Do It in Japan.* Morton Grove, IL: Albert Whitman, 2002.

Ende, M. *The Neverending Story.* New York: Dutton Books, 1997.

Frank, A. *The Anne Frank Diary.* Upper Saddle River, NJ: Prentice Hall, 1993.

Leedy, L. *Mapping Penny's World.* New York: Henry Holt, 2000.

Miranda, A. *Night Songs.* New York: Simon & Schuster, 1993.

Naidoo, B. *Journey to Jo'burg: A South African Story.* New York: HarperTrophy, 1988.

Showers, P. *Listening Walk.* New York: HarperTrophy, 1993.

UNIT

VII

Affective Areas

24

Improving Self-Concept

25

Developing Interests

26

Suggestions for Parents

Unit Introduction

Affective areas . . . those factors that influence feelings or emotions. The three factors identified in this unit are self-concept, interests, and parents.

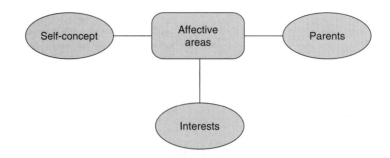

Bloom (1976) wrote that as much as 25 percent of all achievement can be attributed to the affective domain. Franken (1994) identified self-concept as the basis for motivated behavior. Alexander and Jetton (2000) summarized research on interests. They concluded that attention to elements of text, students' involvement in reading, and academic engagement are all associated with interest (Alexander and Jetton 2000).

The importance of parental involvement cannot be overestimated. The National Education Association (9/10/2002) identified a number of different meanings of parental involvement, ranging from reading to your child to becoming an advocate for better education. The summary of research presented by the NEA connects the impact of parental involvement with increased reading success, students staying in school longer, increased overall academic performance, reduced absenteeism, improved behavior, and more positive parental attitudes toward schools.

Improving Self-Concept

Description

Self-concept . . . how one perceives his/her abilities, value, self-worth, and identity.

As much as 25 percent of all achievement can be attributed to the affective domain according to Bloom (1976). You may have some students who do not see any value in themselves. They seem to have little or no self-worth. You may have some students who are so discouraged that they have given up. Instead of trying, they spend their time daydreaming or creating disturbances to get attention—even if negative.

Reinforcement Activities

1. **Success.** Provide many experiences that end in success for the student.
2. **Frequent praise.** Each student should be praised at least once a day. With older students, the praise should be conveyed quietly so that peer embarrassment does not occur.
3. **Something unique.** Teach the student something unique that the other students in the class do not know. Then let him/her demonstrate it to the class (like, how to put an egg into a bottle without breaking it).
4. **Dramatizing success.** Use charts that illustrate small steps of progress so students can visually see their gains. Charts might include graphs, trees with leaves, bookworms, thermometer charts, or a spaceship going to the planets.
5. **Me posters or collages.** The student can bring in a picture of himself/herself, mount it on construction paper, cut positive descriptive words from the paper, then paste the words around the picture.
6. **Me mobiles.** Students can make mobiles of themselves by using actual pictures of drawings.
7. **Time lines.** Have students create time lines of important events in their lives. Select five important positive events, put each event on a separate

index card (5 by 7 in.), then attach the cards to a string and hang them in the room.

8. **Silhouettes.** Have the student stand between a light and piece of black construction paper, then trace the student's silhouette (head). After the silhouette is drawn and cut out, the student can mount it on brightly colored paper. Finally, she/he can cut and paste positive words that describe him or her around the silhouette.

9. **Sharing success.** Ask students to close their eyes and picture a large movie screen in front of them. Then have them picture a time in their lives when they were really happy and successful at something. Ask questions such as "Where are you?" "Whom are you with?" "What are you doing?" "How do you feel?" "What did you accomplish?" "Who saw you doing this?" Then have students open their eyes and share their experiences.

10. **Success journal.** At the end of the class or day have students share their successes—large or small. These can be written in a daily success journal.

11. **Things I like to do.** Have students make a list of 10 things they like to do.

12. **Self poems.** Have the student write his/her name vertically down a sheet of paper. Then have the student write a positive self-descriptive word after each letter.

    *P*roud
    *A*ble
    *T*all

13. **Favorite color poems.** Students can write poems about their favorite colors:

    Yellow looks like _____,
    feels like _____,
    sounds like _____,
    smells like _____, and
    tastes like _____.
    Yellow is my favorite color.

14. **Favorite recipes.** Have students write the directions for cooking their favorite recipes. These can be placed into a favorite recipe book.

15. **Self-made commercial.** Just as there are commercials on TV to persuade people to purchase products, students can make self-commercials that emphasize their positive attributes. These commercials can be videotaped.

16. **Assistants.** Give students the opportunity to volunteer to help younger students. For example, they might practice reading a story until it's read "perfectly," then read it to a kindergarten class.

Developing Interests

Description

Interest . . . a motivational element in learning; the tendency to select, choose, or attend to something because of inquisitiveness, a feeling of its importance, or the like.

Literature circle . . . an organizational structure that provides the opportunity for students to select books from a collection identified by the teacher. Students meet in small temporary groups at a scheduled time to discuss their chosen books. Literature focus units are similar to literature circles except that one book is read by the entire class and the teacher assumes a more directive role.

You may have some students in your class who simply refuse to read, or express a desire not to read. This lack of interest in reading may be the result of requiring students to read material that is too difficult, students lacking confidence in their reading ability, an overdependence on using word attack skills, students with a limited range of interests, or requiring students to read a lot of material outside their fields of interest.

Developing students' interests is not a clear-cut, simple task. Rather, it is as complex as the students with whom you work. There is no substitute for the interest and excitement that you express and share with students about books. There is also no substitute for the interest and excitement students share with each other about a book. Remember to provide time for this sharing.

The building of successful experiences and self-confidence contribute to building interests, especially those of students who may have experienced difficulty or failure in reading. Providing experiences related to, but going beyond, reading the story and answering end-of-the-selection questions also contributes to building interest.

Generic activities as well as more specific activities, especially activities for incorporating writing into your reading program, follow. These represent their primary classifications. Some activities, however, may be related to more than one area. The 100 activities are arranged as follows:

Generic, 1–14	Drama, 28–32
Listening, 15–20	Art, 33–42
Speech, 21–27	Writing, 43–100

Reinforcement Activities: Developing Interests

1. **Identifying interests.** You can identify a student's interests by using an interest inventory. (See the inventory at the end of this chapter.)
2. **Providing easier reading materials.** If the student is reading without your assistance, be certain the material being read is at an independent level. If the student is engaged in instruction, be certain the material is no harder than the student's instructional level indicates it should be.
3. **Teaching students to select books.** Teach the student how to select a book for independent reading. Guide students into counting 100 consecutive words in the book. The student should then read this 100-word passage. If there are three or more unknown words, the book is too difficult.
4. **Charts.** Develop attractive charts on which students can keep a record of the books they have read. Bookworms, space ships, and mobiles are good starters.

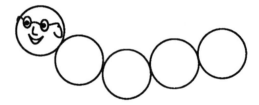

5. **Awards.** Give students awards for reading a specific number of books. These awards might include stickers, items that students collect, and books.
6. **Objects.** Bring in objects or conduct an experiment that makes students think and question. For example, you might do a demonstration in which an egg falls into a bottle that has an opening smaller than the egg's size. Then introduce students to books related to the activities you have just completed.
7. **Posting book lists.** Put on the board a short list of books that you think your students will enjoy reading.
8. **Silent reading time.** Provide a time each day when students and anyone else in the room, including teacher and aides, must read. This SSR (sustained silent reading) is a time during which students read books of

their own choice. Provide other times during the day when students have an opportunity to read, rather than do more workbook pages.

9. **You might be a book master.** Prepare questions around favorite books you have read to students and/or students' favorite books. Students answer questions about these books.

10. **The world of books.** Books have settings in many different locations. Place a large map in the room. Have students tag (or mark) the setting (location) on the map.

11. **Library corner.** Establish a library corner in a section of your classroom. Students should be allowed to go to this corner at designated times during the day.

12. **Reading tub or chair.** Provide a special place where individual students may go to read. This may be a rocking chair, an overstuffed pillow, or an old bathtub.

13. **Monthly topics.** Set up a display of books, posters, and pictures about a specific topic each month. Change the topic each month.

14. **Varying materials.** Allow students to read a variety of nontextbook materials. Such materials might include driver's manuals, cartoons, cookbooks, poetry, hobby books, newspapers, and magazines.

15. **Reading aloud.** Read parts of stories aloud to students to stimulate their interest. Stop at an interesting or exciting point.

16. **Speakers.** Ask students' parents or other community members to talk and share information about their work or hobbies.

17. **Listening stations.** Make audiotapes of books to which students may listen.

18. **Popular music.** Generate opportunities for students to study the music and lyrics of popular music. They can study the lyrics' meanings, read about the musicians, and examine the music's characteristics.

19. **Watching movies.** Encourage students to watch a movie about a specific book. Compare the movie to the book.

20. **Closed-caption TV.** With permission, use a prerecorded closed-caption TV program (adapted to grade level). Introduce the vocabulary ahead of time. Run the program without the sound and stop at critical points for discussion.

21. **Book discussion groups.** Several students may read books related to the same topic. Encourage them to form discussion groups and discuss how the topic was handled by various authors.

22. **Commercials.** Urge students to plan and present commercials to "sell" their books to other students to read.

23. **Read to younger students.** Allow students to spend time reading to younger students.

24. **Buddy reading.** Permit students to read the interesting parts of books to each other.

25. **Demonstrating.** Provide students with the opportunity to demonstrate something they have learned from a book.

26. **Conferences.** Each week try to spend a couple of minutes with each student in a discussion of the book she/he is reading.
27. **Acting.** Allow students to role-play parts of the story.
28. **Bags of books.** Students take brown bags, decorate them, and fill them with artifacts that represent the books they have read. Students tell the class how the artifacts represent the content of their books.
29. **Pantomime.** Students are very clever in the ways they pantomime story events. They can pantomime an event while other students guess the event.
30. **Flannel stories.** Using a flannel board and flannel pieces, students can retell stories to their friends.
31. **Book parade.** Let students dress as characters in their favorite books. Have a parade of these book characters, and have other students guess who their character is.
32. **Puppets.** Use puppet plays put on by students to stimulate interest in books. There are many kinds of puppets–sock, paper bag, stick, paper plate, finger, and papier mache. Vary the types of puppets used.
33. **Mobiles.** Construct mobiles depicting the characters and/or events from a story.
34. **Soap carvings.** Use soap, a metal spoon, a dull metal or plastic knife, and a newspaper. Using the newspaper as a desk or table cover, students can carve an item or scene from a story.
35. **Quilt making.** Use squares of fabric. Have students draw important characters, items, or places from their book on the fabric squares. Students then stitch or glue the squares together and explain each illustration.
36. **Collages.** Have students use cuttings of words and/or pictures from newspapers and/or magazines and construct a collage depicting the book read.
37. **Bookmarks.** Use illustrations and sayings to make bookmarks that represent the content of the book read.
38. **Book jackets.** Post the book jackets of newly acquired books on a bulletin board.
39. **Place mats.** Students might enjoy illustrating the sequence of events, main idea, or a scene from the story. These illustrations can be laminated and used as place mats.
40. **Medallions.** Students can create medallions by taking a plastic lid, illustrating a symbol for the story, placing the plastic on foil, and baking it at 350° F for about three minutes. You can then punch a hole in the medallion for hanging.
41. **Dioramas.** Provide a shoe box in which the student, by using clay and actual objects, can construct a scene related to the story.
42. **Games.** Challenge students to develop and construct a game that teaches important information they have learned from their reading.

43. **Ads.** Creative students will enjoy writing ads for magazines, the yellow pages, or newspapers related to the book(s) read.

44. **Advice columns.** Sometimes books lend themselves to the giving of advice. Students can write advice columns.

45. **Announcements.** Has there been a wedding, anniversary, birth, birthday, move, or other event in the story? Students can write an announcement for the occasion.

46. **Apologies.** Has a character done something or made an error for which an apology is due? Students can write the apology.

47. **Autobiographies.** Students can pretend to be a character and write an autobiography for the character.

48. **Awards.** Was an award given in the story? Should an award, in the student's opinion, have been given? Students can write and design this award.

49. **Bedtime stories.** Did the book contain a very young child as a character? Have your students write a bedtime story for this very young child or sibling.

50. **Biographies.** After students have read biographies of other characters' lives, they might write a personal biography.

51. **Book reviews.** Do students like or dislike the books they are reading? Writing a book review can be a good way to convey this information.

52. **Bulletins.** Students might write brief notices or bulletins about new books they have read from the library, movies based on books, etc.

53. **Bumper stickers.** Bumper stickers decorate many cars. Have students design a clever bumper sticker for a book they have read.

54. **Calendar quips.** Did the story take place during a certain month? During what month was the major character born? The students might write a calendar quip for this month based on the story.

55. **Calorie charts.** Students have just read a book about nutrition, food, or an overweight character. Let them develop a calorie chart for meals they think the character would like or should eat.

56. **Campaign speeches.** What kind of speech do students think the character would make if she/he were running for president of the United States or class president? Students should write a speech for this character and present it to the class.

57. **Cartoons.** Students might enjoy making a cartoon based on a book read.

58. **Cereal boxes.** Students can design a box for the cereal a character might like to eat. Or, if they have just finished reading a book on designing or advertising, they might create a new cereal and design its packaging.

59. **Complaints.** A character is dissatisfied with something, the student did not like the book, or students have read the book and viewed the movie, but did not like the movie. Have students write a complaint not insulting to the person reading it.

60. **Critiques.** Students can write their likes and dislikes of a book read. What could the author have done to improve the book?

61. **Crossword puzzles.** Students can construct crossword puzzles using words from a factual book or several narrative books the students have read.

62. **Data sheets.** After reading a book, students can perform an experiment or collect information and keep a data sheet on it.

63. **Diaries.** Students can create a diary they think a character might have kept.

64. **Directions.** Perhaps an element of the story involved giving directions for getting from one place to another or doing something. Students can try writing a series of directions for getting from one place to another or doing something.

65. **Directories.** Students might prepare directories of places where one can get information on the care of pets, healthful eating habits, recreational activities in the area, or other topics pertinent to the story topic.

66. **Editorials.** Students might write editorials expressing their views on a topic that was covered in the story.

67. **Epitaphs.** Did a mean or evil person die in the story? Did a good, honest person die in the story? Have students write epitaphs that could have been printed on these characters' gravestones.

68. **Excuses.** Did the story contain an episode where the character did not do something he/she was supposed to do? Have students write an excuse the person may have given.

69. **Explanations.** Inspire students to write an explanation on how to do something after reading a story in which explanations were given. Students might explain how to use a curling iron, how to tie a knot, or how to make an ice cream sundae.

70. **Fables.** After students have read fables and have understood that a fable uses animals as characters, that the animals do not have special names. and that they teach a lesson or end in a moral, have them write their own.

71. **Fairy tales.** Students can be given the opportunity to write fairy tales after reading several and realizing that they begin with "Once upon a time . . . ," contain elements of magic, and end with "They lived happily ever after."

72. **Greeting cards.** Greeting cards can be designed for many different occasions. Students can design greeting cards that one character might have given to another.

73. **Horoscopes.** Did something really good or very bad happen to a character in the story? Students might write what they think the character's horoscope was for the day.

74. **How-to guidebooks.** There are many how-to guidebooks on the market. Students might enjoy reading some dealing with hobbies, sports, or the like. They can then write their own guidebooks. ("How to Collect Stamps").

75. **Interviews.** If students read a story or poem with a major theme (such as happiness, loneliness, or rainy-day activities), they can interview

people to find their feelings on this topic. They might also write interview questions they could ask a character in their story, then write the answers they think the character would give to their questions.

76. **Letters to author.** Encourage students to write a letter to the author. Have them tell what they liked about the book and ask any questions they may have about the book or author.

77. **Mysteries.** A student's sense of mystery can be aroused after reading a mystery. Encourage students to rewrite a mysterious scene or create their own mystery.

78. **Myths.** Myths were once used to explain things that we now can explain through science. Let students create their own myths after reading several.

79. **Newscasts.** Report a story as though it were happening today. To do this, students must write the script the newscaster will read.

80. **Notes by students.** Allow students to write notes about a recently read book. These notes should be posted for other students to read.

81. **Nursery rhymes.** Since many parodies have been written of rhymes, students might use known nursery rhymes as takeoffs for writing their own.

82. **Opinions.** Students might enjoy writing about why they liked or disliked a book, character, or scene.

83. **Problem solutions.** Students might identify how they would solve a problem highlighted in a book, or how their solution would differ from that of the author or character.

84. **Product description.** Students might view a product and write a description of it. They might invent a product and describe it.

85. **Proverbs.** Ben Franklin wrote many proverbs. After reading some, students might write their own.

86. **Puppet shows.** Puppet shows can be written to retell a story.

87. **Questionnaires.** Before students survey people, they need to develop a questionnaire. They might also develop questionnaires they think story characters might have written.

88. **Reading shirts.** Students wear shirts to school with favorite passages from books they have read written on them (could be taped, glued, sewed). Students read each other's shirts and make a list of books they would like to read.

89. **Rebuttals.** Students might take an opposite viewpoint from that of a story character and write a rebuttal to statements made by the character.

90. **Reviews.** Students can write about why they think a book is good or bad.

91. **Riddles.** An enjoyable activity involves having students write riddles to stump others. These riddles might be about books they have read.

92. **Slogans.** Give students the opportunity to develop their own slogans.

93. **Story extensions.** After students have finished reading a book, have them continue the plot by writing, explaining, or illustrating what might happen next if the story were continued.

94. **TV commercials.** Can students sell a product, or better still, their book, on TV? Give them the opportunity to write commercials and then videotape them.
95. **Tall tales.** Tall tales are part of our American literary heritage. After reading several, have students try to write even taller tales.
96. **Tongue twisters.** "Peter Piper picked a peck . . ." is one tongue twister. How many more can students write? It's a great activity for teaching alliteration.
97. **Travel folders.** After reading a story that takes place in a particular or imaginary location, students might design a travel folder. What is the weather? What recreational activities are around? How do the hotels look?
98. **Trivia questions.** Students might write trivia questions about selections they read and play a game such a "Jeopardy."
99. **Weather reports and forecasts.** Imaginary weather forecasts can be written for stories. Students might even like to track the local weather and write the evening news weather forecast script.
100. **Writing books.** Have students write, illustrate, and bind their own books. These books can be placed in the library corner for others to read.

Literature Circles

The following guidelines can be used in working with literature circles:

1. Introduce a limited number of books to your students using a book talk or allowing students to look through a book display. Tompkins (2003) suggests introducing five or six books. You will need multiple copies (five or six) of the same text to allow students to make selections.
2. Students select one of these books and form groups based on the book chosen.
3. Students then read the book or a book section, depending on its length, independently or with a partner.
4. After the section is read, students meet in groups to discuss their books.
5. Students take turns at roles they will assume during the literature circle time. This helps to keep the discussions smooth, efficient, and literary. One student might be responsible for keeping the discussion moving along. Another student might identify and read back memorable or important sections of the book. A third student might make connections between the text and real world. A fourth student might begin discussions by presenting a brief summary of the reading. A fifth student might draw a picture related to the selection. A sixth student might be responsible for identifying five or six words from the selection and sharing their meanings with the group (Tomkpins 2003; Daniels 1998). Students are responsible for keeping the discussions moving along and meaningful.
6. Students use written or illustrated notes to keep the discussion moving.
7. Groups change as the teacher changes book selections.

Interest Inventory

Student's name: _____ Grade: _____

Age: _____ Examiner: _____ Date: _____

1. Do you have any brothers and sisters? What are their names? How old are they?
   _____
   _____

2. What do you like to do with your brother(s)/sister(s)? _____
   _____

3. Do you have any special things you like to do with your parent(s) (mother, father)? _____
   _____

4. Do you have any pets? What kind(s)? _____
   _____

5. Do you like sports? What sports do you like? Do you play on any teams?
   _____

6. What are your favorite TV programs? What makes these your favorite? How much time do you spend watching TV every day? _____
   _____

7. Do you like to use computers? What computer programs do you like to use?
   _____
   _____

8. What are your favorite movies or videos? Why are these your favorites?
   _____

9. Do you belong to any clubs or have any hobbies? Tell me about them.
   _____

10. If a friend came to visit you, what would you do with him/her? _____
    _____

11. Where would you like to take a friend or visitor? Why? _____
    _____

12. What would you like to be as an adult (when you grow up)? _____
    _____

13. What is your favorite subject? What do you like best about (name of subject)?
    _____
    _____

14. Do you like to read? Do you have any favorite books or stories? What are they?
    _____
    _____

15. What things make you feel happy? _____
    _____

16. What are the three things you like best about yourself? _____
    _____

17. Is there anything you do not like about yourself? Would you like to tell me about it? _____
    _____

18. If you could do any three things you wanted, what would they be? _____
    _____

19. If you could have three wishes, what would they be? _____
    _____

20. Is there anything else you would like to tell me so that I can get to know you better? _____
    _____

26

Suggestions for Parents

Description

Occasionally parents ask, "What may I do to help?" Since you as the teacher would like to convey some ideas to them, the following may prove helpful in answering this question.

Generic Activities

1. Read to your child.
2. Provide a quiet place where your child can work and read.
3. Talk to your child about items of interest you have seen in the newspaper or in magazines.
4. Label items. Post signs, words, and notes for your child to read.
5. Permit your child to read the grocery list and locate items in the store.
6. Play reading-related games, such as letter or word bingo, "Concentration" with letters or words, and "Scrabble."
7. Arrange mixed-up sentences to make a story.
8. Help your child write stories or books.
9. Read poetry to your child and assist your child in memorizing it.
10. Encourage your child to find and circle known words in the newspaper. Circle the compound words. Circle the words with the short *a* vowel (or some other) sound.
11. Allow your child to help prepare a dish for dinner by reading and following a recipe.
12. Reading directions for making things such as models develops a sense of purpose for the act of reading.
13. Place children's books and magazines around the house.
14. Place a limit on the amount of time your child may spend watching TV. Use TV programs as discussion points to get your child interested in books.
15. Use puppets for storytelling.

16. Be sure to help your child select books she/he can read. These should be easy enough so that your child knows 99 percent of the words without your help.
17. Put your child's name on mailing lists. If mail comes in your child's name, he/she will be more likely to try reading it.
18. Don't compare your child with other children in the family. Remember that she/he is a unique individual with specific likes, dislikes, and abilities.
19. Encourage your child to read to younger siblings or children in the neighborhood.
20. Explain the meaning of words to your child. Use actual objects or pictures whenever possible.

More Specific Activities

1. Play letter identification with license plates. Your child must identify the letters of the alphabet in order by finding them on license plates while riding in the car.
2. Play the buying game. You start by saying, "I'm going to Boston, and I am going to buy . . ." Turns are taken identifying items that begin with *b*. "I'm going to buy beans, bananas," and so on. On another round you might use a different consonant. "I'm going to Milwaukee and I'm going to buy . . ." Turns are taken identifying items that begin with *m*. "I'm going to buy mittens, mice," and so on.
3. Save packaging from grocery items so that your child can play going shopping. Then, when actually shopping at the grocery, ask your child, "What can contains pears?" "What can contains peas?" "What box contains? (name) crackers?"
4. Do finger plays with your child to reinforce story sequence. Two books containing finger plays are

   Marc Brown. *Finger Rhymes.* New York: Dutton, 1980.
   Tom Glazer. *Do Your Ears Hang Low?* New York: Doubleday, 1980.

5. Try word hunts around the house. (The word's difficulty depends on the age and reading achievement of the child.) Give the child a paper bag and name several words he/she should try to find *(peas, toothpaste, polyester, soap, cotton, salt)*. The child puts the objects containing these words into the paper bag.
6. Let your child identify letter names or spell words using alphabet cereal.
7. See how many words your child can make out of the names of states you are going to visit on a vacation. Or see how many words she/he can make out of the names of other siblings in the family.
8. Start telling a story and have your child finish it.

9. Gather some popular, colorful shopping magazines. Allow your child to find pictures of items that begin with a certain consonant sound. Then paste them onto construction paper.
10. Ask your child to tell the most important thing that happened in a TV show he/she was watching.
11. Suggest that your child find a word that begins with each letter of his or her name. For example, if your child's name is *Joe,* he might find *jump, old,* and *egg;* if it is *Jane,* she might find *jewel, apple, night,* and *early.*
12. Plan a picnic and make a list with your child of the food and other items you will need to take along with you.
13. Let your child help you address greeting cards.
14. Challenge your child to think of facts about items. For example, you might say, "Think of three facts about tomatoes." Other vegetables, fruits, animals, or the like may be used.
15. Using the newspaper, let your child find an advertisement. Then let your child tell you what the ad wants you to buy or believe. Explain what the advertiser did to try to get you to buy it (or believe it).
16. Have your child write four safety rules for riding bicycles.
17. Write the names of 10 friends (or relatives) in alphabetical order.
18. Prompt your child to write or find words that describe your car, house, dog, or any other objects, animals, or people.
19. Together with your child, make a list of all the plants and flowers in your backyard.
20. Tell your child to use each letter of his/her name for this activity. Then, using each letter, find words that tell what she/he can eat or do.
21. Motivate your child to help you plan the family vacation by writing to local chambers of commerce to obtain information on places you are going to visit. Older children can help plan the routes.
22. Encourage your child to make a travel journal of places visited.
23. Your child can write six questions about things to learn while on your trip (or just learn in general).
24. Cut off captions from newspaper photos and have your child match the photos and captions.
25. Looking through newspapers and magazines, have your child find words that tell

   - Something he/she likes to eat.
   - Places he/she would like to go.
   - Things he/she would like to do.
   - People he/she would like to meet.

26. Have your child cut out articles from newspaper or magazines and underline

   - Action words.
   - Nouns.
   - Describing words.

27. Using newspapers and magazines, let your child cut and paste on construction paper words that contain

- Suffixes.
- Prefixes.
- Prefixes and suffixes.

28. Make compound word puzzles for your child to complete. Write compound words such as *bedroom, mailbox, and cowboy* on index cards. Cut the index cards apart and have your child put them together to form the compound words.
29. Play games such as "Scrabble" that require children to use their spelling skills.
30. If you own videotaping equipment and your child has finished reading a book, videotape her or him acting out the plot.

Activities for Parents of ESL Students

Parents of ESL students may fear and be confused by the school system in the United States. Some parents view the school system as producing individuals who are self-centered and who do not respect their parents. This is contrary to their view that children should be responsible to and for their families.

Parents of ESL students often do not participate in PTA/PTO organizations or other school-related activities because they feel that the school administrators and teachers are responsible for establishing policies. They view their participation as interference. This nonparticipation, however, does not mean that these parents are not interested in their children's progress or school activities.

To involve parents of ESL students, try the following:

1. Encourage and use parents as school volunteers for various school functions. These activities might involve painting, planting, telling students about their jobs, and assisting with instructional activities.
2. Participation in multicultural activities can give parents a chance to share cultural characteristics and celebrations that are important to them.
3. Conduct meetings, whenever possible, in the parents' language(s).
4. Encourage parents to help plan school activities or parent meetings.
5. When talking to parents, emphasize the unique characteristics and positive qualities of their students.
6. Reduce written contact with parents of ESL students and increase direct, personal contact. In some cultures, a note from school is seen as something negative and students are punished by their parents for having had a note sent home. As a result, students will not show their parents the note.
7. Ask parents what skills or activities they or their children have that they might like to share.

Parent (Guardian) Interview

Parent's name: _____ Date: _____

Address: _____

City, state: _____ Zip code: _____

Home phone: _____ Work phone: _____

Interviewer: _____

1. How old is (child's name)? When was he/she born? Where? _____
    _____

2. Was there anything unusual about (name's) birth (premature,
    complications)? _____

3. Do you remember how old (name) was when she/he spoke her or his first
    word? _____

4. Is any other language spoken in your home? What language? Is (name of
    language) or English spoken more often at home? _____
    _____

5. Does (name) have any known health problems? Does he/she wear
    glasses? Have difficulty hearing? _____

6. Does (name) have any brothers or sisters? What are their ages?
    _____

7. How does (name) get along with his/her brother(s) and/or sister(s)?
    _____

8. How old was (name) when she/he first started attending school?
    _____

9. How many different schools has (name) attended? Where were they
    located? _____
    _____

10. How does (name) feel about school? What does he/she like best about
    school? Least?

11. Was (name) ever retained in school? In what grade(s)? How did (name)
    react to being retained? _____

12. What does (name) enjoy doing when she/he is not in school?
    _____

13. What does (name) like to do with his or her friends? How does he or she
    get along with other children?
    _____

14. Does (name) watch TV? How much time does she/he spend watching TV
    each day? What are his/her favorite TV programs?
    _____

15. Does (name) read when at home? How much time is spent reading each
    day?
    _____

16. Do you read to (name)? How often do you read to (name)?

    _____

17. What things do you think (name) is best at doing?

    _____

18. If you had three wishes for (name), what would they be?

    _____

19. Has (name) ever been tutored? When? Where? How did (name) feel about being tutored?

    _____

20. Can you think of anything else that would assist us in helping (name)?

    _____

UNIT

Specialized Approaches

Kinesthetic Method

Neurological Impress Method

Reading Recovery Method

Language Experience

Unit Introduction

Various methods and approaches have been developed to assist challenged readers. The following map represents the methods discussed in this unit.

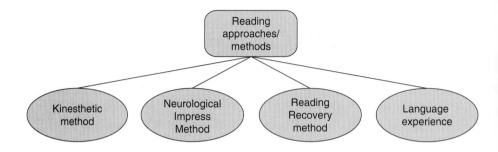

Kinesthetic Method

The kinesthetic method is a multisensory method for learning sight vocabulary. This method was developed by Grace Fernald (1943) and is also called the V.A.K.T. (visual, auditory, kinesthetic, tactile) and tracing method. It is used with students who have severe reading disabilities.

The kinesthetic method uses the senses of touch, sight, and hearing to assist students in learning new words. The student watches you as you write the word, hears you say it, says the word himself/herself, feels the movement of the hand and fingers as she/he traces the word, feels the texture of the crayon while tracing the word, sees his or her hand movement while tracing, and hears himself/herself saying the word as she/he is tracing it.

There are four stages to the kinesthetic method.

Stage 1: Tracing

1. Write a word selected by the student with a crayon on a piece of paper (about 3 by 8 in.). Say the word while you write it.
2. Have the student trace the word with his/her finger. The student pronounces the syllables while tracing them. Tracing should be repeated until the student can reproduce the kinesthetic motions of making the word. (Note: Phonics are not used.)
3. On a piece of paper, the student writes the word from memory. (If the student writes the word incorrectly, go back to step 2.)
4. The student writes the word three times without a mistake.
5. Have the student use the word in context.
6. Write or type the word on an index card (3 by 5 in.) and put it in his/her word bank box.

Stage 2: Writing—No Tracing

1. The student selects a word.
2. The teacher writes the word on an index card (3 by 5 in.) and pronounces it as s/he writes it.
3. The student looks at the word, says it aloud, then reads it silently three times.
4. Next, the student writes the word from memory. If the student makes a mistake, s/he goes back to step 3.
5. Have the student use the word in a sentence. Type the sentence and have the student read it silently, then orally.
6. File the word in the student's word bank box.

Stage 3: Teacher Does Not Print the Word

1. The student looks at the word in print.
2. The teacher pronounces the word.
3. The student looks at the word and pronounces it two times. Then the student writes the word three times from memory and without error. If an error is made, go back to step 2.
4. Write or type the word on an index card (3 by 5 in.) and have the student add it to his/her word bank box.

Stage 4: Independence

1. The student no longer writes the word.
2. The student looks at the word and tries to figure it out based on other words s/he has learned.

28

Neurological Impress Method

The Neurological Impress Method (NIM) was developed by R. O. Heckelman (1969) and is a multisensory approach for helping to expose students to the reading process.

NIM is a simple technique that teacher aides and parents can learn to use. It is successful in part because of the amount of material students read. Heckelman estimates that students can read about 2,000 words in one sitting. Begin by using selections of about 200 words. The steps to the procedure are as follows.

Step 1: Presenting

During this step the student does not have a book and does not see the printed material. The reader sits across from the student and reads to the student. The reader clearly pronounces the words and reads with expression. The student looks at the reader's face at this stage. This material will be read to the student about three times.

Step 2: Interpretation

Heckelman states that the reader puts, or retells, the story in the language the student understands. The reader expands on what was read by relating it to the experiential background of the student. The reader explains the story, puts it in words the student would use, and gestures and pantomimes when telling the story. The student still does not see the printed material.

Step 3: Rereading the Story

In this step the reader reads the story to the student rapidly and without expression. Heckelman states that the reader is modeling silent reading. This rereading is repeated two or three times at faster speeds. It is during this stage that the student is memorizing the material. The student still has not seen the printed material.

Step 4: Echo Reading

Heckelman states that the reader begins with small segments and gradually increases the length. After the reader reads a portion of the story, the student repeats what has been read. The reader may read a phrase at a time, a sentence at a time, or more. The length will depend on the student's capacity to remember and repeat what the reader has just finished reading aloud. This step is repeated two or three times with the student subvocalizing. The student does not see the story during this step.

Step 5: Rereading the Story with Expression

This is similar to step 1. The reader reads the selection aloud with expression only once. The student still does not see the story.

Step 6: Echoing and Reading

The reader moves to the side of the student and reads a phrase into the student's ear. The student echos or repeats the phrase. Then the reader holds the book in front of the student. Synchronizing voice and finger pointing, the reader points to the words she/he is reading aloud while the student looks at the words and repeats what is being read. Notice that this is the first time the student sees the story.

Step 7: Synchronized Reading

In this step the student holds the book. The reader reads into the student's ear and points to the written material. As the student reads along with the reader, the reading rate should be increased as the oral reading continues.

As a guideline, you should begin reading the material at a level slightly lower than the student can read with ease. Then move ahead with more difficult materials as quickly as possible. Do not spend much time on material that is too easy.

Heckelman states that a student, after two hours of instruction, might be reading materials two grade levels higher than his/her beginning level. After 12 hours of instruction the student might be reading materials four levels above his/her starting level.

These sessions should be conducted in a one-to-one setting. They should last approximately 15 minutes and should be conducted on consecutive days until a total of at least 12 hours has been devoted to the procedure.

Note that significant gains are not achieved if students listen to the story on tape. The one-to-one teaching situation produces the most significant results.

29

Reading Recovery Method

The Reading Recovery method was developed as a result of the extensive research of Marie Clay and her colleagues at the University of Auckland during the mid-1970s. The program's purpose is to identify and detect early reading difficulty of the lowest-achieving six-year-olds and provide highly specialized instruction in reading and writing. Strong emphasis is given to the use of phonemic awareness and contextual information. While having very successful results in New Zealand, it also has been successfully used in Great Britain, Canada, Anguilla, Bermuda, and the United States. Research on Reading Recovery indicates that it has an 80 percent success rate with students who complete the lessons (Reading Recovery Council of North America 2007; Reading Recovery, New Zealand, 2007).

Teachers in the Reading Recovery program must complete an intensive one-year professional development program. The curriculum of this program involves literacy theory and practice in Reading Recovery teaching strategies, and diagnostic observation of children's concepts of print and reading. Lessons, conducted behind one-way viewing windows, are observed by colleagues and feedback is given. Site visitations are conducted by lead teachers who provide feedback and ongoing assistance to Reading Recovery teachers.

The student diagnostic component of Reading Recovery has six elements:

1. **Letter identification:** identifying 54 different characters, upper- and lowercase letters, and variant forms.
2. **Word test:** reading the 20 most frequently occurring words in beginning reading books.
3. **Concepts about print:** demonstrating knowledge about reading a book and the printed page (familiarity with a book; identifying a word and sentence on a page; showing where to begin reading)
4. **Writing vocabulary:** writing all the words known in 10 minutes.
5. **Dictation test:** writing a story dictated by the teacher.
6. **Text reading level:** determining the student's reading level based on a series of books of increasing difficulty.

The Reading Recovery lesson is highly structured and sequenced. The student and teacher sit side-by-side to facilitate observation and interaction. The lesson components are as follows.

Step 1: Writing Practice of High-Frequency Words

The student uses a dry erase or chalkboard and practices writing one or more high-frequency words. This practice helps students gain fluency in reading and writing.

Step 2: Reading Familiar Books

The student rereads familiar books, books the student has read successfully in the past. Reading these books lets the student engage in fluent reading. It also provides the opportunity to practice strategies that are being learned. Approximately 400 little books of increasing difficulty are used in the Reading Recovery Program.

Step 3: Rereading a Recently Introduced Book

The student rereads a book introduced during the previous lesson. This allows the teacher to observe the student's reading and take running records. Teaching points are identified during this stage.

Step 4: Working with Letters and Words

Plastic letters are used on a magnetic board or chalkboard to teach letter names and word analysis strategies. This provides a kinesthetic experience for students in forming words. As students manipulate these letters, they practice forming words rapidly.

Step 5: Writing a Story or Message

The student dictates a short story or message. After the message is dictated, the student uses knowledge of phoneme and grapheme relationships to write the individual letters for the sounds heard in the words. The teacher acts as an aid in helping the student write the words correctly. This step helps the student attach meaning to writing and the printed page. It also helps the student identify a relationship between the spoken sound and its written representation (phoneme–grapheme relationship).

Step 6: Rearranging the Story

The teacher rewrites and then cuts apart the student's story into sentences. The student is given the task of rearranging and reading the sentence strips in the correct sequence. This step helps the student reinforce and develop phoneme–grapheme relationships, develop the comprehension skill of sequencing, and use problem solving.

Step 7: Introducing a New Book

The teacher has the student preview or explore a new book. During the previewing phase the student looks at pictures and discusses their possible meaning in the story. The student also previews new words that are important in the story.

Step 8: Reading the New Book

With the help and support of the teacher, the student reads the new book. During this reading the student uses problem-solving strategies to read the book.

Step 9: Rereading the New Book

The student rereads the new book to gain fluency and reinforce new words.

Sources for Further Reading

Clay, M. M. (1985). *The Early Detection of Reading Difficulties,* 3rd ed. Auckland, NZ: Heinemann.

Dinner, M. C. (1993). *Reading Recovery Research, 1986–1992: Citations and Abstracts from the ERIC Database.* Bloomington, IN: ERIC Clearinghouse on Reading and Communication Skills. [ED 376 449]

Dyer, P. C. (1992). "Reading Recovery: A Cost-Effectiveness and Educational Outcomes Analysis." *Spectrum: Journal of Research in Education, 10* (1), pp. 110–119.

Pollock, J. S. (1994). *Reading Recovery Program 1992–93. Elementary and Secondary Education Act—Chapter 1, Final Evaluation Report.* Columbus Public Schools, Ohio. Department of Program Evaluation. [ED 376 437]

30

Language Experience

For students who experience difficulty in reading, especially in terms of developing a sight vocabulary and understanding comprehension as a part of reading, language experience activities offer a personalized and meaningful instructional format. With the language experience approach, comprehension is ensured and student motivation is readily facilitated. (See Chapter 1.)

The most common sequence of steps for implementing a language experience lesson includes the following:

1. Provide students with a personalized experience (like popping popcorn, holding a lizard, baking, taking a field trip, playing a game, or listening to a story).
2. Have students talk about their experience.
3. Use leading questions to help students generate a story. Initially, try to keep the story limited to about eight sentences.
4. Write students' contributions on a chart, thus creating a chart story.
5. When reading the chart story aloud to the students, be certain to point to each word and emphasize the left-to-right movement and return sweep. You may want to read the story aloud several times, depending on your students.
6. Have students engage in repeated readings of the story, either individually or chorally. The number of repeated readings used will depend on the individual or the group of students.
7. Extend the story with related activities (matching words, matching phrase cards, sequencing sentence strips, sequencing words, or engaging in phonics activities.)
8. Type and duplicate the story and give each student a copy.

If you are working with a disabled reader, follow the same steps. We do not recommend correcting the usage of a severely disabled reader before writing his/her story during the initial stage of instruction. The student will remember his/her original words and make an incorrect association between the print and the word she/he remembers.

In working one-to-one with a disabled reader, you might actually type, or input on computer, the story as the student dictates. To do this, follow these steps:

1. Have the student sit or stand on either side of you, but make sure she/he can see the keys of the typewriter striking the paper in front, or the computer monitor.
2. Type as the student speaks. With less mature readers, pause at shorter intervals for reflection.
3. After an appropriate length, stop and give encouragement. You should read back the story, pointing to each word.
4. You and the student read the selection orally together. In this way, if the student stumbles or has difficulty, your voice will carry him/her along. Point to the words, but make sure the student is following along with you.
5. Finally, let the student "read alone' and praise him/her when she/he is finished. If the student stumbles on a word, provide the word immediately.

The best ideas for language experience are personal experiences (a student's hobby, family life, pets, or the like). Sometimes, however, off-the-beaten-path topics may stimulate a student. The following topics might be stimulating to students:

Making School More Interesting
Late at Night
Making Money
Leftovers on the Dinner Table
I Just Won $1,000
My Favorite _____
How to Really Find Out About Someone
My New Pet _____
This Time Next Year
All About Fixing _____
Adventures with My Computer
The Happiest Person
What My Refrigerator Is Fed
Training _____
What Cats Talk About
Help!!
I Love My _____
If I Were Invisible
Going Bass Fishing
Saturday Morning
How to Wash a Car

Winning a Baseball Game
My Best Friend
Walking Home Alone
A Summer Trip to Whynotland
My Favorite Monsters
Life 500 Years from Now
What's in My Favorite Garbage Can
The Story of the $100 Bill
All About Owning a Dinosaur

Speakers of Other Languages

Unit Introduction

English as a second language (ESL) learners or, as they are sometimes called, "limited English proficient" (LEP) students, are the focus of this unit. ESOL refers to "English for speakers of other languages."

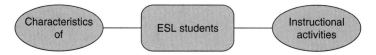

Some people have preferred to define LEP as "language enriched pupils" because these students speak one language and are now broadening or enriching their backgrounds by learning another language—English. No matter what label is placed on these students, their numbers are rapidly increasing.

Students acquire two types of communication skills: basic interpersonal communication skills (BICS) and cognitive/academic language proficiency skills (CALPS). Basic interpersonal communication skills (BICS) are the language we use in conversations or communication with friends. This language is cognitively undemanding. This differs from cognitive/academic language proficiency skills (CALPS), which are cognitively demanding. CALPS involve school (or similar) tasks requiring the use of reading, writing, and problem solving (Chamot and O'Malley 1994; Curtain and Pesola 1994). We cannot assume that a student who has attained good BICS has attained the more advanced CALPS. An understanding of student characteristics and the integration of ESL strategies into instruction will facilitate the development of CALPS.

Au (2000), in her summary of multicultural education and literacy research, writes that "the problem of improving the literacy achievement of students of diverse backgrounds is complex" (p. 839). Some guidelines can, however, be identified in literature. Teachers should understand the culture and language of ESL learners. Teachers should engage students in the use of authentic literacy activities that involve purposeful communication with an audience. They should provide opportunities for students to have challenging experiences with written texts. And they should use multicultural literature books (Au 2000).

31

Characteristics of ESL Students

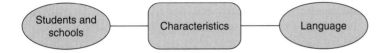

Description

ESL students . . . students who speak languages other than English when they enter school.

Language interference . . . language patterns of a student's first language that affect (or interfere) with reading, writing, and speaking a second language (in this case English).

Native country . . . the country in which the student was born and attended school.

Characteristics of ESL Students/Schools in Native Countries

Although each student is different, the following provides you with some general characteristics of ESL students who may be in your class:

1. Students may be silent much of the time because they are translating from English to their first language.
2. Students may misinterpret the body language of people around them. For example, the "thumbs-up" signal and pointing are seen as very rude in some cultures.
3. Hispanic students may look down when addressing an adult because looking down is seen as a sign of respect. Requiring a student to look directly at you when speaking is telling him/her to be disrespectful to you.
4. Students may rely on a teacher's gestures for understanding. Therefore, it is important for teachers to be consistent in their use of gestures. It is also important to be sure the gestures you use are not viewed as a sign of disrespect.
5. Students may have had very little formal classroom experience because of political or economic conditions in their native countries.

6. Students' social language skills may be more advanced than their academic language skills. That is, students may be able to speak English to their peers, but they may have difficulty reading and writing English.
7. Students' writing may contain the syntactic structure of their first language, and they may experience variations from day to day in their ability to write in English.
8. ESL students (especially Haitian) may be accustomed to learning by rote, in which all materials are memorized and then recited.
9. Audiovisual materials and computers are almost nonexistent in some countries, especially Haiti.
10. Communication is usually from the teacher to the student, not student to teacher.
11. Students may be unable to participate in extracurricular activities because their families do not have the money to pay for them.
12. Students may be absent frequently because they are expected to help with family matters such as paying bills, translating for their parents, or caring for siblings. Or they may be late because it is polite to arrive late in some Hispanic cultures.

Language Interference

Several examples of language interference are listed here. In the same manner that Spanish and Creole have unique characteristics, so does nonstandard English (often referred to as Black English or Ebonics). As you test or observe the oral reading of students of diverse backgrounds, think about the part language interference may be playing.

Language Interferences of Spanish

Phonology

1. No short vowel sounds.
2. Consonant sound substitutions

English		Spanish Substitution	
b	(box)	v	(vox)
j	(jet)	y	(yet)
j	(jet)	ch	(chet)
m	(Sam)	ng	(sang)
n	(run)	ng	(rung)
s	(sell)	z	(zell)
sh	(ship)	ch	(chip)
th	(than)	d	(Dan)
th	(they)	s	(say)
w	(wait)	g	(gate)

3. Difficulty with final consonant sounds because only a limited number occur in Spanish. Consonants that cause difficulty: *b, g, h, k, m, p, s,* and *v.*
4. Difficulty with final consonant digraphs. Consonant digraphs that cause difficulty: voiced *th,* unvoiced *th, sh,* and *ch.*
5. Difficulty with certain initial consonant blends: *sk, sm, sn, sp, st, scr, shr, spl, spr,* and *str.*

Grammar

1. In Spanish *no* is used to mean both "not" and "no."

   English: She did not go.
   Spanish: She no go.

2. The words *do, does,* and *did* are not used to form questions.

   English: Did you go shopping?
   Spanish: You go shopping? (raising intonation)

3. *To be* is not used to express temperature, age, or state of being.

   English: I am 18 years old.
   Spanish: I have 18 years.

4. The prepositions *in* and *on* are not used. Instead, *en* is used.

   English: The pot is on the stove.
   Spanish: The pot is en the stove.

5. The comparative and superlative suffixes *er* and *est* are not used. Instead, *more* and *the most* are used.

   English: John is the biggest.
   Spanish: John is the most big.

6. Articles are used with professional titles.

   English: I saw Dr. Lynn.
   Spanish: I saw the Dr. Lynn.

Language Interferences of Haitian or Creole

Phonology

1. No short vowel sounds.
2. Consonant sound substitutions.

English		Creole Substitution	
r	(ripe)	w	(wipe)
sh	(shin)	ch	(chin)
th	(think)	sh	(sink)
th	(them)	z	(zem)
n	(run)	ng	(rung)

3. Difficulty with final consonant digraphs because only a limited number are used in Creole. Difficulty with *b, f, g, h, k, m, p, s,* and *v.*
4. Difficulty with final consonant digraphs: unvoiced *th,* voiced *th, sh,* and *ch.*
5. Difficulty with certain initial consonant blends: *sk, sm, sn, sp, st, scr, shr, spl, spr,* and *str.*

Grammar

1. Plurals are not made by adding *s.* Instead *yo* is placed after the noun.
2. There are no variant forms of pronouns (such as *they, them, their, he, she, it*). *He* is used to refer to males, females, and objects.
3. The verb *to be* is not used.
4. Definite articles *(the)* are used after nouns, not before.

Language Interferences of Black English

Phonology

1. The final consonants *d, t,* and *k* are omitted.

English	Black English
told	tol
lift	lif
risk	ris

2. Plural and past tense endings are omitted.

English	Black English
rocks	rock
boots	boot
stopped	stop
barked	bark

3. The *r* and *l* sounds are omitted at the ends of words.

English	Black English
tore	toe
door	doe
stool	stoo
mail	may

4. Various consonant sounds are substituted for *th.*

English	Black English
this	dis (the sound of *d* at the beginning)
mother	muver (the sounds of *v, dd,* or *tt* in the middle)
	mudder
	mutter
with	wif (the sound of *f* at the end of words)

Grammar

1. Double negatives are used.

   English: I don't have any bananas.
   Black English: I don't have no bananas.

2. *S* is added to irregular plurals.

   English: men, feet
   Black English: mens, feets

3. The root word is used for third-person agreement.

   English: John walks every morning.
   Black English: John walk every morning.

4. The pronouns *they* and *them* are substituted for *their* and *those.*

   English: They carried their balloons.
                        Send me those letters.
   Black English: They carried they balloons.
                        Send me them letters.

5. Omissions and substitutions are made for the verb *to be.*

   English: Sam is running
                        Sam is tired. (at this time)
                        Sam is tired. (all the time)
                        They (we, you) were running.
   Black English: Sam running.
                        Sam be tired.
                        Sam bes tired.
                        They (we, you) was running.

6. The word *done* is substituted for *have.*

   English: I have completed my homework.
   Black English: I done my homework.

S. J. Crawley and L. Mountain, *Strategies for Guiding Content Reading* (New York: Allyn and Bacon, 1995) pp. 269–272; reprinted with permission. Also adapted from J. R. Harber and J. N. Beatty, *Reading and the Black English–Speaking Child* (Newark, Del.: International Reading Association, 1978); and N. R. Bartel, J. J. Grill, and D. N. Bryen. "Language Characteristics of Black Children: Implications for Assessment," *Journal of School Psychology, 11,* 351–364.

Teaching ESL Students

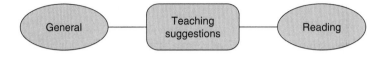

General — Teaching suggestions — Reading

Description

General suggestions . . . encompass those teaching behaviors or strategies that facilitate overall learning.

Reading suggestions . . . encompass those teaching activities and strategies that facilitate learning tasks involving reading, writing, and problem solving.

General Suggestions

1. Recognize that ESL students will be apprehensive about talking aloud in front of the class and maybe in groups.
2. Students may avoid requesting help.
3. Include the student in class activities.
4. Provide daily reviews.
5. Be sure to expect the same classroom behavior from ESL students as other students.
6. Identify trade books in other languages to supplement learning.
7. Read aloud to students.
8. Put labels around the classroom.
9. Provide ESL students with buddies who can assist them (especially in becoming oriented to the school setting and classroom procedures), serve as translators and interpreters, and help students with learning tasks.
10. Speak to the beginning ESL student in simple sentences and follow regular grammatical structures such as N–V or N–V–N. Avoid explaining things in compound and compound-complex sentences.
11. Be consistent in classroom routines and expectations.
12. Speak slowly; use wait time to allow ESL students to translate from their first language to English.
13. Use actual hands-on experiences; use visuals when hands-on experiences are not possible.

14. Encourage ESL students to describe the differences between their cultures and American culture.
15. Have students work in heterogeneous groups so that other students can serve as resources for the ESL student. Cooperative learning helps students in the socialization process as well as decreasing anxiety when speaking alone in front of the class.
16. Write clearly. Remember, the writing systems in some countries differ from that of the United States.
17. Use transparencies when possible so that the student sees the visual while hearing the auditory.
18. Use a variety of methods and modalities when presenting a lesson.
19. Use drama and role playing whenever possible.
20. Provide materials that are relevant to the student's culture and American culture.
21. Provide opportunities for students to talk about their home experiences and experiences in their first country.
22. Be careful to use wait time for students to respond.
23. Develop programs where parents can learn literacy skills and parenting skills.
24. Encourage students to share what happened at school with their parents.
25. Praise and encourage students when they do their best work in school and attempt to make meaningful contributions to the class.
26. Create a nonthreatening atmosphere that allows the student to experiment with English and be praised for success.

Suggestions for Reading/Literacy

1. Ascertain the student's knowledge of concepts of print, letter awareness, and phonemic awareness. (See Unit I for additional suggestions.)
2. Use patterns in words to teach decoding skills.
3. Use songs to teach vocabulary and pronunciation.
4. Maintain a picture file to help students make connections between the spoken and printed word.
5. Encourage students to read silently, especially prior to oral reading.
6. Semantic mapping before reading and for discussion purposes helps students organize information. (See Chapter 8 for additional graphic organizers.)
7. Demonstrations can illustrate the meaning of words to students.
8. The use of K–W–L (know–want to learn–learned) helps students activate prior knowledge, set purposes for reading, and review what was learned.
9. Encourage students to write in journals. Learning logs, personal journals, and reading logs are several different kinds of journals that may be successfully used with students.
10. Permit students to use computers or typewriters when writing.

11. Incorporate the language experience approach into classroom activities.
12. Integrate real-life experiences into reading and writing whenever possible.
13. Reciprocal teaching is a dialogue between teachers and students. The teacher and students alternate roles in asking and answering questions by each other. The teacher encourages students to answer questions that involve predicting, summarizing, and critical reading.
14. PQP (praise, question, polish) is a cooperative activity in which students reflect on each other's writing and identify what they like about it, raise any questions that could be answered to clarify the writing, and then indicate the punctuation, spelling, or grammatical structures that should be changed to "polish" the writing.
15. Emphasize the importance of reading to their parents daily.
16. Teach students reading games they can teach and play with their parents.
17. Read easy books to students.
18. Read multicultural books involving the student's first culture.
19. Encourage students to share books about their culture with the class.
20. Tape-record books for the ESL student to listen to.
21. Use computer programs in which words are highlighted as a narrator reads the selection. Pictures in these programs provide help in understanding concepts.
22. Provide opportunities to create "About Me" or "This Is My Story" books. In these books students share their customs, feelings about living in a new country, and so on.
23. Use the activities for fluency in Chapter 13 (big books, repeated reading, choral and antiphonal reading, echo reading, paired reading, radio reading, readers' theater, Neurological Impress Method).

Major Word Analysis Generalizations

Phonics

Consonant sounds: Speech sounds that are restricted. The air stream is obstructed by constrictions on the speech organs. This is why you hear the *uh* sound when trying to make the sound of individual consonants.

b	ball	j	jet	p	pie	v	vine
c	car	k	kite	q	quail	w	wagon
d	deer	l	lamb	r	river	x	xylophone
f	fish	m	monkey	s	sun	y	yellow
g	gate	n	nickel	t	tuba	z	zipper
h	hat						

Consonant blends: Two or more letters that are combined or blended together so that each sound is heard. The letters used to write these sounds are called *clusters*.

Initial Blends:

l blends		*r* blends		*s* blends		Other clusters	
bl	blanket	br	bridge	sc	scare	qu	queen
cl	closet	cr	crib	sk	skate	dw	dwarf
fl	flag	dr	drink	sl	slice	tw	twin
gl	glass	fr	fry	sm	smile	chr	chrome
pl	plate	gr	grass	sn	snow	phr	phrase
sl	sled	pr	prize	sp	spill	shr	shrink
		tr	tree	st	stone	thr	three
		wr	wreath	sw	sweet		
		thr	three	scr	scream		
				spl	splash		
				spr	spring		
				squ	squash		
				str	string		

Ending Blends:

ct	act	nd	bend
ft	raft	nk	junk
ld	fold	nt	sent
lp	help	rd	yard
lt	malt	rk	work
mp	lamp	sk	risk
		st	fast

Consonant digraph: Two letters that are not alike but produce one sound (phoneme) that is different from the sound of the two letters.

Initial Consonant Digraphs:			Final Consonant Digraphs:		
sh	/sh/	ship	ck	sack
ch	/ch/	chip	gh	cough
	/k/	chorus	ng	wing
	/sh/	chef		
ph	/f/	phone		
th	(voiced)	them		
th	(unvoiced)	thimble		
wh	/hw/	why		

Silent consonants: In words containing two similar, adjacent consonants, the first consonant is sounded and the second is silent.

bb	rubber	ff	ruffle	mm	summer	rr	barrel
cc	raccoon	gg	egg	nn	funny	ss	boss
dd	ladder	ll	yellow	pp	floppy	tt	mitten

The following are combinations of two unlike letters in which the sound of only one letter is heard:

kn	/n/	knit	- ck	/k/	back
gn	/n/	gnaw	- dg(e)	/j/	fudge
igh	/i/	frighten	- lm	/m/	calm
ps	/s/	psycho	- mb	/m/	lamb
wr	/r/	wrap	- tch	/ch/	witch

Hard and soft <c> and <g>: When the consonants <c> and <g> are followed by the vowels <e>, <i>, or <y>, they usually have their soft sounds—that is, the sound of /s/ and the sound of /j/.

\<c\> /s/	\<c\> /k/	\<g\> /j/	\<g\> /g/
cent	cat	gentle	game
cereal	cake	giant	goat
city	coat	gym	gutter
cite	corn		
cycle	cut		

Vowel sounds: Speech sounds that are relatively unrestricted. There is a relatively free passage of breath through the larynx and oral cavity. That is why you can keep making a long or short vowel sound until you "run out of breath."

Short Vowel Sounds:		**Long Vowel Sounds:**	
a	apple	a	ape
e	egg	e	eagle
i	igloo	i	ice
o	otter	o	oboe
u	umbrella	u	mule

Vowel generalizations

1. A single vowel in a syllable followed by a consonant usually has its short sound unless it is followed by \<i\>, \<r\>, or \<w\> (V–C pattern: b*a*t, *i*n).
2. If there is an open syllable (a vowel at the end of the syllable), the vowel usually has its long sound (C–V pattern: m*e,* sp*i*-der).
3. Words that end in vowel–consonant–*e* usually have a silent \<e\>, and the vowel has its long sound (V–C pattern: hate, dime, rope).
4. When the vowels \<ai\>, \<ay\>, \<ea\>, \<ee\>, and \<oa\> appear together in a word, the first vowel usually has the long sound and the second vowel is silent (V–V pattern: maid, bait, may, hay, eat, feat, tree, free, oak, oat).
5. If \<y\> follows a consonant in a one-syllable word, it usually has the long \<i\> sound (my, fry). In words containing two or more syllables, the \<y\> usually has the long \<e\> sound (baby).
6. A vowel followed by \<r\> or \<l\> is r-controlled. It is not long or short.

\<ar\>	\<er\>	\<ir\>	\<ur\>	\<or\>	\<al\>
/är/	/ûr/	/ûr/	/ûr/	/ô/	/ô/
car	her	bird	burn	born	ball
lard	were	fir	fur	word/ur/	halt

7. The vowel sound in an unstressed syllable is the *schwa:* a very short or softened short vowel sound.

about	fable	pencil	rayon	circus

Vowel digraphs: Vowel pairs that make a single sound.

ai (train)	ea (reach)	ie (piece)	oa (goat)
ay (hay)	ea (weather)		oo (look)
	ee (meet)		oo (spoon)
	ei (freight)		ou (rough)
	ei (ceiling)		ow (row)

Vowel diphthongs: a unison of two vowels that produce a sliding sound.

au (Paul)	ew (new)	oi (coil)
aw (saw)		oy (toy)
all (fall)		ou (pout)
		ow (how)

Structural Analysis

Forming suffixes:

When adding a suffix that begins with a vowel to a word ending in <e>, drop the final <e> before adding the suffix.

rake	raked	raking	raker
wise	wiser	wisest	

When adding a suffix to a word ending in a <y> that is preceded by a consonant, change the <y> to <i> and add the suffix. If the suffix begins with an <i>, do not change the <y> to <i>.

dirty	dirtied	dirtier	dirtiest	dirtying

If the word ends in a vowel + <y>, do not change the <y> to <i>.

play	player	playing
monkey	monkeying	

Double the final consonant before adding an ending that begins with a vowel if the word contains one vowel and ends with a consonant.

hop	hopper	hopping
swim	swimmer	swimming

Forming plurals:

In general, plurals are formed by adding <s>.

cat	cats	house	houses
cap	caps	moon	moons

Add <es> to words ending in <s>, <ss> <sh>, <ch>, and <x>.

bus	buses	church	churches
class	classes	fox	foxes
bush	bushes		

If a word ends in a consonant + <y>, form the plural by changing the <y> to <i> and adding <es>.

baby   babies

Syllabication:

Each syllable must contain a vowel sound. There are as many syllables as vowel sounds. Divide syllables between compound words.

cow-boy   fire-fly

Divide syllables between two like consonants.

bat-tle   lad-der   trol-ley

Divide syllables between two unlike consonants if they are located between two vowels.

har-den   lim-ber

Generally, do not divide between consonant digraphs or consonant blends.

preach-er   a-pron

A consonant plus <le> usually forms the final syllable.

ea-gle   nee-dle   ca-ble   sim-ple

Prefixes and suffixes usually form separate syllables.

un-known   fear-less   dis-ap/point-ment

Accent generalizations:

The first syllable of a compound word generally is stressed, or accented.

box'-wood   mail'-box

The first syllable of a two-syllable word generally is stressed.

mea'-sles   sal'-ad

In words containing prefixes or suffixes, the stress generally falls on or within the root word.

fight'-ing   re-gret'

In words that contain two like consonants, the stress usually falls on the syllable containing the first like consonant.

bat′-tle   mis′-sive

If two vowels occur together in the last syllable of a two-syllable word, this last syllable generally contains the stress.

en-root′   at-tain′   ar-oid′

APPENDIX B

Word Lists
for Word Analysis Elements

Initial Consonants

b

baboon   baby   back   bacon   bad   badge   bag   bait   ball   ballet   balloon
banana   bar   bark   barn   basket   bass   bat   bath   bear   bed   been   bell
bend   berry   best   bib   bicycle   big   bike   bird   board   boat   bone
bonus   bottle   box   bubble   buffalo   builder   bulletin   bunny   bus   butter
button   buy

hard c

cab   cabinet   cactus   cage   cake   calf   call   came   camel   camp   camera
canary   candle   candy   cane   card   carrot   cast   castle   cave   cob
coin   cold   comb   come   comic   continent   continue   cook   cork   corn
count   cousin   cow   cub   cup   cut

soft c

cease   cedar   ceiling   celery   cell   cellar   cement   censor   census   cent
center   central   ceramic   cereal   certain   cider   cinema   cinnamon   circle
circus   cite   citizen   citrus   city   civil   cycle   cyclone   cylinder   cymbal

d

dab   dad   damp   dance   dark   dart   dash   date   day   dead   deal   dear
den   dent   dentist   desk   dice   did   diet   dill   dime   dimple   dinosaur
dip   dirty   disc   dish   dive   divide   do   doctor   does   dog   doll   dollar
domino   done   donkey   donut   door   dot   double   down   dud   dug   dull
dummy   duplicate   dust

f

face   fact   faith   fall   family   fan   fantastic   far   farm   farmer   farther
fast   fat   fear   fed   feet   fence   fiddle   fifteen   fig   fill   fin   find   finger

fire first fish fit five fix flag food foot for fork forty foul found fourteen fox fudge full fume funny

hard g

gab gag gain gallon gamble game garbage garden gas gate gave gear gift gig girl give go goat goblin goes gold gone good gopher gorilla got gut

soft g

gee gel gelatin gem Gemini gender gene general genetics gens gentle gentry giant gibber gibe gigantic gin ginger giraffe gist gym gyp Gypsy

h

hack had hail hair half hallow ham hammer hammock hand hard has hat hatch have hay he head hear heart hedge help hem hen her here hid hide high hill hinge hip hippo hit hockey hog hold holiday home hook hoop hop hope horn horse house hug human humming hurt husband hut

j

jabber jack jacket jag jail jam jar jaw jazz jeans jeep jelly jet jewel jiffy jiggle jitter job jog join joke jolly jolt joy juggle judge judo juice jumble jumbo jump June jungle junk jury just

k

kale kangaroo karate keel keen keep keg kennel kept kernel ketchup kettle key kick kid kidnap kill kiln kilo kilt kind kindle king kink kiss kite kitty kiwi koala

l

lab label labor lace lack lad ladder ladybug lag lake lamb lamp land lantern lap large last late laugh lavatory leaf lean leap leave led leg lemon leopard let letter lettuce lick lid life lift light like lily limb lime limp line lion lip list lit litter little live lizard llama load loaf loan lobby lobster local locker lofty log loin lone long look loon loop lot love low lucky lug lumpy lunch lung lurk *m*

machine mad made magic magician magnet mail mailman main
man mantle many map march mare mars mask mat match math
may me mean meat melon mend men mercury mere merry met
metal mice mid middle milk mirror mist mix mold mole mom
money monkey mood moon moose mop moral moth mother
mountain mouse mouth much mud mug munch muscle mushroom
music mustache my

n

nab nag nail name nap napkin narrow nasty nation nature naval
navy near neat neck necklace need needle nerve nest net never
new newspaper next nibble nice nick nickel niece night nimble
nine nip no noble noise noon north nose not notation note noun
now number nun nurse nut

p

pace pack pad page paid pail pain paint pajamas palm pan
panda panther paper parade park parrot party pass pasta paste pat
patch paw peach peanut pear peg pen penny people pepper
period pet piano pickle picnic picture pie pig pillow pin pink
pint pipe pit pizza pocket poem poetry point poke pole police
pony poodle popcorn pull pumpkin pupil puppy purple purse
puzzle

q

quack quail quake quarrel quart quarter queen question quick quiet
quilt quip quit quite

r

rabbit raccoon race rack radio radish raft rag rail rainbow
raincoat raisin rake ram ran ranch range rank rat rattle rap rare
rate read ready rear reason red reindeer remainder rent report rest
rib rid ride rig right rim ring rip river road roam rob robe
robot rocket roller rooster root rose rot round routine row rub
rubber rug ruler ruin run rust

s

sack sad safe sag said sail sailor sake salt same sample sand
sandwich sang sap sat satin sauce save savor saw say sea seal
seam search seasonal seat second seed seek seesaw self sell sent
sentence serve set seven sick side sign signal sing sister sit six
so soap sob sock soda soft some soon sound soup south sub
subtract suit sum sun sunny super supper

t

tab table tack tag tail take tale tall tame tan tank tap tape tar
taste tax taxi tea teacher team tear tease teddy teepee telephone
tell ten tennis tent test tide tie tiger tight tile tilt time tin
title toad toast today toe together told tomorrow too took tool
tooth top tot toy tuba tug tumble turkey turn turtle tutor tux

v

vacuum vail valentine valid valley value van vary vase vault veil
velvet verb very vest veto vice view villa virus vine violet
violin visit vital vivid vocal voice void volcano volley volt vote
vulture

w

wag wagon waist wait wake walk wall wallet walrus wand wane
want war warn was wash watch water watermelon wave wax
way wear weasel web wed wee weekday weld well went were
wet wig wild wildcat will win windmill window wish wit witch
wolf woman wood wool word work worm would

x

xylophone

y

yak yammer yang yank yap yard yarn yawn yea year yeast yell
yellow yen yes yet yield yoga yogurt yolk yonder you
young your yo-yo yummy

z

zany zap zeal zebra zenith zero zesty zigzag zinc zipper zippy
zither zombie zone zoo

Initial Consonant Blends

l-blends

bl

blab   black   blacken   blackboard   blackout   blame   bland   blank   blanket
blare   blaze   bleach   bleak   bleed   blemish   blend   bless   blight   blimp
blink   blip   bliss   blister   blizzard   blob   block   blond   blood   bloom
blossom   blot   blouse   blow   blubber   blue   blueberry   bluff
blunt   blush   bluster

cl

clack   clad   claim   clam   clamber   clamp   clan   clang   clank   clap
clarinet   clarity   clash   clasp   class   clatter   claw   clay   clean   clear
clench   clerk   clever   click   client   cliff   climate   climb   clinic   clink
clip   cloak   clobber   clock   clod   clog   clone   clop   close   closet   clothes
cloudy   clout   clown   club   clue   clumsy   cluster   clutch

fl

flabby   flag   flaky   flair   flank   flannel   flap   flare   flash   flask   flat
flatter   flaunt   flavor   flea   fleck   flee   fleece   fleet   flesh   flew   flex
flick   flicker   flier   flies   flight   flimsy   flinch   fling   flint   flip   flipper
flirt   flit   float   flock   flood   floor   flop   floppy   floral   flour   flow
flower   flown

gl

glacial   glacier   glad   glade   glamor   glance   gland   glare   glass   glaze
gleam   glee   glen   glib   glide   glider   glimmer   glimpse   glint   glisten
glitch   glitter   gloat   glob   global   globe   gloomy   glorify   glory   gloss
glove   glow   glue   glum

pl

place   placement   placid   plague   plaid   plain   plan   plane   planet   plank
plant   plantation   plaque   plaster   plastic   plate   plateau   platform   platoon
platter   play   plaza   plea   pleasant   please   pleasure   pleat   pledge   plenty
pliers   plight   plod   plop   plot   plow   pluck   plug   plumber   plummet
plump   plunder   plunger   plunk   plural   plus   plush   ply

r-blends

br

brace   bracelet   brag   braid   braille   brain   bran   branch   brand   brash
brass   brave   bravo   brawl   bray   bread   breakfast   breast   breath   breeze
brew   bribe   brick   bridal   bride   bridge   brief   brilliant   bring   brisk
brittle   broad   broccoli   brochure   broil   broke   bronco   bronze   brook
broom   broth   brother   brought   brow   brown   brownie   bruise   brunch
brush   brutal   brute

cr

crab   crack   crackle   cradle   craft   crafty   cram   cramp   crane   crank
crash   crate   crave   crawl   crayon   crazy   creak   crease   create   creative
credit   creep   crept   crevice   crew   crib   cricket   cried   crime   criminal
crimp   cringe   crinkle   cripple   crisis   crisp   critic   crocodile   crook   crop
cross   crow   crowd   crown   crumb

dr

draft   drag   dragon   drain   dramatic   drank   drape   drapery   drastic   draw
drawer   drawl   dread   dream   dreary   dredge   dress   drew   drier   drift
drill   drink   drip   drive   drool   droop   drop   drought   drove   drowsy
drug   drum   drunk

fr

fraction   fracture   fragile   fragment   frail   frame   freckle   free   freedom
freeway   freeze   freight   frenzy   fresh   freshman   fret   friction   friend
fright   frigid   frisk   frivolous   frog   frolic   from   front   frosting   frown
frozen   frugal   fruit

gr

grab   grace   gracious   grade   graduate   grain   gram   grammar   grandfather
granola   grant   grape   grass   grate   grave   gravel   gravity   gray   grease
great   greed   green   greet   grew   grey   grid   grief   grieve   grin   grind
gristle   grit   groan   grocery   groom   gross   grouch   ground   group   grove
grow   gruff   grumpy   grunt

pr

practice   prairie   praise   prance   prank   preach   precede   precise   preen
president   press   pressure   pretend   pretty   prevent   price   pride   prim
primary   prime   primp   prince   princess   principal   print   prior   prize
produce   program   prom   promise   prompt   prong   proof   proper   protect
protein   protest   proud   provoke

tr

trace track tractor trade tradition trail trailer train trait trample
trance trap trapeze trash travel tray treat treaty tree tremor
triangle tribe tribute trick trickle tricky trifle trigger trim trinket
trip troll troop trophy tropic trot trouble true trumpet trunk trust
truth

s-blends

sc

scab scald scale scallop scalp scamper scan scant scar scarf
scarlet scary scatter scavenger scold scope scorch score scorn
scorpion scout scowl scuff sculpt scurry

scr

scrabble scrap scrape scratch scream screech screen screw scribe
scrimp script scrod scroll scrub scruff scrumptious

sm

small smart smash smatter smear smell smelt smile smirk smite
smith smock smog smoke smoky smolder smooth smother

sn

snack snaffle snafu snag snail snake snap snare snarl
snatch sneak sneer sneeze snicker sniff sniffle snip
snipe snob snook snoop snoot snooze snore snorkel snort snout
snow snubby snuff snug snuggle

sp

spa space spacious spackle spade spaghetti spall span spangle
spaniel spank spanner spar spare spark sparkle sparrow sparse
spasm spat spatter spatula spawn spay speak spear special species
specific specify specious speck spectrum speech speed spell spend
spent spice spider spike spill spin spinach spindle spine spinner
spiral spirit spit spoil sponge spoof spooky spool spoon sport
spot spur

spr

sprain sprat sprawl spray spread spree sprig spring sprinkle sprint
sprocket sprout spruce sprung

st

stab   stable   stack   stadium   staff   stag   stage   stagger   stain   stair   stake stale   stalk   stall   stallion   stammer   stamp   stance   stand   standard stanza   staple   star   starch   stare   stark   start   starve   stash   state   static station   statue   status   stave   stay   steady   steak   steal   steam   steed steep   steer   stem   stencil   step   stick   stiff   still   sting   stink   stint   stir stock   stomach   stone   stoop   stop   storage   stork   storm   story   stout stove   student   studio   study   stuff   stumble   stump   stupid

str

straddle   strafe   straggle   straight   strain   strait   strake   strand   stranger strap   strategy   strath   straw   stray   streak   stream   street   strength strenuous   stress   stretch   strew   strick   strickle   strict   stride   strike string   strip   stripe   strive   strobe   stroke   stroll   stroller   strong   stroud strove   struck   structural   struggle   strung   strut

sw

swab   swaddle   swag   swallow   swam   swamp   swan   swank   swap swarm   swash   swat   sway   swear   sweat   sweep   sweet   swell   swelter swerve   swift   swig   swim   swindle   swine   swing   swipe   swirl   swish switch   swivel   swizzle   swoon   swoop   sword   sworn   swum

Other Blends (Clusters)

tw

twaddle   twain   twang   tweed   tweezer   twelve   twenty   twice   twiddle twig   twilight   twill   twin   twine   twinge   twinkle   twirl   twist   twit twitch   twitter   twixt

qu

quack   quad   quag   quail   quaint   quake   quality   qualm   quarrel   quart quarter   queen   quell   quench   quest   question   quibble   quick   quiet quill   quilt   quip   quit   quiz   quote

shr

shrank   shred   shriek   shrill   shrimp   shrine   shrink   shrivel   shrub   shrug

thr

thrash   thread   threaten   three   threw   thrift   thrill   thrive   throat   throb throne   throw   thrush

Final Consonant Blends

-ft

cleft   draft   left   raft

-ld

bald   bold   build   child   cold   field   fold   gold   held   hold   mild   mold   old   sold   told   weld   wild   world

-lp

help   gulp   kelp   scalp   yelp

-lt

belt   dealt   fault   felt   malt   melt   salt   welt

-mp

bump   camp   champ   clump   cramp   damp   dump   hump   jump   lamp   lump   plump   pump   rump   stamp   stump   thump   tramp   trump

-nd

around   background   band   behind   bend   bind   blind   end   find   found   friend   grand   hand   kind   land   lend   mound   pond   pound   round   sand   second   send   sound   spend   stand   understand

-nk

bank   blank   blink   brink   bunk   chunk   clank   drank   drink   dunk   flank   frank   honk   hunk   ink   junk   link   mink   pink   plank   plunk   prank   rank   rink   sank   shrink   shrunk   sink   skunk   spank   stink   stunk   sunk   tank   thank   think   trunk   wink

-nt

ant   aunt   bent   front   pent   plant   rent   sent   tent   went

-rd

bard   bird   board   card   cord   hard   heard   herd   hord   lard   sword   toward   word   yard

-rk

bark   clerk   dark   fork   hark   jerk   lark   mark   park   perk   shark   spark   stark   stork   work

-sk

ask   brisk   desk   dusk   husk   mask   mollusk   musk   risk   task   tusk

-st

artist   beast   best   boast   breakfast   breast   cast   chest   coast   crest   cyst
digest   fast   feast   first   fist   forest   host   jest   jist   just   last   list   most
must   past   pest   post   rest   roast   test   toast   trust

Initial Consonant Digraphs

ch /ch/

chafe   chaff   chain   chair   chalice   chalk   challenge   chamber   champ
chance   change   channel   chat   chap   chapter   charcoal   charge   chariot
charity   charm   chart   chase   chat   cheap   cheat   check   checker   cheddar
cheek   cheep   cheer   cheese   cherish   cherry   chest   chew   chick   chicken
chide   chief   child   chili   chill   chime   chimney   chimp   chimpanzee
chin   chirp   chive   chocolate   choice   choke   chop   chore   chow   chuck
chunk   church   churn

ch /k/

chameleon   chaos   character   charisma   chemical   chemist   chiropractor
choir   cholesterol   choral   chorale   chord

ch /sh/

chagrin   chaise   chalet   chandelier   chaparral   chapeau   charlotte   chateau
chauffeur   chef   chemise   chevron   chic   chiffon   chivalry   chute

ph /f/

phantom   phase   pheasant   phew   philander   phobia   phoney   photo
physics

sh

shabby   shack   shackle   shad   shade   shadow   shaft   shag   shake   shale
shall   shallow   sham   shame   shampoo   shamrock   shank   shape   shapely
share   shark   sharp   shatter   shave   shawl   she   shear   shed   sheep   sheet
shelf   shell   sheriff   shield   shift   shin   ship   shirk   shirt   shiver   shoal
shock   shoe   shone   shook   shop   short   shot   shout   shove   shovel
show   shuck   shudder   shun   shut   shuttle   shy

th (unvoiced)

thank   thatch   thaw   theater   theft   theme   theory   thermos   thick   thicket
thief   thigh   thimble   thin   thing   think   third   thirst   thirty   thistle   thong
thorn   thousand   thud   thug   thumb   thump   thunder

th (voiced)

than   that   the   thee   their   them   then   thence   there   these   they   thine
this   thou   though   thus   thyself

wh /hw/

whack   whale   wham   whammy   whang   wharf   what   wheat   wheel
wheeze   when   where   whether   whey   which   whiff   while   whim
whimper   whimsical   whip   whirl   whisk   whisker   whisper   whit   white
whittle   whiz   whoops   whopper

Final Consonant Digraphs

-ch

approach   attach   beach   bench   birch   branch   breach   bullfinch   bunch
clench   church   clinch   coach   detach   drench   each   enrich   finch   grinch
inch   leach   lunch   lurch   march   mulch   ostrich   ouch   peach   pinch
poach   punch   rich   search   such   teach   torch   touch

-ck

aback   attack   barrack   beck   black   block   brick   buck   check   chuck
clack   crack   click   cock   clock   cluck   deck   dock   duck   flack   fleck
flick   flock   hick   hock   jack   kick   knack   lack   lick   lock   luck   mock
neck   tuck   o'clock   pack   peck   pick   pluck   prick   quack   rack   rock
shack   slick   snack   sock   tack   tick   track   trick   whack   wick

-ng

among   bang   belong   ding   fang   flung   gang   gong   hang   hung
oblong   pang   ping   prolong   prong   rang   ring   sang   sing   sling   song
strong   strung   stung   sung   swing   tang   thong   throng   twang
wrung   wing   zing

-sh

ambush anguish ash astonish bash blush brandish brush bush cash clash crush dish establish famish fish flash flush fresh gnash gush harsh hash hush lush mash mesh push plush rash rush sash smash stash trash

Two Similar Consonants

bb

babble bubble dabble ebb gobble hobby rabbit ribbon rubber wobble

cc

acclaim accord accumulate occasion occupy occur raccoon

dd

add caddy daddy forbidden griddle hidden ladder middle odd paddle puddle saddle sudden

ff

affair bluff buff coffee cuff differ efface effort fluff giraffe huff jiffy offend offer puff ruff scuff sheriff sluff snuff

gg

egg gaggle giggle goggle waggle wiggle

ll

all alloy balloon bell belly bill call cell collect dell doll dollar ellipse fellow follow gallon gallop hello lollipop lullaby million pill roll silly skillet small spell swallow thrill village wall yell yellow

mm

ammonia bummed common crammed dimmer drummer glimmer grammar hammer hammock mammal shimmer slamming slimmest summer trimmer tummy

nn

annex annoy annual banned bunny dinner flannel funnel granny minnow nanny penny running skinny tunnel

pp

apparatus apparel appeal apple floppy happen happy hippo opponent pepper puppet puppy slipper whipped zipper

rr

arraign array arrest arrive arrogant arrow barrel berry carrot cherry ferry merry mirror parrot squirrel

ss

across bass bliss boss brass chess class cross dress floss fuss glass gloss hiss kiss loss mass massage message pass possible press scissors stress tassel

tt

attain batter better bottom butter button cotton cutter flatter kitten letter litter little mitten pretty rattle tattle

Silent Consonant Combinations

dg(e)

badge bridge budge dodge edge fudge hedge judge ledge lodge midget nudge pledge ridge sledge wedge

(i)gh

blight bright fight flight fright height light might night right sigh slight tight

kn

knack knave knead knee knew knickers knife knight knit knob knock knoll knot know knowledge knuckle

lm

alm balm calm elm embalm palm qualm realm

mb

bomb climb comb crumb dumb lamb limb numb plumb thumb

tch

batch catch ditch dutch fetch hatchet hitch hutch latch
match notch patch pitch watch witch

Vowel Digraphs

ai

aid bait bail braid chain daily fail faint faith frail gain gait
grain hail jail laid lain maid mail nail paid pail pain paint
quail raid rail rain raise raisin sail saint stain tail taint train
vain wail wait

ay

bay bayonet bray cay clay day daylight delay fay fray gray hay
jay lay layer may nay parlay pay play ray relay say slay spay
stay stray tray way

ea (reach)

beach beacon bead beagle beak beam bean beast bleach breach
cheap clean deacon each feast feat gear glean heal heap heat
leaf leak leap lease leave meal mean measles meat neat peach
peal peat please reach read real ream reason sea seal seam
season seat steal tea teach team veal weak weasel wheat

ea (weather)

breakfast cleanser dead deaf feather head health heather heaven
heavy lead leather meadow measure pleasure spread sweater thread
treasure wealth weapon weather

ee

agree beef beep beetle cheek cheese deed deem deep eel feet
fleet geese heel jeep keep keen leek meed meek needle peek
peep queen reef reel seed seek seem seen seep seethe sheep
sleep speech speed steep sweet teem teeny wee weed week weep

ei (ceiling)

ceiling conceive either leisure neither perceive receipt receive seize
sheik veil

ei (freight)

beige   eight   lei   neigh   neighbor   reign   reindeer   sleigh   weigh   weight

ie (piece)

achieve   belief   chief   diesel   field   fiend   grief   grieve   lief   lien
medieval   niece   piece   pier   prairie   siege   thief   thievish   wield   yield

oa

approach   boast   boat   broach   cloak   coach   coal   coast   coat   coax
croak   float   foam   gloat   goad   goal   goat   groan   load   loaf   loan
moan   moat   oaf   oak   oat   poach   roach   road   roam   roast   soak   soap
throat   toad   toast

oo (look)

book   brook   cook   cookie   crooked   dogwood   foot   good   goody   gook
hood   hoof   hook   look   misunderstood   nook   rookie   shook   soot   stood
took   whoop   wood

oo (spoon)

baboon   balloon   bamboo   bloom   blooper   boom   boon   booth   boost
booze   brood   broom   caboose   cartoon   coo   cool   coon   coop   droop
food   foolish   goober   goose   groove   hoop   hoot   igloo   kangaroo   loom
loon   loop   looser   loot   maroon   mood   moon   moose   mushroom
noodle   noose   pooch   poodle   pool   raccoon   roof   root   rooster   saloon
scoop   shampoo   shoot   smooth   spool   spoon   stool   tool   tooth   zoo

ou (rough)

cousin   curious   double   enormous   enough   envious   trouble   tough   young

ow (low)

arrow   below   billow   blow   blown   bowl   crow   elbow   fellow   flow
follow   glow   grow   harrow   known   low   mellow   mow   owe   owing
own   pillow   row   show   slow   snow   sorrow   sow   stow   swallow
throw   thrown   tomorrow   tow   willow

Vowel Diphthongs

au (Paul)

applause auburn audio audit auger augment August aunt
aura auspice austere authentic author auto autumn caught cauldron
caulk cause caustic clause daughter daunt dauphin faucet fault
faun fraud gaudy gauze haul haunt laud launch launder laurel
maudlin mauve naughty pauper pause sauce saucer taught vault

aw (saw)

awe awful awkward bawl brawl caw claw crawl dawn draw
drawer drawn fawn flaw hawk hawthorn jaw law lawn lawyer
Mohawk paw pawl pawn raw saw shawl slaw sprawl straw
tawny thaw yawn

all (fall)

all allspice ball ballplayer call callable fall fallout gall hall
hallway install mall pall scald small spall squall stall tall tallest
wall walled wallet

ew (new)

anew askew blew brew chew clew crew dew drew few flew grew
hew hewn jewel knew new newly news newscaster pew renew
screw shrew shrewd skew spew stew threw view whew yew

oi (coil)

anoint appoint asteroid avoid boil boisterous broil coil coin choice
despoil foible foil hoist join joist loin loiter moist noise oil
point poise poison soil spoil toil turmoil voice void

oy (toy)

ahoy alloy annoy boy convoy decoy destroyer disloyal employ
enjoy hoy joy loyal ploy royal soy toy voyage

ou (pout)

about account aloud amount announce blouse bounce bound cloud
clout couch count crouch devour doubt flour flout foul found
ground grout hound hour house loud mound mount mouse mouth
noun ouch ounce our out pouch pound pout proud round route
scour scout shout sour sprout thou trounce trout wound

ow (how)

allow brow brown chow clown cow crowd crown dower down
drown endow flower fowl gown how howl jowl now owl
plow pow powder power prow prowl rowdy scow shower town
vow vowel wow

Common Phonograms (Rimes)

ab	cab, crab, dab, drab, gab, grab, jab, stab
able	able, cable, table, stable
ace	ace, brace, face, grace, lace, pace, place, race, space, trace
*ack	back, black, clack, crack, hack, jack, knack, lack, pack, rack, sack, slack, smack, snack, stack, tack, track
add	add, bad, brad, cad, clad, dad, fad, gad, glad, had, lad, mad, pad, plaid, sad
ade	blade, fade, glade, grade, jade, made, shade, spade, trade, wade
ag	bag, brag, crag, drag, flag, gag, hag, jag, lag, nag, rag, sag, shag, slag, snag, stag, swag, tag, wag
age	age, cage, page, rage, sage, stage, wage
aid	aid, afraid, braid, laid, maid, paid, raid
*ail	bail, fail, hail, jail, mail, nail, pail, quail, rail, sail, snail, trail, wail
*ain	brain, chain, drain, gain, grain, lain, main, pain, plain, rain, slain, sprain, stain, strain, train, twain, vain
air	air, chair, fair, flair, glair, hair, lair, pair
*ake	bake, brake, cake, drake, fake, flake, lake, make, quake, rake, sake, shake, snake, stake, take, wake
*ale	ale, bale, dale, gale, hale, kale, male, pale, sale, scale, stale, swale, tale, vale, wale, whale
alk	balk, chalk, stalk, talk, walk
all	all, ball, call, fall, hall, small, stall, tall, wall
am	am, cam, clam, cram, dam, ham, jam, swam
*ame	blame, came, dame, fame, flame, frame, game, lame, name, same, shame, tame
amp	camp, champ, clamp, cramp, damp, gramp, lamp, ramp, scamp, stamp, tamp, tramp, vamp
*an	an, ban, began, bran, can, clan, fan, man, pan, plan, ran, scan, span, tan, than, van
and	and, band, bland, brand, gland, grand, hand, land, rand, sand, stand, strand

ane	bane, cane, crane, lane, mane, pane, plane, sane, vane, wane
ang	bang, clang, fang, gang, hang, pang, rang, sang, slang, sprang, tang
*ank	bank, blank, clank, crank, flank, frank, hank, lank, plank, prank, rank, sank, shank, shrank, spank, tank, thank, yank
ant	ant, chant, grant, pant, plant, rant, slant
*ap	cap, chap, clap, flap, gap, hap, lap, map, nap, pap, rap, sap, scrap, slap, snap, strap, tap, trap, wrap
ape	ape, cape, drape, grape, nape, scrape, shape, tape
ar	bar, car, char, far, jar, mar, par, scar, star, tar
ard	bard, card, chard, guard, hard, lard, yard
are	bare, blare, care, dare, fare, flare, glare, hare, mare, pare, rare, scare, share, square, stare
ark	ark, bark, dark, hark, lark, mark, park, shark, spark, stark
arm	alarm, arm, charm, farm, harm
art	apart, art, cart, chart, dart, heart, mart, part, smart, start, tart
*ash	ash, bash, brash, cash, clash, crash, dash, flash, gash, hash, lash, mash, rash, sash, slash, smash, thrash, trash
ast	bast, blast, cast, last, mast, past, vast
aste	baste, haste, paste, taste, waste
*at	at, bat, cat, chat, fat, flat, gnat, hat, mat, pat, plat, rat, sat, slat, spat, sprat, that, vat
*ate	ate, bate, crate, date, fate, gate, grate, hate, late, mate, plate, rate, skate, slate, state
*aw	caw, claw, draw, flaw, gnaw, jaw, law, paw, raw, slaw, squaw, straw, taw, thaw
awn	dawn, draw, lawn, yawn
*ay	bay, bray, clay, day, dray, fay, flay, fray, gay, gray, hay, jay, lay, may, play, pray, ray, say, slay, spay, spray, stay, stray, sway, tray, way
ea	flea, lea, pea, plea, sea, tea
each	beach, bleach, breach, each, peach, preach, reach, teach
ead	bread, dread, head, lead, read, spread, stead, thread, tread
eak	beak, bleak, creak, freak, leak, peak
eal	deal, heal, meal, peal, seal, squeal, steal, teal, veal, weal, zeal
eam	beam, bream, cream, dream, gleam, ream, scream, seam, steam, stream, team
ean	bean, clean, dean, glean, mean, wean
ear	clear, dear, ear, fear, hear, near, rear, smear, spear
east	beast, east, feast, least, yeast
*eat	beat, bleat, cheat, eat, feat, heat, meat, neat, peat, pleat, seat, teat, treat, wheat

eck	beck, check, deck, fleck, neck, peck, speck, wreck
ed	bed, bled, bred, fed, fled, led, red, shed, sled, sped, ted, wed
ee	bee, fee, flee, free, glee, knee, lee, see, spree, tee, thee, three, tree
eed	bleed, breed, creed, deed, feed, freed, greed, heed, need, reed, seed, speed, steed, tweed, weed
eek	cheek, creek, leek, meek, reek, seek, sleek, week
eel	eel, feel, heel, keel, kneel, peel, reel, steel, wheel
eem	deem, seem, teem
een	green, keen, preen, queen, screen, seen, sheen, spleen
eep	asleep, cheep, creep, deep, keep, peep, seep, sheep, sleep, steep, sweep, weep
eer	beer, cheer, deer, steer
eet	feet, fleet, greet, meet, sheet, sleet, street, sweet
eeze	breeze, freeze, sneeze, squeeze
eg	beg, dreg, egg, keg, leg, peg, skeg
eld	geld, held, meld, weld
*ell	bell, cell, dell, dwell, ell, fell, hell, knell, quell, sell, shell, smell, spell, swell, tell, well, yell
elp	help, kelp, whelp, yelp
elt	belt, dwelt, felt, knelt, melt, pelt, smelt, spelt, welt
em	gem, hem, stem, them
en	den, fen, glen, hen, ken, men, pen, ten, then, when, wren, yen
ench	bench, blench, clench, drench, quench, stench, trench, wench, wrench
end	bend, blend, end, fend, friend, lend, mend, rend, send, spend, tend, trend, vend, wend
ent	bent, blent, cent, dent, lent, meant, pent, rent, sent, spent, tent, vent, went
ept	crept, kept, slept, swept, wept
ess	bless, chess, cress, dress, guess, less, mess, press, stress, tress
*est	best, chest, crest, guest, jest, lest, nest, pest, quest, rest, test, vest, west, wrest, zest
et	bet, fret, get, jet, let, met, net, pet, set, wet, yet
ew	chew, few, flew, grew, knew, mew, new, pew, stew
ib	bib, crib, fib, glib, jib, nib, rib, sib, squib
*ice	dice, ice, lice, nice, price, rice, slice, spice, splice, twice, vice
*ick	brick, click, crick, flick, kick, lick, nick, pick, prick, quick, rick, sick, slick, stick, thick, tick, trick, wick
id	amid, bid, did, forbid, grid, hid, kid, lid, mid, quid, rid, skid, slid, squid
*ide	bide, bride, chide, glide, guide, hide, pride, ride, side, slide, stride, tide, wide

ie	die, lie, pie, tie, vie
ief	belief, brief, chief, fief, grief, lief, thief
ife	fife, knife, life, rife, strife, wife
ift	drift, gift, lift, rift, shift, swift, thrift
ig	big, brig, dig, fig, gig, jig, pig, prig, rig, sprig, swig, twig, wig
igh	high, nigh, sigh, thigh
*ight	bright, fight, flight, light, might, night, right, sight, tight
ike	alike, bike, hike, like, pike, spike, strike
ild	child, mild, wild
ile	bile, file, mile, pile, rile, smile, stile, tile, vile, while, wile
ilk	bilk, ilk, milk, silk
*ill	bill, chill, dill, drill, fill, gill, grill, hill, ill, kill, mill, pill, quill, rill, shrill, sill, skill, spill, squill, still, swill, thrill, till, trill, twill, will
im	brim, dim, glim, grim, him, limb, prim, rim, skim, slim, swim, trim, vim, whim
ime	chime, crime, dime, grime, lime, mime, prime, slime, time
imp	blimp, crimp, gimp, imp, limp, primp, scrimp, shrimp, skimp
*in	bin, chin, din, fin, gin, grin, in, kin, pin, shin, sin, skin, spin, thin, tin, twin, win
ind	behind, bind, blind, find, grind, hind, kind, mind, rind, wind
*ine	brine, chine, dine, fine, line, mine, nine, prine, shine, shrine, sine, spine, swine, tine, trine, twine, vine, whine, wine
*ing	bring, cling, ding, fling, king, ping, ring, sing, sling, spring, sting, string, swing, thing, wing, wring
*ink	blink, brink, clink, drink, ink, kink, link, pink, shrink, sink, slink, stink, think, wink
int	dint, flint, footprint, glint, hint, lint, mint, print, splint, sprint, squint, stint, tint
*ip	chip, clip, dip, drip, flip, grip, hip, lip, nip, pip, quip, rip, scrip, ship, sip, skip, slip, snip, strip, tip, trip, whip
ipe	gripe, pipe, ripe, snipe, stipe, stripe, swipe, tripe, wipe
ire	dire, fire, hire, ire, mire, shire, sire, spire, squire, tire, wire
irl	girl, swirl, twirl, whirl
irt	dirt, flirt, shirt, skirt, squirt
ish	dish, fish, swish, wish
isk	brisk, disk, frisk, risk, whisk
iss	bliss, hiss, kiss, miss
ist	gist, grist, hist, list, mist, twist, whist, wrist
*it	bit, chit, fit, flit, grit, hit, it, kit, knit, lit, pit, quit, sit, slit, smitten, spit, split, sprit, tit, twit, whit, wit, writ

ite	bite, cite, kite, mite, quite, rite, site, smite, spite, sprite, trite, white, write
ive	arrive, dive, drive, five, hive, live, shrive, strive, thrive, wive
ive	give, live
ix	fix, mix, six
oad	goad, load, road, toad
oast	boast, coast, roast, toast
oat	afloat, bloat, boat, coat, float, gloat, goat, moat, oat, throat
ob	bob, cob, dob, job, knob, lob, mob, rob, sob
obe	globe, lobe, probe, robe
*ock	block, clock, cock, crock, dock, flock, frock, knock, lock, rock, shock, smock, sock, stock, tock
od	clod, cod, god, mod, nod, pod, prod, rod, sod, tod
ode	abode, bode, code, lode, mode, node, ode, rode, strode
oe	doe, floe, foe, hoe, roe, sloe, woe
oft	croft, loft, oft, soft
og	bog, clog, cog, dog, flog, log, frog, grog, hog, job, log, nog, slog
oil	boil, broil, coil, foil, oil, soil, spoil, toil
*oke	awoke, broke, choke, coke, joke, poke, smoke, spoke, stoke, stroke, woke, yoke
old	bold, cold, fold, gold, hold, mold, old, scold, sold, told
ole	bole, hole, mole, pole, role, sole, stole
olt	bolt, colt, dolt, jolt, molt
ome	chrome, dome, gnome, home
ond	blond, bond, fond, pond
ong	along, belong, long, prong, song, strong, thong, throng, wrong
ood	good, hood, stood, wood
ook	book, brook, cook, crook, hook, look, nook, rook, shook, took
ool	cool, drool, fool, pool, school, spool, tool
oom	bloom, boom, broom, gloom, groom, loom, room
oon	coon, croon, moon, noon, soon, spoon
oop	coop, droop, hoop, loop, scoop, stoop, swoop, troop
oot	boot, hoot, loot, moot, shoot, toot
*op	chop, crop, drop, flop, hop, lop, mop, pop, prop, shop, slop, sop, stop, top
ope	cope, elope, grope, hope, mope, pope, rope, scope, slope, tope, trope
*ore	bore, core, fore, gore, lore, score, shore, snore, sore, store, swore, tore, wore
ork	cork, fork, pork, stork

orm	form, norm, storm
orn	adorn, born, corn, horn, morn, scorn, shorn, sworn, thorn, torn, worn
ort	fort, port, short, sort, sport
ose	arose, chose, close, nose, pose, prose, rose, those
oss	boss, cross, dross, floss, gloss, joss, loss, moss, toss
ost	cost, frost, lost
*ot	blot, cot, dot, got, hot, jot, knot, lot, not, plot, pot, rot, shot, tot, trot
ote	cote, dote, mote, note, quote, rote, smote, tote, vote, wrote
ouch	couch, crouch, ouch, pouch, slouch
oud	cloud, loud, proud, shroud
ought	bought, brought, fought, ought, sought, thought, wrought
ound	bound, found, ground, hound, mound, pound, round, sound, wound
our	dour, flour, hour, our, scour, sour
ouse	blouse, douse, grouse, house, louse, mouse, spouse
out	about, bout, clout, flout, grout, knout, lout, out, pout, rout, scout, snout, spout, sprout, stout, tout, trout
ove	above, dove, glove, love, shove
ove	clove, cove, dove, drove, grove, hove, Jove, rove, shrove, stove, strove, wove
ow	bow, brow, chow, cow, how, now, plow, prow, row, scow, vow, wow
owl	cowl, fowl, growl, howl, jowl, owl, prowl, scowl, yowl
own	brown, clown, crown, down, drown, frown, gown, town
own	blown, flown, grown, known, mown, own, shown, sown
ox	box, cox, fox, lox, ox, pox, sox
oy	ahoy, boy, cloy, coy, goy, hoy, joy, ploy, soy, toy, troy
ub	bub, blub, chub, club, cub, drub, dub, grub, hub, hubbub, nub, pub, rub, scrub, shrub, stub, sub, tub
*uck	buck, chuck, cluck, duck, luck, muck, pluck, puck, ruck, shuck, struck, stuck, suck, truck, tuck
ud	bud, cud, dud, mud, scud, spud, stud, sud, thud
udge	budge, drudge, fudge, grudge, judge, nudge, sludge, smudge, snudge, trudge
uff	bluff, buff, chuff, cuff, duff, fluff, gruff, guff, huff, luff, muff, puff, ruff, scruff, scuff, snuff, stuff, tuff
*ug	bug, chug, drug, dug, hug, jug, lug, mug, plug, pug, rug, shrug, slug, smug, snug, thug, tug
ull	cull, dull, gull, hull, lull, mull, null, scull, skull
um	bum, chum, drum, glum, gum, hum, mum, plum, rum, scum, scrum, slum, strum, sum, swum

umble	bumble, fumble, humble, jumble, mumble, rumble, stumble, tumble
*ump	bump, chump, clump, crump, dump, frump, grump, gump, hump, jump, lump, mumps, plump, pump, rump, slump, stump, thump, trump
un	bun, dun, fun, gun, nun, pun, run, spun, stun, sun, tun
unch	brunch, bunch, crunch, hunch, lunch, munch, punch, scrunch
ung	bung, clung, dung, flung, hung, lung, rung, slung, sprung, stung, sung, swung, wrung, young
*unk	bunk, chunk, drunk, dunk, flunk, funk, hunk, junk, plunk, punk, shrunk, skunk, slunk, spunk
unt	blunt, brunt, bunt, grunt, hunt, punt, runt, shunt, stunt
up	cup, hiccup, makeup, pup, sup, teacup, tup, up
ur	blur, burr, cur, fur, knur, slur, spur
urn	burn, churn, spurn, turn, urn
ush	blush, crush, flush, gush, hush, lush, mush, plush, rush, slush, thrush, tush
usk	busk, dusk, husk, musk, rusk, tusk
ust	adjust, bust, crust, dust, gust, just, lust, must, rust, thrust, trust
ut	but, cut, glut, gut, hut, jut, mut, rut, scut, shut, slut, smut, strut, tut

---

*Most common phonograms identified by Wylie and Durrell (1970).

APPENDIX D

Developing a Teaching Kit

Description

Teaching kit . . . an organizational system that contains unused supplementary reading materials, book lists, and tests.

The materials in a teaching kit might include teacher or commercially prepared phonic and comprehension games, including the popular file folder variety, and pages from reading workbooks of varying instructional levels. All these materials will be filed by skill area. Once you identify a student's weakness, you will have a ready source for targeting instruction. It is important to remember that skills instruction in isolation is not effective. Students must apply the skills in meaningful context.

How to Construct the Kit

1. Identify the decoding, comprehension, study skills, and affective areas you will need for remedial instruction. Then organize your materials under familiar word analysis headings.
2. Collect enough file folders for each skill area you identified. Label these folders according to skill.
3. Search for materials to place in the file folders. They may be found in discount stores, instructional materials storage areas, and closets.
4. Color code the sheets and activities according to difficulty. Red might be for grade one, blue for grade two, and so on. Then place them in the appropriate folders.
5. File the folders in a cardboard box that has been covered with contact paper, or in a file cabinet.

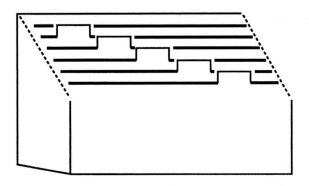

6. If the worksheets are nondisposable, you may laminate the sheets, place them between page protectors, and cover them with exposed X-ray film. You might also obtain exposed X-ray film from a radiology technologist at your nearest hospital. Then have your student use a nonpermanent marker for recording answers.

7. For scoring, decide whether you or the student will check the answers. Some teachers attach pocket card holders on the file folder with the answers recorded on index cards (3 by 5 in.). Students retrieve the appropriate answer card for self-correction of the skill sheet. Other teachers, who prefer a little tighter control on scoring, retain their own correct-response guide in notebook format on or near their desk.

8. Following correction, the nondisposable skill sheet is returned to the appropriate folder, and student notations on the transparent covering are then erased with a paper towel, sponge, or cloth before storing.

Award-Winning Books

Caldecott Medal Books

The Caldecott Medal is presented annually by the Melcher family in honor of Randolph Caldecott, one of the most famous English illustrators of children's books. The medal is awarded to an American illustrator for the most distinguished picture book for children. Book title, illustrator, and year of the award are listed below.

Flotsam, Wiesner, 2007

The Hello, Goodbye Window, Raschka, 2006

Kitten's First Full Moon, Henkes, 2005

The Man Who Walked Between the Towers, Gerstein, 2004

My Friend Rabbit, Rohmann, 2003

The Three Pigs, Wiesner, 2002

So You Want to Be President, Small, 2001

Joseph Had a Little Overcoat, Taback, 2000

Snowflake Bentley, Azarian, 1999

Rapunzel, Zelinsky, 1998

Golem, Wisniewski, 1997

Officer Buckle & Gloria, Rathmann, 1996

Smokey Night, Diaz, 1995

Grandfather's Journey, Say, 1994

Mirette on the High Wire, McCully, 1993

Tuesday, Wiesner, 1992

Black and White, Macaulay, 1991

Lon Po Po: A Red-Riding Hood Story from China, Young, 1990

Song and Dance Man, Gammell, 1989

Owl Moon, Schoenherr, 1988

Hey, Al, Egielski, 1987

The Polar Express, Van Allsburg, 1986

Saint George and the Dragon, Hyman, 1985

The Glorious Flight, Provensens, 1984

Shadow, Brown, 1983

Jumanji, Van Allsburg, 1982

Fables, Lobel, 1981

Ox-Cart Man, Cooney, 1980

The Girl Who Loved Wild Horses, Goble, 1979

Noah's Ark, Spier, 1978

Ashanti to Zulu: African Traditions, Dillons, 1977

Why Mosquitoes Buzz in People's Ears, Dillons, 1976

Arrow to the Sun, McDermott, 1975

Duffy and the Devil, Zemach, 1974

The Funny Little Woman, Lent, 1973

One Fine Day, Hogrogian, 1972

A Story—A Story, Haley, 1971

Sylvester and the Magic Pebble, Steig, 1970

The Fool of the World and the Fling Ship, Shulevitz, 1969

Drummer Hoff, Emberly, 1968

Sam, Bangs & Moonshine, Ness, 1967

Always Room for One More, Hogrogian, 1966

May I Bring a Friend? Montresor, 1965

Where the Wild Things Are, Sendak, 1964

The Snowy Day, Keats, 1963

Once a Mouse, Brown, 1962

Baboushka and the Three Kings, Sidjakov, 1961
Nine Days to Christmas, Ets, 1960
Chanticleer and the Fox, Cooney, 1959
Time of Wonder, McCloskey, 1958
A Tree Is Nice, Simont, 1957
Frog Went A-Courtin', Rojankovsky, 1956
Cinderella, Brown, 1955
Madeline's Rescue, Bemelmans, 1954
The Biggest Bear, Ward, 1953
Finders Keepers, Mordvinoff, 1952
The Egg Tree, Muhous, 1951
Song of the Swallows, Politi, 1950

The Big Snow, Haders, 1949
White Snow, Bright Snow, Duvoisin, 1948
The Little Island, Weisgard, 1947
The Rooster Crows, Petershams, 1946
Prayer for a Child, Jones, 1945
Many Moons, Slobodkin, 1944
The Little House, Burton, 1943
Make Way for Ducklings, McCloskey, 1942
They Were Strong and Good, Lawson, 1941
Abraham Lincoln, d'Aulaires, 1940
Mei Li, Handforth, 1939
Animals of the Bible, Lathrop, 1938

Newbery Medal Books

The Newbery Medal is presented annually by the Melcher family in honor of John Newbery, a British bookseller and the first publisher of children's books. The medal is awarded to an American author who makes the most distinguished contribution to children's literature. Book title, author, and year of the award are listed below.

The Higher Power of Lucky, Patron, 2007
Criss Cross, Perkins, 2006
Kira-Kira, Kadohata, 2005
The Tale of Despereaux: Being the Story of a Mouse, a Princess, Some Soup, and a Spool of Thread, DiCamillo, 2004
Crispin: The Cross of Lead, Avi, 2003
A Single Shard, Park, 2002
A Year Down Yonder, Peck, 2001
Bud, Not Buddy, Curtis, 2000
Holes, Sachar, 1999
Out of the Dust, Hesse, 1998
The View from Saturday, Konigsburg, 1997
The Midwife's Apprentice, Cushman, 1996
Walk Two Moons, Creech, 1995
The Giver, Lowry, 1994
Missing May, Rylant, 1993
Shiloh, Naylor, 1992
Maniac Magee, Spinelli, 1991
Number the Stars, Lowry, 1990

Joyful Noise: Poems for Two Voices, Fleischman, 1989
Lincoln: A Photobiography, Freedman, 1988
The Whipping Boy, Fleischman, 1987
Sarah, Plain and Tall, McKinley, 1986
The Hero and the Crown, McKinley, 1985
Dear Mr. Henshaw, Cleary, 1984
Dicey's Song, Voigt, 1983
A Visit to William Blake's Inn: Poems for Innocent and Experienced Travelers, Willard, 1982
Jacob Have I Loved, Paterson, 1981
A Gathering of Days: A New England Girl's Journal, 1830–32, Blos, 1980
The Westing Game, Raskin, 1979
Bridge to Terabithia, Paterson, 1978
Roll of Thunder, Hear My Cry, Taylor, 1977
The Grey King, Cooper, 1976
M. C. Higgins, the Great, Hamilton, 1975
The Slave Dancer, Fox, 1974
Julie of the Wolves, George, 1973

Mrs. Frisby and the Rats of NIMH, O'Brien, 1972

Summer of the Swans, Byars, 1971

Sounder, Armstrong, 1970

The High King, Alexander, 1969

From the Mixed-Up Files of Mrs. Basil E. Frankweiler, Konigsburg, 1968

Up a Road Slowly, Hunt, 1967

I, Juan de Pareja, de Trevino, 1966

Shadow of a Bull, Wojciechowska, 1965

It's Like This, Cat, Neville, 1964

A Wrinkle in Time, L'Engle, 1963

The Bronze Bow, Speare, 1962

Island of the Blue Dolphins, O'Dell, 1961

Onion John, Krumgold, 1960

The Witch of Blackbird Pond, Speare, 1959

Rifles for Watie, Keith, 1958

Miracles on Maple Hill, Sorensen, 1957

Carry On, Mr. Bowditch, Latham, 1956

The Wheel on the School, De Song, 1955

And Now Miguel, Krumgold, 1954

Secret of the Andes, Clark, 1953

Ginger Pye, Estes, 1952

Amos Fortune, Free Man, Yates, 1951

The Door in the Wall, de Angeli, 1950

King of the Wind, Henry, 1949

The Twenty-One Balloons, du Bois, 1948

Miss Hickory, Bailey, 1947

Strawberry Girl, Lenski, 1946

Rabbit Hill, Lawson, 1945

Johnny Tremain, Forbes, 1944

Adam of the Road, Gray, 1943

The Matchlock Gun, Edmonds, 1942

Call It Courage, Sperry, 1941

Daniel Boone, Daugherty, 1940

Thimble Summer, Enright, 1939

The White Stag, Seredy, 1938

Roller Skates, Sawyer, 1937

Caddie Woodlawn, Brink, 1936

Dobry, Shannon, 1935

Invincible Louisa, Meigs, 1934

Young Fu of the Upper Yangtze, Lewis, 1933

Waterless Mountain, Armer, 1932

The Cat Who Went to Heaven, Coatsworth, 1931

Hitty, Her First Hundred Years, Field, 1930

The Trumpeter of Krakow, Kelly, 1929

Gay-Neck, Mukerji, 1928

Smoky, the Cowhorse, James, 1927

Shen of the Sea, Chrisman, 1926

Tales from Silver Lands, Finger, 1925

The Dark Frigate, Hawes, 1924

The Voyages of Doctor Doolittle, Lofting, 1923

The Story of Mankind, Van Loon, 1922

Coretta Scott King Award

The Coretta Scott King Award has been given annually since 1970 to commemorate the life of Dr. Martin Luther King, Jr., and honor his widow Coretta Scott King. A task force of the American Library Association selects authors and illustrators of African descent for their distinguished books in promoting the understanding and appreciation of the American dream. Below, *author* indicates the author award, and *illustrator* the illustrator award.

2007

Author—Draper, Sharon. *Copper Sun.*

Illustrator—Nelson, Kadir. *Moses: When Harriet Tubman Led Her People to Freedom;* text by Carole Boston Weatherford.

2006

Author—Lester, Julius. *Day of Tears: A Novel in Dialogue.*

Illustrator—Collier, Bryan. *Rosa;* text by Nikki Giovanni.

2005

Author—Morrison, Toni. *Remember: The Journey to School Integration.*

Illustrator—Nelson, Kadir. *Ellington Was Not a Street;* text by Ntozake Shange.

2004

Author—Johnson, Angela. *The First Part Last.*

Illustrator—Bryan, Ashley. *Beautiful Blackbird.*

2003

Author—Grimes, Nikki. *Bronx Masquerade.*

Illustrator—Lewis, E. B. *Talkin' About Bessie: The Story of Aviator Elizabeth Coleman.*

2002

Author—Taylor, Mildred D. *The Land.*

Illustrator—Pinkney, Jerry. *Goin' Someplace Special;* text by Doreen Rappoport.

2001

Author—Woodson, Jacqueline. *Miracle's Boys.*

Illustrator—Collier, Bryan. *Uptown.*

2000

Author—Curtis, Christopher Paul. *Bud, Not Buddy.*

Illustrator—Pinkney, Brian. *In the Time of the Drums;* text by Kim L. Siegelson.

1999

Author—Johnson, Angela. *Heaven.*

Illustrator—Wood, Michael. *i see the rhythm;* text by Toyomi Igus.

1998

Author—Draper, Sharon M. *Forged by Fire.*

Illustrator—Steptoe, Javaka. *In Daddy's Arms I Am Tall: African Americans Celebrating Fathers;* text by Alan Schroeder.

1997

Author—Myers, Walter Dean. *Slam.*

Illustrator—Pinkney, Jerry. *Minty: A Story of Young Harriet Tubman;* text by Alan Schroeder.

1996

Author—Hamilton, Virginia. *Her Stories.*

Illustrator—Feelings, Tom. *The Middle Passage: White Ships Black Cargo.*

1995

Author—McKissack, Patricia and Frederick. *Christmas in the Big House, Christmas in the Quarters.*

Illustrator—Ransome, James. *The Creation;* text by James Weldon.

1994

Author—Johnson, A. *Toning the Sweep.*

Illustrator—Feelings, Tom. *Soul Looks Back in Wonder.*

1993

Author—McKissack, Patricia. *Dark Thirty: Southern Tales of the Supernatural.*

Illustrator—Wilson, K. A. *Origin of Life on Earth: An African Creation Myth;* text by David A. Anderson.

1992

Author—Bryan, Ashley. *All Night All Day.*

Illustrator—Ringgold, Faith. *Tar Beach.*

1991

Author—Taylor, Mildred D. *Road to Memphis.*

Illustrator—Dillon, Leo and Diane. *Aida;* text by Leontyne Price.

1990

Author—McKissack, Patricia and Frederick. *A Long Hard Journey: The Story of the Pullman Porter.*

Illustrator—Gilchrist, Jan Spivey. *Nathaniel Talking;* text by Eloise Greenfield.

1989

Author—Myers, Walter Dean. *Fallen Angels.*

Illustrator—Pinkney, Jerry. *Mirandy and Brother Wind;* text by Patricia McKissack.

1988

Author—Taylor, Mildred D. *The Friendship.*

Illustrator—Steptoe, John. *Mufaro's Beautiful Daughters: An African Tale.*

1987

Author—Walter, Mildred Pitts. *Justin and the Best Biscuits in the World.*

Illustrator—Pinkney, Jerry. *Half a Moon and One Whole Star;* text by Crecent Dragonwagon.

1986

Author—Hamilton, Virginia. *The People Could Fly: American Black Folktales.*

Illustrator—Pinkney, Jerry. *The Patchwork Quilt;* text by Valerie Flournoy.

1985

Author—Myers, Walter Dean. *Motown and Didi.*

Illustrator—No award given.

1984

Author—Clifton, Lucille. *Everett Anderson's Goodbye.*

Illustrator—Cummings, Pat. *My Mama Needs Me;* text by Mildred Pitts Walter.

1983

Author—Hamilton, Virginia. *Sweet Whispers, Brother Rush.*

Illustrator—Magubane, Peter. *Black Child.*

1982

Author—Taylor, Mildred D. *Let the Circle Be Unbroken.*

Illustrator—Steptoe, John. *Mother Crocodile: An Uncle Amadou Tale from Senegal;* text adapted by Rosa Guy.

1981

Author—Poitier, Sidney. *This Life.*

Illustrator—Bryan, Ashley. *Beat the Story-Drum, Pum-Pum.*

1980

Author—Myers, Walter Dean. *The Young Landlords.*

Illustrator—Byard, Carole. *Cornrows;* text by Camille Yarbrough.

1979

Author—Davis, Ossie. *Escape to Freedom: A Play about Young Frederick Douglass.*

Illustrator—Feelings, Tom. *Something On My Mind;* text by Nikki Grimes.

1978

Author—Greenfield, Eloise. *African Dream.*

Illustrator—Byard, Carole. *African Dream.*

1977

Author—Haskins, James. *The Story of Stevie Wonder.*

Illustrator—No award given.

1976

Author—Bailey, Pearl. *Duey's Tale.*

Illustrator—No award given.

1975

Author—Robinson, Dorothy. *The Legends of Africania.*

Illustrator—Temple, Herbert. *The Legends of Africania.*

1974

Author—Mathis, Sharon Bell. *Ray Charles.*

Illustrator—Ford, George. *Ray Charles.*

1973

Author—Robinson, Jackie, as told to Alfred Duckett. *I Never Had It Made: The Autobiography of Jackie Robinson.*

1972

Author—Fax, Elton C. *Seventeen Black Artists.*

1971

Author—Rollins, Charlemae. *Black Troubadour: Langston Hughes.*

1970

Author—Patterson, Lillie. *Dr. Martin Luther King Jr., Man of Peace.*

Boston Globe—Horn Book Awards

The Horn Book Awards were first presented in 1967. They began by presenting awards in two fields of outstanding picture book and outstanding fiction and poetry. In 1976 a third award, nonfiction, was added. Because of their more advanced reading levels, the nonfiction books are not listed here.

2007

Fiction—*The Astonishing Life of Octavian Nothing, Traitor to the Nation, Volume 1: The Pox Party,* Anderson.

Picture Book—*Dog and Bear: Two Friends, Three Stories,* Seeger.

2006

Fiction—*The Miraculous Journey of Edward Tulane,* DiCamillo, author; Ibatouline, illustrator.

Picture Book—*Leaf Man,* Ehlert.

2005

Fiction—*The Schwa Was Here,* Schusterman.

Picture Book—*Traction Man Is Here!,* Grey.

2004

Fiction—*The Fire Eaters,* Almond.

Picture Book—*The Man Who Walked Between the Towers,* Gerstein.

2003

Fiction—*The Jamie and Angus Stories,* Fine, author; Dale, illustrator.

Picture Book—*Big Momma Makes the World,* Root, author; Oxenbury, illustrator.

2002

Fiction—*Lord of the Deep,* Salisbury.

Picture Book—*"Let's Get a Pup," Said Kate,* Graham.

2001

Fiction—*Carver: A Life in Poems,* Nelson.

Picture Book—*Cold Feet,* DeFelice, author; Parker, illustrator.

2000

Fiction—*The Folk Keeper,* Billingsley.

Picture Book—*Henry Hikes to Fitchburg,* Johnson.

1999

Fiction—*Holes,* Sachar.

Picture Book—*Red-Eyed Tree Frog,* Cowley, author; Bishop, illustrator.

1998

Fiction—*The Circuit: Stories from the Life of a Migrant Child,* Jimenez.

Picture Book—*And If the Moon Could Talk,* Banks, author; Hallensleben, illustrator.

1997

Fiction—*The Friends,* Yumoto, author; Hirano, translator.

Picture Book—*The Adventures of Sparrowboy,* Pinkney.

1996

Fiction—*Poppy,* Avi, author; Floca, illustrator.

Picture Book—*In the Rain with Baby Duck,* Hest, author; Barton, illustrator.

1995

Fiction—*Some of the Kinder Planets,* Wynne-Jones.

Picture Book—*John Henry,* Lester, author; Pinkney, illustrator.

1994

Fiction—*Scooter,* Williams.

Picture Book—*Grandfather's Journey,* Say.

1993

Fiction—*Ajeemah and His Son,* Berry.

Picture Book—*The Fortune Tellers,* Alexander, author; Hyman, illustrator.

1992

Fiction—*Missing May,* Rylant.

Picture Book—*Seven Blind Mice,* Young.

1991

Fiction—*The True Confessions of Charlotte Doyle,* Avi.

Picture Book—*The Tale of the Mandarin Ducks,* Patterson, author; L. and D. Dillon, illustrators.

1990

Fiction—*Maniac Magee,* Spinelli.

Picture Book—*Lon Po Po: A Red Riding Hood Story from China,* Young.

1989

Fiction—*The Village by the Sea,* Fox.

Picture Book—*Shy Charles,* Wells.

1988

Fiction—*The Friendship,* Taylor.

Picture Book—*The Boy of the Three-Year Nap,* Snyder, author; Say, illustrator.

1987

Fiction—*Rabble Starkey,* Lowry.

Picture Book—*Mufaro's Beautiful Daughters,* Steptoe.

1986

Fiction—*In Summer Light,* Oneal.

Picture Book—*The Paper Crane,* Bang.

1985

Fiction—*The Moves Make the Man,* Brooks.

Picture Book—*Mama Don't Allow,* Hurd.

1984

Fiction—*A Little Fear,* Wrightson.

Picture Book—*Jonah and the Great Fish,* Hutton.

1983

Fiction—*Sweet Whispers, Brother Rush,* Hamilton.

Picture Book—*A Chair for My Mother,* Williams.

1982

Fiction—*Playing Beatie Bow,* Park.

Picture Book—*A Visit to William Blake's Inn: Poems for Innocent and Experienced Travelers,* Willard, author; A. and M. Provensen, illustrators.

1981

Fiction—*The Leaving,* Hall.

Picture Book—*Outside Over There,* Sendak.

1980

Fiction—*Conrad's War,* Davies.

Picture Book—*The Garden of Abdul Gasazi,* Van Allsburg.

1979

Fiction—*Humbug Mountain,* Fleischman.

Picture Book—*The Snowman,* Briggs.

1978

Fiction—*The Westing Game,* Raskin.

Picture Book—*Anno's Journey,* Anno.

1977

Fiction—*Child of the Owl,* Yep.

Picture Book—*Granfa' Grig Had a Pig and Other Rhymes without Reason,* Goose, author; Tripp, editor.

1976

Fiction—*Unleaving,* Walsh.

Picture Book—*Thirteen,* Charlip and Joyner.

1975

Fiction—*Transport 7-41-R,* Degens.

Picture Book—*Anno's Alphabet,* Anno.

1974

Fiction—*M. C. Higgins, The Great,* Hamilton.

Picture Book—*Jambo Means Hello,* M. Feelings, author; T. Feelings, illustrator.

1973

Fiction—*The Dark Is Rising,* Cooper.

Picture Book—*Kind Stork,* Pyle, author; Hyman, illustrator.

1972

Fiction—*Tristan and Iseult,* Sutcliff.

Picture Book—*Mr. Grumpy's Outing,* Burningham.

1971

Fiction—*A Room Made of Windows,* Cameron.

Picture Book—*If I Built a Village,* Mizumura.

1970

Fiction—*The Intruder,* Townsend.

Picture Book—*Hi, Cat!* Keats.

1969

Fiction—*A Wizard of Earthsea,* Le Guin.

Picture Book—*The Adventures of Paddy Pork,* Goodall.

1968

Fiction—*The Spring Rider,* Lawson.

Picture Book—*Tiki Tiki Tembo,* Mosel, author; Lent, illustrator.

1967

Fiction—*The Little Fishes,* Haugaard.

Picture Book—*London Bridge Is Falling Down,* Spier.

The E. B. White Read Aloud Award

This recent award was established in 2004 in recognition of reading aloud as a pleasurable experience at all ages, and to honor books reflecting read aloud standards emulated in E. B. White's books such as *Charlotte's Web, The Trumpet of the Swan,* and *Stuart Little.* In 2006 the award was expanded into two categories, one for picture books and one for older readers.

2007

Picture Book—*Houndsley and Catina,* Howe, author; Gay, illustrator.

Older Readers—*Alabama Moon,* Key.

2006

Picture Book—*If I Built a Car,* Van Dusen.

Older Readers—*Each Little Bird That Sings,* Wiles.

2005

Wild About Books, Sierra, author; Brown, illustrator.

2004

Skippyjon Jones, Schachner.

Theodor Seuss Geisel Award

Another recent award is the Theodor Seuss Geisel Award which began in 2006. It is to honor U.S. authors and illustrators of books for beginning readers who demonstrate creativity and imagination.

2007

Zelda and Ivy: The Runaway, Kvasnosky.

2006

Henry and Mudge and the Great Grandpas, Rylant, author; Stevenson, illustrator.

Schneider Family Book Award

The Schneider Family Book Award began in 2004. It honors an author or illustrator of a young children's book, middle school book, and teen book that focuses on the disability experience of a child or young adult.

2007

Young Children—*The Deaf Musicians,* Seeger, author; Christie, illustrator.

Middle School—*Rules,* Lord.

Teen—*Small Steps,* Sachar.

2006

Young Children—*Dad, Jackie, and Me,* Uhlberg, author; Bootman, illustrator.

Middle School—*Tending to Grace,* Fusco.

Teen—*Under the Wolf, Under the Dog,* Rapp.

2005

Young Children—*My Pal Victor/Mi Amigo, Victor,* Bertrand, author; Sweetland, illustrator.

Middle School—*Becoming Naomi León,* Ryan.

Teen—*My Thirteenth Winter: A Memoir,* Abeel.

2004

Young Children—*Looking Out for Sarah,* Lang.

Middle School—*A Mango Shaped Space,* Mass.

Teen—*Things Not Seen,* Clements.

American Indian Youth Services Literature Award

The American Indian Youth Services Literature Award was established in 2006. It honors the best writing and illustrations by and about American Indians. There are three categories of awards: picture book, middle school, and young adult.

2006

Picture Book—*Beaver Steals Fire: A Salish Coyote Story,* Confederated Salish and Kootenai Tribes, author; Sandoval, illustrator.

Middle School—*The Birchbark House,* Erdrich.

Young Adult—*Hidden Roots,* Bruchac.

The Pura Belpré Award

The Pura Belpré Award was established in 1996 to honor a Latino/Latina writer and illustrator for the exceptional portrayal, affirmation, and celebration of the Latino culture in literature for children and youth.

2006

Narrative—*The Tequila Worm,* Canales.

Illustration—*Doña Flor: A Tall Tale About a Giant Woman with a Great Big Heart,* Colón.

2005

2004

Narrative—*Before We Were Free,* Alvarez.

Illustration—*Just a Minute: A Trickster Tale and Counting Book,* Morales.

2003

2002

Narrative—*Esperanza Rising,* Ryan.

Illustration—*Chato and the Party Animals,* Guevara.

2001

2000

Narrative—*Under the Royal Palms: A Childhood in Cuba,* Ada.

Illustration—*Magic Windows,* Garza.

1999

1998

Narrative—*Parrot in the Oven: Mi Vida,* Martinez.

Illustration—*Snapshots from the Wedding,* Garcia.

1997

1996

Narrative—*An Island Like You: Stories of the Barrio,* Cofer.

Illustration—*Chato's Kitchen,* Guevara.

Sydney Taylor Book Award

The Sydney Taylor Book Award was established in 1968 to recognize the best in Jewish children's literature. Awards are given for books that authentically portray the Jewish experience.

2007

Young Readers—*Hanukkah at Valley Forge,* Krensky, author; Harlin, illustrator.

Older Readers—*Julia's Kitchen,* Ferber.

Teen Readers—*The Book Thief,* Zusak.

2005–2006

Young Readers—*Sholom's Treasure: How Sholom Aleichem Became a Writer,* Silverman, author; Gerstein, illustrator.

Older Readers—*Confessions of a Closet Catholic,* Littman.

2004

Older Readers—*Real Time,* Kass.

2003

Young Readers—*Bagels from Benny,* Davis, author; Petricic, illustrator.

Older Readers—*Who Was the Woman Who Wore the Hat?* Patz.

2002

Young Readers—*Chicken Soup by Heart,* Hershenhorn, author; Litzinger, illustrator.

Older Readers—*Hana's Suitcase: A True Story,* Levine.

2001

Young Readers—*Rivka's First Thanksgiving,* Rael, author; Kovalski, illustrator.

Older Readers—*Sigmund Freud: Pioneer of the Mind,* Reef.

2000

Young Readers—*Gershon's Monster: A Story for the Jewish New Year,* Kimmel, author; Muth, illustrator.

Older Readers—*The Key Is Lost,* Vos.

1999

Young Readers—*The Peddler's Gift,* Schur, author; Root, illustrator.

Older Readers—*Speed of Light,* Rosen.

1998

Younger Readers—*Nine Spoons,* Stillerman, author; Gerber, illustrator.

Older Readers—*Stones in Water,* Napoli.

1997

Younger Readers—*When Zaydeh Danced on Eldridge Street,* Rael, author; Priceman, illustrator.

Older Readers—*When Jesse Came Across the Sea,* Hest, author; Lynch, illustrator.

1996

Younger Readers—*Shalom, Haver: Goodbye Friend,* Sofer.

Older Readers—*When I Left My Village,* Schur, author; Pinkney, illustrator.

1995

Young Readers—*Star of Fear, Star of Hope,* Hoestlandt, author; Kang, illustrator.

Older Readers—*Dancing on the Bridge of Avignon,* Vos.

1994

Younger Readers—*The Always Prayer Shawl,* Oberman, author; Lewin, illustrator.

Older Readers—*The Shadow Children,* Schnur, author; Tauss, illustrator.

1993

Young Readers—*The Uninvited Guest,* Jaffe, author; Savadier, illustrator.

Older Readers—*Sworn Enemies,* Matas.

1992

Young Readers—*Something from Nothing,* Gilman.

Older Readers—*Letters from Rifka,* Hesse.

1991

Young Readers—*Cakes and Miracles: A Purim Tale,* Goldin, author; Weihs, illustrator.

AND

Daddy's Chair, Lanton, author; Haas, illustrator.

1990

Young Readers—*The Chanukkah Guest,* Kimmel, author; Carmi, illustrator.

Older Readers—*My Grandmother's Stories,* Geras, author; Jordan, illustrator.

1989

Young Readers—*Berchick,* Blanc, author; Dixon, illustrator.

Older Readers—*Number the Stars,* Lowry.

1988

Young Readers—*The Keeping Quilt,* Polacco.

Older Readers—*The Devil's Arithmetic,* Yolen.

1987

Young Readers—*The Number on My Grandfather's Arm,* Adler, author; Eichenbaum, photographer.

Older Readers—*The Return,* Levitin.

1986

Young Readers—*Joseph Who Loved the Sabbath,* Hirsh, author; Grebu, illustrator.

Older Readers—*Beyond the High White Wall,* Pitt.

1985

Young Readers—*Brothers,* Freedman.

Older Readers—*Ike and Momma and the Seven Surprises,* Snyder.

1984

Young Readers—*Mrs. Moskowitz and the Sabbath Candlesticks,* Schwartz.

Older Readers—*The Island on Bird Street,* Orlev.

1983

Young Readers—*Bubby, Me, and Memories,* Pomerantz.

Older Readers—*In the Mouth of the Wolf,* Zar.

1982

Young Readers—*The Castle on Hester Street,* Heller.

Older Readers—*Call Me Ruth,* Sachs.

1981

Young Readers—*Yussel's Prayer,* Cohen, author; Deraney, illustrator.

Older Readers—*The Night Journey,* Lasky.

1980

A Russian Farewell, Fisher.

1979

Ike and Momma and the Block Wedding, Snyder.

1978

The Devil in Vienna, Orgel.

1977

Exit From Home, Heyman.

1976

Never to Forget, Meltzer.

1975

Waiting for Mama, Moskin.

1974

NO HONOR AWARDED

1973

Uncle Misha's Partisans, Suhl.

1972

NO HONOR AWARDED

1971

NO HONOR AWARDED

1970

The Year, Lange.

1969

Our Eddie, Ish-Kishor.

1968

The Endless Steppe, Hautzig.

Trade Books for Challenged Readers

American Guidance Service, Inc. (AGS)

(A division of Pearson Learning Group)

145 S. Mt. Zion Road

P.O. Box 2500

Lebanon, IN 46052

Phone: (800) 328-2560

E-mail: agsmail@agsnet.com

Web site: www.agsglobe.com

Reading Skills for Life

Includes high-interest stories for struggling readers. Initial instruction includes letter/sound alphabet and phonetic awareness. Teacher's guide includes activities that address a variety of learning styles.

✓ Reading Level: Six reading levels, nonreaders through Grade 6

✓ Interest Level: Ages 6–12

AGS Classics Classroom Reading Plays

Features 24 plays for oral reading practice. These include British literature such as *Treasure Island* and *A Christmas Carol,* as well as American literature, including *Moby Dick, The Call of the Wild,* and *Tom Sawyer.*

Note: AGS's titles of illustrated classics for middle school, high school, ABE, and ESL students are too numerous to mention here.

✓ Reading Level: Grades 3–4

✓ Interest Level: middle school, high school, ABE, ESL

Continental Press

520 E. Bainbridge Street

Elizabethtown, PA 17022-2299

Phone: (800) 233-0759

Fax: (888) 834-1303

Web site: www.continentalpress.com

Backpack Novels

Features 12 fictional stories of real-life dilemmas and challenges that are touched with humor. Among the titles: *Laptop Detectives* and *Ming Ling and the Country Western Band.*

✓ Reading Level: Grades 4–5   ✓ Interest Level: Ages 6–12

Curriculum Associates

P.O. Box 2001

North Billerica, MA 01862-0901

Phone: (800) 225-0248 (US)

(978) 667-8000 (Canada)

Fax: (800) 366-1158

E-mail: info@CAinc.com

Web site: www.curriculumassociates.com

Passageways Anthology I Series

This series includes four nonfiction titles for reluctant readers. Photos, illustrations, and graphics are included. Theme based with content area topics. Teacher's guide available.

✓ Reading Level: Grades 2–5   ✓ Interest Level: Grades 4–8, Adult, ESL

Globe Fearon

(A division of Pearson Learning Group)

145 S. Mt. Zion Road

P.O. Box 2500

Lebanon, IN 46052

Phone: (800) 321-3106

Fax: (800) 393-3156

Web site: www.pearsonlearning.com

Pacemaker Classics
Titles feature high-interest adaptations of classic literature including *The Adventures of Sherlock Holmes, Silas Marner, Little Women,* and similar titles. Study guide and read-along audio cassettes available.

✓ Reading Level: Grades 3–4   ✓ Interest Level: Grades 5–12, ABE, ESL

Uptown Downtown Series
Suspense and reality stories about an urban teenager dealing with family, friends, danger, and the like. There are eight titles in this series.

✓ Reading Level: Grades 2–3   ✓ Interest Level: Grades 9–12, ESL

Sportellers
Eight titles focusing on the drama of a different sport. Subplots explore conflicts and challenges of young athletes. Softcover.

✓ Reading Level: Grades 2–3   ✓ Interest Level: Grades 6–12, ABE, ESL

Matchbook Five-Minute Thrillers
Twenty titles in 16-page minibooks are presented in unique matchbook format. Answer key and audio cassettes available.

✓ Reading Level: Grade 3   ✓ Interest Level: Grades 6–12, ABE, ESL

Quick Reads
High-interest, nonfiction text. Builds cross-curricular vocabulary and background knowledge. Audio CD also available.

✓ Reading Level: Grades 2–5   ✓ Interest Level: Grades 6–12

Fastbacks
Seventy-four fast-paced, short novels of motivation. Emphasis is on reading for pleasure. Areas of interest include mystery, sports, and romance. Softcover. The follow-up *Double Fastback* has the same RL and IL skill checks. Cassettes are available.

✓ Reading Level: Grades 4–5   ✓ Interest Level: Grades 6–12, ABE

Caught Reading Plus
This is a combined work text and novel-oriented reading program. It is sequenced from preliteracy through reading level 4. Assessments are available for each of the booklets on seven levels. Presented in softcover.

✓ Reading Level: Preliteracy–   ✓ Interest Level: Grades 6–12, ABE, ESL
                  Grade 4

Bestsellers

Available in four sets, each with 10 titles covering mystery, science fiction, suspense, and adventure. Students read about young adult characters they can relate to. Teacher's guide, answer keys, and skill check cards are available.

✓ Reading Level: Grades 2–4   ✓ Interest Level: Grades 6–12, ABE, ESL

High Noon Books

(A division of Academic Therapy)

20 Commercial Blvd.

Novato, CA 94949-6191

Phone: (800) 422-7249

Fax: (888) 287-9975

Web site: www.academictherapy.com

Sound Out Chapter Books

Written for students with minimal reading skills. Set A begins with single-syllable words.

✓ Reading Level: Grade 1   ✓ Interest Level: Ages 7–11

Starting Gate Series

Story topics are on contemporary, relevant subjects for young people and adults, such as computers, recreation, work, and so forth.

✓ Reading Level: Grade 1   ✓ Interest Level: Ages 11–18 and over

Riddle Street Mystery Series, Sets 1 and 2

Five titles are included in each set. Reproducible activity workbooks are available.

✓ Reading Level: Grade 1   ✓ Interest Level: Ages 9–16

Other series available:

Reading Level 1

Win, Lose or Draw Sports Series

Tom and Ricky Mystery Series

Reading Level 2

Trailblazers Series

Trade Route Explorers

The High Seas

Postcards From America

Postcards From South America

Postcards From Europe

Large selection of books with low reading level, high–interest level.

Incentives for Learning
111 Center Avenue Suite 1
Pacheco, CA 94553
Phone: (888) 238-2379
Web site: www.IncentivesForLearning.com

Tom and Ricky Mysteries
Single-plot, fast-paced stories involving two 14-year-olds. Five books in each of the six sets. Softcover.

✓ Reading Level: Grade 1   ✓ Interest Level: Grades 4–12, Adult, ESL, LD

Reading Power Series
Sports-oriented topics are featured with thirty 24-page, full-color titles, including superstars Hulk Hogan, Terrell Davis, Marion Jones, Kobe Bryant, Derek Jeter, and many more. Hardcover.
Note: There are two other *Reading Power Series* collections with interest and reading levels similar to 2.2. Diverse topics are designed to attract remedial readers.

✓ Reading Level: Grade 1   ✓ Interest Level: Grades 4–12, Adult

Mystery, Adventure, Science Fiction Collections
The 10 titles in each of these areas of interest feature teens in thrilling situations.

✓ Reading Level: Grades 2–4   ✓ Interest Level: Grades 4–12, Adult

Jamestown Education
(A division of Glencoe/McGraw-Hill)
P.O. Box 543
Blacklick, OH 43004-9902
Phone: (800) 872-7323
Fax: (614) 860-1877
Web site: www.jamestowneducation.com

Goodman's Five Star Stories
Titles feature high–interest level, multicultural anthologies from around the world. Teacher's notes include answers for the series. Included works: *Travels, More Travels, Adventures, More Adventures, Chills, More Chills, Surprises, More Surprises.*

✓ Reading Level: Grades 1–4   ✓ Interest Level: Grades 4–12

The Contemporary Reader

Diverse nonfiction stories for low-level readers. Stories include 14 popular themes involving current issues. Teacher's guide and audiocassettes available.

✓ Reading Level: Grades 2.5–5   ✓ Interest Level: Grades 6–12

Livewire—Real Lives

This series includes 25 high-interest biographies, including Michael Jordan, Tom Cruise, Sitting Bull, and Mother Theresa. Books are color-coded to identify readability. Teacher's guide included.

✓ Reading Level: Grades 2–5   ✓ Interest Level: Grades 10–12

Pearson Learning Group

145 S. Mt. Zion Road
P.O. Box 2500
Lebanon, IN 46052
Phone: (800) 321-3106
Fax: (800) 393-3156
Web site: www.pearsonlearning.com

MC Comics: The Action Files

These skill-based comics are designed for ESL, below-level, and reluctant readers. High-interest, nonviolent adventure, colorful pictures, and multicultural characters. Includes six sets of four comics, each with teacher's guide.

✓ Reading Level: Grades 1.5, 3–5   ✓ Interest Level: Grades 4–6, ESL

The "Joy Chapters" (author Joy Cowley)

These stories offer support in reading for students who no longer relate to small picture books. Longer stories are divided into chapters and age appropriate pictures support the test.

✓ Reading Level: Grades 2–4   ✓ Interest Level: Grades 4–6, ESL

Domine Biography Series

This series contains stories of eighteen people who have overcome adversity to succeed. Bill Gates, Cesar Chavez, and Venus and Serena Williams are among the people featured. Each title contains a table of contents and glossary of challenging words.

✓ Reading Level: Grades 3–4   ✓ Interest Level: Varies

Perfection Learning Corporation

1000 North Second Avenue

P.O. Box 500

Logan, IA 51546-0500

Phone: (800) 831-4190

Fax: (800) 543-2745

Web site: www.perfectionlearning.com

Cover to Cover: Chapter Books

Topics include high-interest fiction and nonfiction for below grade level readers. Titles include *Wagons Ho!* The diary is of a young girl explaining how her family traveled by Conestoga from Illinois to Oregon City. Similar titles include *Historical Toys,* which explores the evolution of many childhood favorites, such as kites, marbles, and other fun games. Teacher's guide available. Softcover.

✓ Reading Level: Grades 1–4   ✓ Interest Level: Grades 2–6

Cover to Cover: Kooties Club Mysteries

Readers join the five boys in solving intriguing mysteries. Short chapters designed to motivate reluctant readers. Thirteen titles. Teacher's guide available.

✓ Reading Level: Grade 1   ✓ Interest Level: Grades 2–6

Cover to Cover: Chapter 2 Books

Novel-like format with appealing topics written for upper elementary students. Multicultural, with fast-moving chapters. Teacher's guide available.

✓ Reading Level: Grades 1–3   ✓ Interest Level: Grades 4–6

Cover to Cover: Informational Books

These books appeal to readers with relevant topics such as *Service Dogs, Pirates and Privateers in The New World,* and *Child Care: Yeow! I'm in Charge of a Human Being.* All highly engaging and grade appropriate. Teacher's guide available. Softcover or reinforced.

✓ Reading Level: Grades 2–5   ✓ Interest Level: Grades 4–9

Cover to Cover: Novels

All fiction novels are found in mysteries, sports, humor, and the like. Exciting plots are written to engage struggling readers. Books are designed to appeal to middle school students. Topics and themes are also appealing to ESL students. Teacher's guide available.

✓ Reading Level: Grades 2–3   ✓ Interest Level: Grades 4–9, ESL

Note: Perfection Learning has a special catalog, *Hi/Lo Reading,* which offers over 400 titles. Their telephone book–size catalog (Pre K–8) contains titles too numerous to list here.

Saddleback Educational, Inc.

3 Watson
Irvine, CA 92618-2767
Phone   (888) 735-2225
Fax: (888) 734-4010
E-mail: info@sdlback.com
Web site: www.sdlback.com

Hot Sports Readers, Saddleback Classics

80-page stories with activity book. Read-along books include Coretta Scott King and Newbery Award winners. The *Saddleback Classics* introduce developing readers to literature.

✓ Reading Level: 3.5-5   ✓ Interest Level: Grades 5 through Adult

Dolch Sight Word Readers

Readers for beginning, remedial, at-risk, and ESL students contain lists of words to learn and sets of easy reading books of interest to any age.

✓ Reading Level: Varies   ✓ Interest Level: Varies

High–Interest Level Reading Collections

There are six adventure oriented titles in this series involving personal courage, mysteries, overseas adventures, and the like.

✓ Reading Level: Grades 2–4   ✓ Interest Level: Grades 5–10, Adult, ESL

Land and Sea

The nonfiction series features a history of military vehicles, including aircraft carriers, PT boats, and military trucks. There are 16 titles in the series. Reinforced binding.

✓ Reading Level: Grades 3–4   ✓ Interest Level: Grades 3–9, ESL

Serving Your Country

Titles feature behind-the-scenes stories of specialized groups in the military. The 16-book color collection includes *Air Assault Teams, The Blue Angels, Military Police, U.S. Army Rangers, The United States Coast Guard, U.S. Navy Seals,* and more. Reinforced binding.

✓ Reading Level: Grades 3–4   ✓ Interest Level: Grades 3–9, ESL

Saddleback has an extensive catalog of high-interest, low-vocabulary paperbacks. Some have read-along cassettes. All-inclusive areas of interest include monster trucks, motorcycles, classics, chillers, biographies, literature, etc.

Scholastic, Inc.

P.O. Box 7502

Jefferson City, MO 65102

Phone: (800) 724-6527

Fax: (800) 560-6815

Web site: www.scholastic.com

Although Scholastic does not emphasize the high–low in their reading selections, their *Scholastic Reading Inventory* is designed to identify a student's reading level for counseling better book selections. Their *Scholastic Supplementary Materials* catalog is packed with lively, entertaining selections that are categorized by interest. Get on their mailing list.

Steck-Vaughn Company

(Harcourt Achieve Imprint)

6277 Sea Harbor Drive

Orlando, FL 32887

Phone: (800) 531-5015

Web site: www.harcourtachieve.com

Steck-Vaughn Mystery, Adventure, and Science Fiction Collections

The series features intriguing subjects and plots designed to motivate reluctant readers. Ten titles in each area, three glossy magazines, three teacher's guides and a storage box available.

✓ Reading Level: Grades 2–3   ✓ Interest Level: Grades 5–12

True Tales

This is a real-life, high-interest adventure series in geography and science areas for struggling readers. Activities are designed to improve reading skills and reinforce content area concepts and vocabulary. There are three pages of activities after each story for developing vocabulary, comprehension, and map skills. Answer key, soft cover.

✓ Reading Level: Grade 3   ✓ Interest Level: Grades 4–12

Short Classics

The 28-book soft cover series is designed to motivate students to succeed with literary classics. Controlled vocabulary is used while maintaining style. Teacher's guide available.

✓ Reading Level: Grades 4–6   ✓ Interest Level: Grades 4–12

Sundance Publishing

1 Beeman Road

P.O. Box 740

Northborough, MA 01532

Phone: (800) 343-8204

Fax: (800) 456-2419

Web site: www.sundancepub.com

Second Chance Reading

This series has 42 nonfiction books that grab and keep the attention of reluctant readers. Titles include *Motorcycle Madness, Incredible Rescues,* and *What Smells?*

✓ Reading Level: Grades 2–3   ✓ Interest Level: Grades 4–8

The Wright Group/McGraw-Hill

220 E. Danieldale Road

DeSoto, TX 75115-2490

Phone: (800) 648-2970

Fax: (800) 593-4418

Web site: www.wrightgroup.com

A large selection of books for challenged readers. Books are grouped by topic, grade level, and reading level. Leveled library available for classroom with motivating titles. Send for catalog.

The X-Zone Series

Features 48 nonfiction titles with amazing facts, photographs etc.

✓ Reading Level: Grades 2–3   ✓ Interest Level: Grades 4–8

Zaner-Bloser

P.O. Box 16764

Columbus, OH 43216-6764

Phone: (800) 421-3018

Fax: (800) 992-6087

Web site: www.zaner-bloser.com

Trio Books

Six books each of 15 titles; fiction and nonfiction in history, geography, fantasy, and science.

Trio—Red:	Reading Level: Grades 3–5	
	Interest Level: Grades 4–8	
Trio—Green:	Reading Level: Grades 4–6	
	Interest Level: Grades 4–8	
Trio—Blue:	Reading Level: Grades 5–7	
	Interest Level: Grades 4–8	

APPENDIX G

Commercial Books, Kits, and Workbooks for Instruction

Academic Therapy

20 Commercial Boulevard

Novato, CA 94949-6191

Phone: (800) 422-7249

Fax: (888) 287-9975

Web site: www.academictherapy.com

The *Phonics Based Reading Test* offers a quick evaluation of reading skills. Word lists and words are coordinated to the typical sequences of phonics skill acquisition. Test kit includes: manual, stimulus book, and 25 student test booklets in portfolio.

American Guidance Service, Inc. (AGS)

(A division of Pearson Learning Group)

145 S. Mt. Zion Road

P.O. Box 2500

Lebanon, IN 46052

Phone: (800) 328-2560

Web site: www.agsglobe.com

English to Use

This high-interest, user-friendly text includes a writing/speaking skills review as well as learning English as a second language. Social skills activities include how to make introductions and using good manners. Additional activities are available on CD-ROM. The teacher's edition includes activities encouraging real life applications. Answer key.

✓ Reading Level: Grade 3   ✓ Interest Level: Ages 6–12, ABE, ESL

Everyday Writing

The focus is on everyday writing skills, like filling out forms and constructing proper sentences in writing letters. Answer key available.

✓ Reading Level: Grade 3   ✓ Interest Level: Ages 6–12, adult

Discover Health

This is a comprehensive health program for students reading below grade level. Includes full-color and easy-to-read selections with a focus on important health issues facing today's preteens and teens. Additional teacher's support available on CD-ROM, which is written to meet National Health Education Standards.

✓ Reading Level: Grades 3.5–4   ✓ Interest Level: Ages 6–9, ABE, ESL

Continental Press

520 E. Bainbridge Street
Elizabethtown, PA 17022-2299
Phone: (800) 233-0759
Fax: (888) 834-1303
Web site: www.continentalpress.com

Phonics and Word Analysis

The instructional focus is on phonic and structural analysis in decoding for older students in need of remediation. The program is sequential and can stand alone or be supplementary. Teacher's guide available. There are six different sets, one for each reading level 1–6. Interest level for all six reading levels is grades 3–8.

Read Reason Write

Students read high-interest articles that are grade-level appropriate. Questions are clearly labeled so students can monitor their own progress. Graphic organizers structure facts to aid transition to writing. Eight different sets, one for each reading level 1–8.

Listen Read Write

Provides a wealth of comprehension strategies, including prior knowledge, identifying main idea, identifying cause and effect, and more. Gives practical pointers on listening and taking notes. There are six different sets, one for each reading level 3–8.

Vocabulary Links

Students are introduced to new words. Students read a content-related selection in which all the words are used. Students complete activities which reinforce the new words. There are six different sets, one for each reading level 3–8.

Curriculum Associates

P.O. Box 2001

North Billerica, MA 01862-0901

Phone: (800) 225-0248

Fax: (800) 366-1158

Web site: www.curriculumassociates.com

Phonics for Reading

Decoding skills include letter/sound, prefixes/suffixes, and single- to multi-syllabic words. Student's books, teacher guides, and answer keys are available.

First Level: Vowels, consonants, blends, and digraphs

Second Level: Vowel combinations, vowel/*r*, endings, and CVCs

Third Level: Prefixes/suffixes, *c* and *g* sounds, and vowel combinations

✓ Reading Level: Primary   ✓ Interest Level: Grades 1–8, ESL, Adult

Phonics: A Sound Approach

Five-level progression phonics for students needing assistance in word attack skills.

Level A: Consonants, short V, VC, and CVC

Level B: Digraphs and trigraphs, CVCV

Level C: Vowel pairs, C blends, base words with endings, *r*-controlled vowels

Level D: Digraphs, diphthongs, affixes, compounds, and so forth

Level E: Syllable patterns, contractions, and possessives

✓ Reading Level: Primary   ✓ Interest Level: Remedial to Grades 4+,
                                                                        Adult education

Globe Fearon

(A division of Pearson Learning Group)

145 S. Mt. Zion Road

P.O. Box 2500

Lebanon, IN 46052

Phone: (800) 321-3106

Fax: (800) 393-3156

Web site: www.pearsonlearning.com

Quick Reads

Fifteen minutes a day for fluency and comprehension. Each level contains three books which present 18 topics. Read-along audio CD enables student to listen to passages as many times as necessary.

High Noon Books

(A division of Academic Therapy)

20 Commercial Boulevard

Novato, CA 94949-6191

Phone: (800) 422-7249

Fax: (888) 287-9975

Web site: www.academictherapy.com

Basic Angling

Designed for students in need of phonetics, decoding, and spelling training, with basic vocabulary. Can also be used as a supplement to other programs. Includes student's workbook. Teacher manual available.

✓ Reading Level: Beginning ✓ Interest Level: Primary, LD, Adult literacy

Study Book

Breaks down language learning into seven basic levels: short vowels and consonants; vowels and consonants; vowel–consonant–*e; r*-controlled vowels; consonant diagraphs; special syllables and situations; and spelling rules. Includes both sense and nonsense words.

✓ Reading Level: Beginning ✓ Interest Level: Grades 4–12

Workbook

Designed to be used with the above Study Book. Decoding skills learned in Study Book are applied in Workbook.

✓ Reading Level: Beginning ✓ Interest Level: Grades 4–12

Phonetic Remedial Reading Lessons

The program is designed for children who fail by conventional methods. Emphasis for instruction is on single-symbol relationships. Spiral bound.

✓ Reading Level: Beginning through Grade 2 ✓ Interest Level: Varies

Phonetic Pathways

Sequentially organized lessons progress from vowels, blends, and phrases up to sentences in gradual progression. Three-letter words can be used in regular classrooms. Softcover.

✓ Reading Level: Beginning ✓ Interest Level: Grades K–5, remedial

Incentives for Learning

111 Center Avenue, Suite 1

Pacheco, CA 94553

Phone: (888) 238-2379

Web site: www.incentivesforlearning.com

3-Minute Reading Assessments

Helps teachers quickly screen reading problems such as low word recognition, poor fluency rate, and comprehension.

✓ Reading Level: Grades 1–4 and 4–8

Hot Dot Reading Comprehension Kit

After reading a story on the front of a card, student flips it over and answers questions with a Hot Dot pen. Immediate feedback. Each set contains 50 cards ranging in levels from 2.0 to 6.0.

Publisher has many reading comprehension games. Specific-skill series kits all with high interest and low readability level.

Jamestown Education

(A division of Glencoe/McGraw-Hill)

P.O. Box 543

Blacklick, OH 43004-9902

Phone: (800) 872-7323

Fax: (614) 860-1877

Web site: www.jamestowneducation.com

Six Way Paragraphs

High-interest, nonfiction passages teach skills necessary for reading factual material. Questions include main idea, details, conclusions, clarifying devices, subject matter, and vocabulary in context. One hundred passages per book. Diagnostic chart and progress graph in each book.

✓ Reading Levels: Introductory: Grades 1–4

Middle: Grades 4–8

Advanced: Grades 8–12

Jamestown Signature Reading

The program goes beyond teaching specific skills by showing students how and when to apply skills in a variety of texts. Desktop resource available for each level.

Level	Reading Level	Interest Level
Level D:	Grades 2–4	Grades 4–8

Level E:	Grades 3–5	Grades 4–8
Level F:	Grades 4–6	Grades 6–10
Level G:	Grades 5–6	Grades 6–10

McGraw-Hill Contemporary

(A division of SRA)
220 E. Danieldale Road
DeSoto, TX 75115
Phone: (888) 772-4543
Fax: (800) 998-3103
Web site: www.mhcontemporary.com

Contemporary's Reading Basics

The program is primarily for adults who need to improve their basic reading abilities. The lessons are presented in their *Workbook* and stories in their correlating *Reader,* which is designed to practice skills just learned. Pre- and post-tests are given. Students check their work when the lesson is completed.

✓ Reading Levels: Grades 1.6–3.9, 3.6–6.9, 6.6–8.9   ✓ Interest Level: Adult

Reading for Adults

Designed as a total reading experience, the focus is on reading for both information and enjoyment with the aim of developing independent readers. Colorful illustrations are found in 90 book titles, based on adult interest. Tutor guide and teacher's guide available. Interactive CD-ROM program available as a supplement.

Note: Contemporary offers other programs with RLS 4+

National Reading Styles Institute

P.O. Box 737
Syosset, NY 11791
Phone: (800) 331-3117
Fax: (516) 921-5591
Web site: www.nrsi.com

NRSI grew from the work of Dr. Marie Garbo, who developed the *Reading Style Inventory* you have seen or heard about. The institute markets the colored overlays placed over black letters on white paper. The overlays are designed for students experiencing letter or word reversals, tracking problems, and the like. Since not all are helped by the same color overlay, the Colored Overlay Assessment Kits are available. The RSI also identifies a student's learning style for reading. Teaching recommendations are included. You may also wish to inquire about their Power Reading Paks (with audio tapes) and Pic-Wizard vocabulary cards.

New Readers Press

(A division of ProLiteracy Worldwide
U.S. Publishing Division of Laubach Literacy)
1320 Jamesville Avenue
Syracuse, NY 13210
Phone: (800) 448-8878
Fax: (866) 894-2100
Web site: www.newreaderspress.com

The adult education catalog is packed with a variety of materials far too numerous to list here. ABE and ESL teachers should simply call for a current catalog. The "Reading and Writing" section features their phonics-based "Laubach Way to Reading" (RL 0–4). Other programs, including workplace, family literacy, and ESL-oriented materials have convenient RL placements. Catalog icons indicate type of multimedia. Teacher support is available for the program areas of interest to you.

Phoenix Learning Resources, Inc.

910 Church Street
Honesdale, PA 18431
Phone: (800) 228-9345
Fax: (570) 253-3227
Web site: www.phoenixlr.com

Sullivan's Programmed Reading

This is a step-by-step individualized linguistic reading program that provides continuous reinforcement and success for every kind of student. Pupils check their answers by moving a slider down the left column on the page for immediate feedback. The program is designed to ensure success in a colorful format. Teacher's guide and placement test available.

✓ Reading Level: Grades PP–6   ✓ Interest Level: Grades K–6, ESL

Creature Teachers

These 44 self-paced story lessons are designed to develop basic reading, word analysis, and comprehension skills using cassette tapes. Pupil books and teacher's guides available.

✓ Reading Level: Grade 1   ✓ Interest Level: Grades 1–4, ESL

New Practice Readers

Titles include carefully graded articles and books from across the curriculum. There are read-along audiocassettes for books A–D. Teacher's manual includes an informal placement inventory. The easiest four of the seven book levels are described here.

Book A:	Reading Level Grades 2–2.5
Book B:	Reading Level Grades 2.4–3.5
Book C:	Reading Level Grades 3.5–4.8
Book D:	Reading Level Grades 4+

Interest Level (all four): Grades 2–adult, ESL

Conquests in Reading

More than 25 years in publication. Concentrated lessons in word attack and comprehension for remedial students. Teacher's edition for text-workbook and two diagnostic oral reading tests available.

✓ Reading Level: Grades 1–6   ✓ Interest Level: Grades 4–12, Adult, ESL

Saddleback Educational, Inc.

3 Watson
Irvine, CA 92618-2767

Phone:	(888) 735-2225
Fax:	(888) 734-4010
E-mail:	info@sdlback.com
Web site:	www.sdlback.com

Hot Sports Readers, Saddleback Classics

Eighty-page stories with activity book. Many are stories of sports stars. Read-along books include Newbery and Coretta Scott King Award winners. The *Saddleback Classics* introduce developing readers to literature. Extensive catalog.

Dolch Sight Word Readers

For beginning, remedial, at-risk, and ESL students. Contains lists of words to learn and sets of easy-reading books of interest to any age.

Voyager

This is a four-stage program from beginning stages of reading and writing through Ninth-Grade level, using contemporary content. Every book includes phonics with comprehension. Teacher's resource guide and answer keys are available. The four stages are as follows:

Stage	Reading Level	Interest Level
Learning to read	Grades .05–2.5	Grades 9–12, adult, ESL
The emerging reader	Grades 2.0–4.5	Grades 9–12, ESL
Reading to learn	Grades 4.0–7.5	Grades 9–12, ESL
Reading for work and life	Grades 7.0–9.5	Grades 9–12, ESL

Daily Comprehension

The series feature a nonfiction story for each day of the month for all 12 months. Stories were chosen because of their significance on that date. Hands-on activities are comprehension oriented. Answer keys; reproducible.

✓ Reading Level: Grades 3–4   ✓ Interest Level: Grades 3–12, ESL

Comprehension Quickies

These are three-minute reading comprehension activities that may be used for student assessment, remediation, or review. May also be used for those who have trouble reading longer paragraphs. Answer keys; reproducible. Four books, four levels.

✓ Reading Level: Grades 1–4   ✓ Interest Level: Grades 4–8, ESL

Skill Booster Series

The series is designed for students needing practice in understanding such areas as prefixes, suffixes, compounds, contractions, abbreviations, and so on. Answer key; reproducible.

✓ Reading Level: Grades 3–4   ✓ Interest Level: Grades 3–8, ESL

SRA/McGraw-Hill

220 E. Danieldale Road
DeSoto, TX 75115
Phone: (888) 772-4543
Fax: (972) 228-1982
Web site: www.sraonline.com

Specific Skill Series

The series now offers updated reading selections and artwork designed to build reading skill areas, including *Working within Words, Using the Context, Getting the Main Idea,* and so forth. All can be used in regular classes, reading labs, ESL and specialized classes. Short reading passages of student interest are followed by skill exercises. Individualized sets are divided into primary, middle, and upper elementary. Teacher's manual, answer keys. Check SRA's *Multiple Skill Series,* designed to develop one or more reading comprehension areas for individual or group, or whole class instruction. Features a placement test, teacher's manual and blackline, and masters for students in each set.

✓ Reading Level: Varies with set   ✓ Interest Level: Grades Pre-K–8

Open Court Phonics Kit

Kits for K–3, plus intervention program to help students more than one grade level behind in reading. Grades 1 and 2 kits offer help with blending. Grade 3 adds word attack skills.

Reading Reinforcement Skill Text Series

These are theme-based stories with exciting content that boost reading skills of below-average readers. The stories are on eight levels with different themes. Stories are designed to build vocabulary and comprehension. Teacher's edition available for each level.

✓ Reading Level: Grades 1–5   ✓ Interest Level: Grades 1–8

Corrective Reading

This program is designed for students who have not learned in other programs and don't learn on their own. It is for students who misidentify, reverse, or omit words while reading and have poor recall or understanding. Each of two programs is a core program with teacher-guided lesson plans for upper-grade teachers unaccustomed to teaching beginning reading. Workbook and blackline masters available.

✓ Reading Level: Basic   ✓ Interest Level: Grades 4–12

Steck-Vaughn Company

(Harcourt Achieve Imprint)
6277 Sea Harbor Drive
Orlando, FL 32887
Phone: (800) 531-5015
Web site: www.harcourtachieve.com

Steps to Achieve Reading

Specifically designed to bring struggling students to grade level performance. Instruction begins two grades below on-grade reading level. *Three Steps* uses scaffolded approach. Workbook and teacher's guide.

✓ Reading Level: Grades 3–8

Steck-Vaughn Comprehension Skills

The program is designed to develop six skills (facts, sequence, main idea, context, conclusion, and inference) at five reading levels. Writing activities are included in each of the 30 books. Placement tests and answer keys. Teacher's guide includes a placement for each level.

✓ Reading Level: Grades 2–6   ✓ Interest Level: Adult

Vocabulary Connections

The eight-book softcover series concentrates on developing vocabulary in the important content areas. Literature and nonfiction selections provide an appropriate context for instruction. Available in software.

✓ Reading Level: Grades 1–8   ✓ Interest Level: Adult

Multimedia, Including Games, Software, Electronics, and Writing Activities

Academic Therapy Publications

20 Commercial Boulevard

Novato, CA 94949-6191

Phone: (800) 422-7249

Fax: (888) 287-0075

Web site: www.AcademicTherapy.com

Perceptual Activities

Four activities with fifty exercises in each are presented in graduating skill levels. Different mazes encourage visual discrimination and concentration skills. The dot-to-dots enhance fine motor skills. Find-the-word activities help the student discriminate letters while increasing attention span. The finish-the-picture activities give the student a sense of accomplishment of completing a task. Reproducible.

Curriculum Associates

P.O. Box 2001

North Billerica, MA 01862-0901

Phone: (800) 225-0248

Fax: (800) 366-1158

Web site: www.curriculumassociates.com

Quick-Word Handbooks

The Handbook for Beginning Writers, grades 1–2, references 330 words. These words include: weather words, school-related words, and other resources. There are writing lines for students to add personal words.

The Handbook for Everyday Writers for grades 2 and up serves as a personal dictionary. It also includes days, months, number words, and common abbreviations. Also available: *Quick-Word Handbook for Practical Writing* for grades 7 and up. Other handbooks available; see catalog. Some available in Spanish.

Curious Creatures

The Taris Space Down program was designed for the reluctant readers in a life science area in 4th grade and above. High-interest topics; full-color students' books and CD-ROM version of books. Students can work together or alone. One teacher's guide includes five titles: *Bats, Owls, Snakes, Spiders,* and *Wolves.* Jigsaw Pages, Mix and Match, and Create It activities.

✓ Reading Level: Grades 2–3   ✓ Interest Level: Grades 2–8, ESL

Franklin Electronic Publishers

One Franklin Plaza
Burlington, NJ 08016-4907
Phone: (800) 525-9673
Fax: (609) 239-5950
Web site: www.franklin.com

Franklin specializes in the small handheld language-master devices, offering an interesting variety of functions that go far beyond the old machines. Some of their catalog offerings:

Speaking Merriam-Webster Dictionary and Thesaurus

Includes more than 100,000 words, 300,000 definitions, and 500,000 synonyms and antonyms. Students can listen to a word's pronunciation. Functions include phonetic spelling corrections, word games, and more, all designed to build confidence and vocabulary.

Speaking Language Master

Features a large screen, keyboard, and spelling correction for 100,000 words. When students see an unfamiliar word, they type in the word, touch the "say" key, and hear the word definition. Grammar guide and headphones.

Spelling Ace Spelling Corrector and Thesaurus

Features Franklin's patented phonetic spell correction. Enter: *jiraf* and get *giraffe.* Interactive word-building games, crossword puzzle solver, and homophone guide (to, too, two).

The Franklin download kit allows you to download e-books from the Internet. Go to their Web site to view a list of titles. Also, e-news can be downloaded with this kit.

Great Source Education Group

(A division of Houghton Mifflin)

181 Ballard Vale Street, Box 7050

Wilmington, MA 01887

Phone: (800) 289-4490

Fax: (800) 289-3994

Web site: www.greatsource.com

Reader's Handbook

A student guide for reading and learning across the curriculum. *Inspiration* software, integrated with the handbook, gives students visual learning that has been effective. Handbook available for grades 3–5, 6–8, and 9–12. CD-ROM available.

High Noon Books

(A division of Academic Therapy)

20 Commercial Boulevard

Novato, CA 94949-6191

Phone: (800) 422-7249

Fax: (888) 287-9975

Web site: www.academictherapy.com

Ann Arbor Tracking Materials

Designed primarily to improve eye movement skills required for reading: short term visual memory, left-to-right directionality, peripheral awareness, word recognition. The materials are appropriate for beginning readers, remedial students, and slow readers at all levels.

Letter Tracking

Teaches alphabet sequence and visual discrimination of letters while correcting reversals.

Word Tracking: High Frequency Words

After completion of these exercises, the student will be familiar with the 500 most frequently used words.

Cursive Tracking

Carefully designed exercises for the student who has difficulty in the transition between manuscript and cursive writing.

See catalog for complete list of Tracking materials.

Clusters

This is a word-building game, including 98 plastic tiles in 10 colors. Pupils create words with vowels, digraphs, and so forth. Tile holders are included for four players.

✓ Reading Level: Primary   ✓ Interest Level: Varies

Syllabification

Players discover that large words are made up from chunks of letters. Plastic tiles contain root words, prefixes, suffixes, etc. The game is designed for up to six players.

✓ Reading Level: Beginning (varies)   ✓ Interest Level: Grades 3–6

Incentives for Learning

111 Center Avenue, Suite 1
Pacheco, CA 94553
Phone: (888) 238-2379
Web site: www.Incentivesforlearning.com

Reading Comprehension Games

Each full-color comprehension game targets a specific reading skill area. Designed for 2–6 players. Two sets with 15 games each.

✓ Reading Level: ✓ Interest Level: Elementary grades
   Grades 2.0–3.5 and 3.5–5.0

Jamestown Education

(A division of Glencoe/McGraw-Hill)
P.O. Box 543
Blacklick, OH 43004-9902
Phone: (800) 872-7323
Fax: (614) 860-1877
Web site: www.jamestowneducation.com

Comprehension Skills

Computerized testing system diagnoses and prescribes placement in Skills Books. Five-part lesson plan and follow-up testing.

National Reading Styles Institute

P.O. Box 737
Syosset, NY 11791
Phone: (800) 331-3117
Fax: (516) 921-5591
Web site: www.nrsi.com

Power Reading Games
Match reading stories with games. Each story in the Nonfiction Power Paks has a follow-up game that practices essential reading skills.

✓ Reading Level: Grades 2–12

NRSI catalog offers equipment for teaching reading including: Telex listening centers, cassette recorder player, CD player, cassette duplicators, microphones, audio card readers, and much more.

Pearson Learning Group

145 S. Mt. Zion Road
P.O. Box 2500
Lebanon, IN 46052
Phone: (800) 321-3106
Fax: (800) 393-3156

Quick Reads technology is offered in both stand-alone and network editions. The package edition includes: books, manual, audio CDs, CD-ROM, office software manual, headsets, training CD, and laminated instruction card.

Perfection Learning Corporation

1000 North Second Avenue
P.O. Box 500
Logan, IA 51546-0500
Phone: (800) 831-4190
Fax: (800) 543-2745
Web site: www.perfectionlearning.com

Blank Books
These are hardcover books (side-sewn for durability) or softcover. Students supply their own illustrations as desired.

D'Nealian or Primary-Ruled Blank Books
Colorful cover with space for the student's name.

Blank Picture Books
Includes 48 pages, 7 by 8 in. Elephants or penguins on cover.

Shaped Blank Books
Six choices, in softcover:

1. Animal: A blank page only
2. Suitcase: Alternative blank with ruled pages.
3. Houses: Ruled on bottom and blank on top
4. Vehicle: Ruled on right-hand pages, blank on left.
5. Cupcake: Alternating blank page with page ruled on bottom and blank on top.
6. Top Hat: Folds on top and creates a long space ruled on bottom and blank on top.

Little Blank Books
Crayons and markers can be used to illustrate covers. Two types, 6 by 8 in. journal and storybook.

Phoenix Learning Group
2349 Chaffee Drive
St. Louis, MO 63146
Phone: (800) 221-1274
Fax: (314) 569-2834

Sold their book division. Now offers only film and videos. Send for catalog.

Saddleback Educational, Inc.
3 Watson
Irvine, CA 92618-2767
Phone: (888) 735-2225
Fax: (888) 734-4010
E-mail: info@sdlback.com
Web site: www.sdlback.com

Reading Comprehension Games
These are high-interest games designed for reluctant readers, with topics like taking a trip around the world, searching for treasure, and so on. Players identify the main idea, details, fact or opinion, etc.

✓ Reading Level: Grades 2–5   ✓ Interest Level: Grades 4–12, Adult, ESL

Reading Blaster Software
Helps students develop grammar and comprehension, etc. CD-ROM.

✓ Reading Level: Grades 1–3, 4–6

Scholastic, Inc.
P.O. Box 7502
Jefferson City, MO 65102
Phone: (800) 724-6527
Fax: (800) 560-6815
Web site: www.scholastic.com

Scholastic now has a *Software Resources for the Classroom* catalog that you may wish to order. While more grade oriented, software such as their Diary Maker (grades 5–9) encourages writing. Order their catalog for system requirements.

Shakean Stations
P.O. Box 68
Farley, IA 52046
Phone: (800) 765-1475
Fax: (800) 765-1475

Smart Start
Twelve file-folder games for reading readiness skills.

✓ Reading Level: Varies   ✓ Interest Level: Grade 1

Reading Unlimited
Twenty-four file-folder games for teaching, reinforcing, or remediating major word attack skills, including alphabet recognition, beginning consonants, sight words, two-letter blends, consonant digraphs, short vowels, long vowels, diphthongs etc.

✓ Reading Level: Varies   ✓ Interest Level: Grades 1–4

Sports of Sorts
Twelve file-folder games with sports themes devoted to different vocabulary and word-building skills, including compound words, antonyms, synonyms, root words, suffixes etc.

✓ Reading Level: Varies   ✓ Interest Level: Grades 3–6

Steck-Vaughn
(Harcourt Achieve Imprint)
6277 Sea Harbor Drive
Orlando, FL 32887
Phone: (800) 531-5015
Web site: www.harcourtachieve.com

Power Up Series

Offers reluctant readers high-interest, low readability materials at four levels. Each level includes: workbook, paperbacks, "Power Up on the Web," audio cassettes, books on CD-ROM, teacher's workbook, and resource binder.

✓ Reading Level: Grades 2.5–5.5   ✓ Interest Level: Grades 5–9

Learning 100 System

This is a fairly large comprehension reading program designed for adults who do not respond to traditional lectures and textbook exercises. There is a computerized *Reading Skills Inventory* for determining an individual's reading level and mastery of comprehension skills. The print-based version automates diagnosis, prescriptions, instruction, and evaluation. Contact their customer service department for more information. There are 10 reading levels from the beginning in the Upward Spiral Language Master program. See catalog for system requirements.

Sundance Publishing

1 Beeman Road
P.O. Box 740
Northborough, MA 01532
Phone: (800) 343-8204
Fax: (800) 456-2419
Web site: www.sundancepub.com

Sundance has a variety of blank books and journal activities designed to help students connect reading and writing, including both hardcover and softcover blank books. Readers' response journals are offered, in which students respond to something they have read by writing about it.

Make sure you check out the numerous catalog listings in *Books for Below-Level Readers,* which include both RL and IL.

Treetop Publishing

P.O. Box 320725
Franklin, WI 53132
Phone: (800) 255-9228
Fax: (888) 201-5916

This is the publishing company that markets the professionally bound *Bare Books, Bare Books Plus,* and now the softcover spiral-bound books you have seen. The originals had blank white covers with white pages sewn into a hard cover. These and the more recent varieties are excellent for the author-artist in your classroom. Many supplementary items are available, even a community puzzle for classroom or school activity. Activity guides with teaching ideas are available from their Web site for primary, intermediate, and high school levels. Any writing or reading activities are energized using this creative format.

The Wright Group/McGraw-Hill

220 E. Danieldale Road

DeSoto, TX 75115-2490

Phone: (800) 648-2970

Fax: (800) 593-4418

Web site: www.wrightgroup.com

Book to Web offers 72 titles which combine reading and technology. Ages 9–14; grades 4–8.

Zaner-Bloser, Educational Publishers

P.O. Box 16764

Columbus, OH 43216-6764

Phone: (800) 421-3018

Fax: (800) 992-6087

Web site: www.zaner-bloser.com

Word Wisdom

Vocabulary for listening, speaking, reading, and writing. Unlock the meaning of new words with context clues. Shows Latin and Greek word roots. Activities include: analogies, word families, semantic mapping, and contextual application. Teacher edition includes CD-ROM; grades 3–8.

In addition to the handwriting you are familiar with, Zaner-Bloser offers writing related story journals that include space for artwork and pictures. You will need their catalog for ordering the type of lined paper and supplies. Be sure to check out their expanded reading offerings, including phonics activities and their leveled trade books. CD-ROM available with certain orders for reading, spelling, and writing.

APPENDIX I

Publishing Companies

Academic Therapy Publications

20 Commercial Boulevard

Novato, CA 94949-6191

Phone: (800) 422-7249

Fax: (888) 287-9975

Web site: www.academictherapy.com

Provides materials for parents and professionals in the field of learning disabilities. Large variety of assessment materials. *How to Write an IEP* also includes data for special education teachers. Large selection of resource materials for teachers. Found in Appendixes G, H.

American Guidance Service, Inc. (AGS)

(A division of Pearson Learning Group)

145 S. Mt. Zion Road

P.O. Box 2500

Lebanon, IN 46052

Phone: (800) 328-2560

Web site: www.agsglobe.com

Offers many books with high-interest, low-reading level. Some books suitable for ABE, ESL. A phone call can connect to product specialists. Field reps can visit schools and offer in-service on products. Found in Appendixes F, G.

Continental Press

520 E. Bainbridge Street

Elizabethtown, PA 17022-2299

Phone: (800) 233-0759

Fax: (888) 834-1303

Web site: www.continentalpress.com

Many test prep materials available, including state-specific for five states. Found in Appendixes F, G.

Curriculum Associates

P.O. Box 2001

North Billerica, MA 01862-0901

Phone: (800) 225-0248

Fax: (800) 366-1158

Web site: www.curriculumassociates.com

E-mail: info@CAinc.com

Offers state-specific Practice and Mastery series for nine states. *Focus Series* offers strategy-specific practice for reading comprehension, including understanding main idea, comparing and contrasting etc. Found in Appendixes F, G, H.

Franklin Electronic Publishers, Inc.

One Franklin Plaza

Burlington, NJ 08016-4907

Phone: (800) 525-9673

Fax: (609) 239-5950

Web site: www.franklin.com

Franklin offers the Pocket Prep, a handheld tutor for SAT preparation. Many products resemble handheld games which receive great student acceptance. Found in Appendix H.

Glencoe

(A division of McGraw-Hill)

P.O. Box 543

Blacklick, OH 43004-0543

Phone: (800) 334-7344

Fax: (614) 860-1877

Glencoe products are found in Appendix F under Jamestown Education.

Globe Fearon

(A division of Pearson Learning Group)

145 South Mt. Zion Road

P.O. Box 2500

Lebanon, IN 46052

Phone: (800) 321-3106

Fax: (800) 393-3156

Web site: www.pearsonlearning.com

The catalog includes products from Domine Press and Dale Seymour Publications. Contains state-specific performance on standardized tests for middle school and high school students. Found in Appendixes F, G.

Great Source Education Group

(A division of Houghton Mifflin)

181 Ballard Vale Street, Box 7050

Wilmington, MA 01887

Phone: (800) 289-4490

Fax: (800) 289-3994

Web site: www.greatsource.com

The catalog lists Great Source resources that qualify for federal funds and grant programs. Also offered are kit resources for each grade level and high-interest level reading instruction for standardized tests. Found in Appendix H.

High Noon Books

(A division of Academic Therapy)

20 Commercial Blvd

Novato, CA 94949-6191

Phone: (800) 422-7249

Fax: (888) 287-9975

Web site: www.academictherapy.com

Materials for students reading below grade level. Independent readers designed so that students can carry around these books without being embarrassed. Other books with readability levels grade 1 through 5. Found in Appendixes F, G, H.

Incentives for Learning

111 Center Avenue, Suite 1

Pacheco, CA 94553

Phone: (888) 238-2379

Web site: www.incentivesforlearning.com

Offers many books with audio cassettes, including read-along books. Spectrum offers state-specific test practice designed for six states' standardized tests. Found in Appendixes F, G, H.

Jamestown Education

(A division of Glencoe/McGraw-Hill)

P.O. Box 543

Blacklick, OH 43004-9902

Phone: (800) 872-7323
Fax: (614) 860-1877
Web site: www.jamestowneducation.com

Motto for Jamestown is: "Helping all readers become better readers." Offers a multitude of approaches and solutions in the reading field. Found in Appendixes F, G, H.

McGraw-Hill Contemporary

(A division of SRA)

220 E. Danieldale Road

DeSoto, TX 75115

Phone: (888) 772-4543
Fax: (800) 998-3103
Web site: www.mhcontemporary.com

Offers a national edition for test prep. Many reading labs available. The McGraw-Hill group includes SRA, Open Court, Reading Mastery, and MacMillan. Found in Appendix G.

National Reading Styles Institute

P.O. Box 737

Syosset, NY 11791

Phone: (800) 331-3117
Fax: (516) 921-5591
Web site: www.nrsi.com

CD available in Windows or Mac formats. You may identify the reading level of any book by typing in words from the book (readability level). Found in Appendixes G, H.

New Readers Press

(A division of ProLiteracy Worldwide
U.S. Publishing Division of Laubach Literacy)

1320 Jamesville Avenue

Syracuse, NY 13210

Phone: (800) 448-8878
Fax: (866) 894-2100
Web site: www.newreaderspress.com

Features materials for adult and young adult education. Multimedia offers diskette, CD-ROM, audio, and video. Found in Appendix G.

Pearson Learning Group

(Includes Globe Fearon, Modern Curriculum Press, Celebration Press,
Dale Seymour Publications, Pearson Early Learning)

145 S. Mt. Zion Road

P.O. Box 2500

Lebanon, IN 46052

Phone: (800) 321-3106

Fax: (800) 393-3156

Web site: www.pearsonlearning.com

Separate catalogs available from each division. Found in Appendixes F, H.

Perfection Learning Corporation

1000 North Second Avenue

P.O. Box 500

Logan, IA 51546-0500

Phone: (800) 831-4190

Fax: (800) 543-2745

Web site: www.perfectionlearning.com

Catalog lists award-winning books: ALA, notable children's books, Caldecott, Coretta Scott King, Newbery, and Orbis Pictus award books suitable for elementary level. Visual materials offered, including audio cassettes and videos with 68 new titles. Found in Appendixes F, H.

Phoenix Learning Group

2349 Chaffee Drive

St. Louis, MO 63146

Phone: (800) 221-1274

Fax: (314) 569-2834

Sold book division and now offers only film and videos. Send for catalog. Found in Appendix H.

Phoenix Learning Resources, Inc.

910 Church Street

Honesdale, PA 18431

Phone: (800) 228-9345

Fax: (570) 253-3227

Web site: www.phoenixlr.com

Offers many high-interest, low-vocabulary books that help develop reading skills. Found in Appendix G.

Rigby

(A division of Steck-Vaughn)
6277 Sea Harbor Drive
Orlando, FL 32887
Phone: (800) 531-5015
Fax: (800) 699-9459
Web site: www.harcourtachieve.com

Large selection of books for reading levels 1–4. Nonfiction series features cats, dogs, bears, hippos, penguins, whales, etc. Rigby collections of books (bookrooms) for individual grade levels. Bookrooms can be enlarged for the entire school district. Not found in Appendixes.

Saddleback Educational, Inc.

3 Watson
Irvine, CA 92618-2767
Phone: (888) 735-2225
Fax: (888) 734-4010
E-mail: info@sdlback.com
Web site: www.sdlback.com

Offers elementary cassette libraries which allow young readers to follow along. Caldecott and Newbery award books in catalog. Found in Appendixes F, G, H.

Scholastic, Inc.

P.O. Box 7502
Jefferson City, MO 65102
Phone: (800) 724-6527
Fax: (800) 560-6815
Web site: www.scholastic.com

Offers large complete catalog with excellent index for quick reference. This may be one of the catalogs to keep on hand for classroom or school library. See catalog for book clubs and software clubs. Found in Appendixes F, H.

School Specialty Publishing

P.O. Box 141487

Grand Rapids, MI 49514-1481

Phone: (800) 417-3261

Web site: www.schoolspecialtypublishing.com

State-specific test prep for six states. The Spectrum Test Prep and Test Practice series encompass grades 1–8. Not found in Appendixes.

Shakean Stations

P.O. Box 68

Farley, IA 52046

Phone: (800) 765-1475

Fax: (800) 765-1475

This company is run by retired teachers. Phone calls can be rerouted to personal cell phones. Found in Appendix H.

SRA/McGraw-Hill

220 E. Danieldale Road

DeSoto, TX 75115

Phone: (888) 772-4543

Fax: (972) 228-1982

Web site: www.sraonline.com

Index of SRA catalog by subject matter and includes grade level and price. Easy to use catalog. Order catalogs from both McGraw-Hill Contemporary and SRA/McGraw-Hill at either phone number. Found in Appendix G.

Steck-Vaughn Company

(Harcourt Achieve Imprint)

6277 Sea Harbor Drive

Orlando, FL 32887

Phone: (800) 531-5015

Web site: www.harcourtachieve.com

Also offers materials for state-specific test preparation for 13 states. Found in Appendixes F, G, H.

Sundance Publishing

1 Beeman Road
P.O. Box 740
Northborough, MA 01532
Phone: (800) 343-8204
Fax: (800) 456-2419
Web site: www.sundancepub.com

Offers 1,000 titles in paperback for grades K–6. A program for below-level readers and grades 2–8, with reading level beginning at grade 1.2, is a Sundance exclusive. Found in Appendixes F, H.

Treetop Publishing

P.O. Box 320725
Franklin, WI 53132
Phone: (800) 255-9228
Fax: (888) 201-5916

A good source for stickers, games, and puzzles, as well as the famous *Bare Books*. Found in Appendix H.

The Wright Group/ McGraw-Hill

220 E. Danieldale Road
DeSoto, TX 75115-2490
Phone: (800) 648-2970
Fax: (800) 593-4418
Web site: www.wrightgroup.com

Outstanding collection of books, including Big Books with rhyme and repetition. This is one of the first catalogs you should order. Great index by readability level and grade level. Quick, easy reference to contents. Found in Appendixes F, H.

Zaner-Bloser, Educational Publishers

P.O. Box 16764
Columbus, OH 43216-6764
Phone: (800) 421-3018
Fax: (800) 992-6087
Web site: www.zaner-bloser.com

The Language Arts and Reading Company. Found in Appendixes F, H.

REFERENCES

Aaronson, S. "Notetaking Improvement: A Combined Auditory, Functional and Psychological Approach." *Journal of Reading* 19, 1975, pp. 8–12.

Adams, M. J. *Beginning to Read: Thinking and Learning about Print.* Cambridge, MA: M.I.T. Press, 1990.

Alexander, P. A., and T. L. Jetton. "Learning from Text: A Multidimensional and Developmental Perspective." In M. L. Kamil; P. B. Mosenthal; P. D. Pearson; and R. Barr (eds.), *Handbook of Reading Research, Vol. III.* Mahwah, NJ: Lawrence Erlbaum Associates, 2000, p. 297.

Allen, R. V. "How a Language Experience Program Works." In E. C. Vilscek (ed.), *A Decade of Innovations: Approaches to Beginning Reading.* Newark, DE: International Reading Association, 1968.

Alvermann, D. E., and S. F. Phelps. *Content Reading and Literacy: Succeeding in Today's Diverse Classrooms,* 3rd ed. Boston: Allyn & Bacon, 2002.

American Federation of Teachers. *Teaching Reading Is Rocket Science: What Expert Teachers of Reading Should Know and Be Able to Do.* Washington, DC: June 1999, Item # 372.

Asch, S. E. "Reformulation of the Problem of Association." *American Psychologist* 24, 1969, pp. 92–102.

Au, K. H. "A Multicultural Perspective on Policies for Improving Literacy Achievement: Equity and Excellence." In M. L. Kamil; P. B. Mosenthal; P. D. Pearson; and R. Barr (eds.), *Handbook of Reading Research, Vol. III.* Mahwah, NJ: Lawrence Erlbaum Associates, 2000.

Bartel, N. R.; J. J. Grill; and D. N. Bryen. "Language Characteristics of Black Children: Implications for Assessment." *Journal of School Psychology* 11, 1973, pp. 351–364.

Bean, T. W., and F. L. Steenwyk. "The Effect of Three Forms of Summarization Instruction on Sixth Graders' Summary Writing and Comprehension." Cited in M. C. McKenna and R. D. Robison, *Teaching through Text: Reading and Writing in the Content Areas,* 3rd ed. Boston: Allyn & Bacon, 1984, p. 147.

Beck, I. L.; M. G. McKeown; R. L. Hamilton; and L. Kucan. *Questioning the Author: An Approach for Enhancing Student Engagement with Text.* Newark, DE: International Reading Association, 1997.

Beers, K. "Probable Passages: A Writing Strategy." *The Reading Teacher* 37, 2003, pp. 496–499.

Betts, E. A. *Foundations of Reading Instruction.* New York: American Book Company, 1946.

Blachman, B. A. "Phonological Awareness." In M. L. Kamil; P. B. Mosenthal; P. D. Pearson; and R. Barr, (eds.). *Handbook of Reading Research: Vol. III.* Mahwah, NJ: Lawrence Erlbaum Associates, 2000.

Blanchowicz, C. L. Z., and P. Fisher. "Vocabulary Instruction." In M. L. Kamil; P. B. Mosenthal; P. D. Pearson; and R. Barr (eds.), *Handbook of Reading Research: Vol. III.* Mahwah, NJ: Lawrence Erlbaum Associates, 2000.

Bloom, B. *Human Characteristics and School Learning.* New York: McGraw-Hill, 1976.

Blum, I. H.; P. S. Koskinen; N. Tennant; E. M. Parker; M. Straub; and C. Curry. "Using Audiotaped Books to Extend Classroom Literacy Instruction into the Homes of Second-Language Learners." *Journal of Reading Behavior* 27 (4), 1995, pp. 535–563.

Carbo, M. "Teaching Reading with Talking Books." *The Reading Teacher* 32, 1978, pp. 267–273.

Carney, J. J.; D. Anderson; C. Blackburn; and D. Blessings. "Preteaching Vocabulary and the Comprehension of Social Studies Materials by Elementary School Children." *Social Education* 48 (3), 1984, pp. 195–196.

Carver, R. P. "Silent Reading Rates in Grade Equivalents." *Journal of Reading Behavior* 21, 1989, pp. 155–166.

Chall, J. S. *Stages of Reading Development.* Orlando, FL: Harcourt, 1996.

Chamot, A. U., and J. M. O'Malley. *The CALLA Handbook: Implementing the Cognitive Academic Language Learning Approach.* New York: Addison-Wesley, 1994.

Clay, M. M. *Becoming Literate: The Construction of Inner Control.* Portsmouth, NH: Heinemann, 1991.

Clewell, S. F., and J. Haldemos. "Organizational Strategies to Increase Comprehension." *Reading World* 22, 1983, pp. 314–321.

Crawley, S. J., and L. Mountain. *Strategies for Guiding Content Reading,* 2nd ed. Boston: Allyn & Bacon, 1995.

Cunningham, P. M. *Phonics They Use: Words for Reading and Writing.* New York: Longman, 1995, p. 297.

Cunningham, P. M., and J. W. Cunningham. "Improving Listening in Content Area Subjects." *National Association of Secondary School Principles Bulletin* 60 (404), 1976, pp. 26–31.

Cunningham, P. M.; J. W. Cunningham; and S. V. Arthur. *Middle and Secondary School Reading.* New York: Longman, 1981.

Curtain, H., and C. A. Pesola. *Languages and Children: Making the Match.* New York: Longman, 1994.

Daniels, H. *Literature Circles: Voice and Choice in the Student-Centered Classroom.* York, ME: Stenhouse Publishers, 1998.

Davey, B. "Think Aloud: Modeling the Cognitive Processes of Reading Comprehension." *Journal of Reading* 27, 1983, pp. 44–47.

Dishner, E. K., and J. E. Readence. "A Systematic Procedure for Teaching Main Idea." *Reading World* 16, 1977, pp. 292–298.

Dolch, E. W. "A Basic Sight Vocabulary." *Elementary School Journal* 36, 1936, pp. 456–461.

Dowhower, S. L. "Effects of Repeated Reading in Second-Grade Transitional Readers' Fluency and Comprehension." *Reading Research Quarterly* 22, 1987, pp. 389–406.

Duke, N. K., and P. D. Pearson. "Effective Practices for Developing Reading Comprehension." In A. E. Farstrup and S. J. Samuels (eds.), *What Research Has to Say about Reading Instruction,* 3rd ed. Newark, DE: International Reading Association, 2002, pp. 205–242.

Durrell, D. "First Grade Reading Success Study: A Summary." *Journal of Education* 40 (3), 1958, pp. 1–24.

Elkonin, D. B. "Reading in the USSR." In J. Downing (ed.), *Comparative Reading.* New York: Macmillan, 1973, pp. 551–579.

Fernald, Grace. *Remedial Techniques In Basic School Subjects.* New York: McGraw-Hill, 1943.

Fountas, I. C., and G. S. Pinnell. *Teaching for All Children.* Portsmouth, NH: Heinemann, 1996.

———. Pinnell. *Leveled Books (K–8): Matching Texts to Readers for Effective Reading.* Portsmouth, NH: Heinemann, 2005.

Franken, R. *Human Motivation,* 3rd ed. Pacific Grove, CA: Brooks/Cole Publishing, 1994.

Geva, E. "Facilitating Reading Comprehension through Flowcharting." *Reading Research Quarterly* 18, 1983, pp. 384–405.

Graves, M. F. "Vocabulary Learning and Instruction." In E. Z. Rothkopf (ed.), *Review of Research in Education* 13, pp. 49–90. Washington, DC: American Educational Research Association, 1986.

Gunning, T. G. *Creating Literacy Instruction for All Children,* 4th ed. Boston: Allyn & Bacon, 2003.

Hanna, P. R.; R. E. Hodges; J. L. Hanna; and E. H. Rudolph. *Phoneme-Grapheme Correspondences as Cues to Spelling Improvement.* Washington, DC: U.S. Office of Education, 1966.

Harber, J. R., and J. N. Beatty. *Reading and the Black English–Speaking Child.* Newark, DE: International Reading Association, 1978.

Heckelman, R. O. "Using the Neurological-Impress Remedial Reading Technique." *Academic Therapy Quarterly* 1 (4), 1969, pp. 235–239.

Heilman, A. W. *Phonics in Proper Perspective,* 8th ed. Columbus, OH: Merrill/Prentice Hall, 1998.

Herber, H., and J. Nelson. "Questioning Is Not the Answer." *Journal of Reading* 18, 1975, pp. 512–517.

Herber, H. L. *Teaching Reading in Content Areas.* Englewood Cliffs, NJ: Prentice-Hall, 1978.

Hoffman, J. "Critical Reading/Thinking Across the Curriculum: Using I-charts to Support Learning." *Language Arts* 69, 1992, pp. 121–127.

Hoffner, H. "An Adapted Language Experience Approach: Helping Secondary Students with Content Area Reading." *Ohio Reading Teacher.* Fall 2003–Spring 2004.

Hofler, D. B. "Outlining—Teach the Concept First." *Reading World* 32, 1983, pp. 176–177.

Holdaway, D. "Shared Book Experiences: Teaching Reading Using Favorite Books." *Theory into Practice* 21, 1982, pp. 293–300.

International Reading Association. *National Reading Association's Summary of the (U.S.) National Reading Panel Report.* Retrieved November 5, 2002, http://www.reading.org/advocacy/nrp/chapter1.html.

Jiganti, M. A., and M. S. Tindall. "An Interactive Approach to Teaching Vocabulary." *The Reading Teacher* 39, 1986, pp. 444–448.

Lyman, F. T. "The Responsive Classroom Discussion: The Inclusion of All Students." In A. Anderson (ed.), *Mainstreaming Digest.* College Park: University of Maryland Press, 1981, pp. 109–113.

Manis, M. *Cognitive Processes.* Belmont, CA: Wadsworth, 1966.

Manzo, A. V. "The ReQuest Procedure." *Journal of Reading* 13, 1979a, pp. 123–126, 163.

———. "The ReQuest procedure." In C. Pennock (ed.), *Reading Comprehension on Four Linguistic Levels.* Newark, DE: International Reading Association, 1979b.

McKenna, M. C., and R. D. Robinson. *Teaching through Text: Reading and Writing in the Content Areas.* Boston: Allyn & Bacon, 2002, p. 64.

McKeown, M. G.; I. L. Beck; R. C. Omanson; and C. A. Perfetti. "The Effects of Long-Term Vocabulary Instruction on Reading Comprehension: A Replication." *Journal of Reading Behavior* 15 (1), 1983, pp. 3–18.

Meyer, B. J.; D. M. Brandt; and G. J. Bluth. "Use of Top-Level Structure in Text: Key for Reading Comprehension of Ninth Grade Students." *Reading Research Quarterly* 16, 1980, pp. 72–103.

Mountain, L. *Early 3 Rs: How to Lead Beginners into Reading, Writing, and Arithme-TALK.* Mahwah, NJ: Lawrence Erlbaum Associates, 2000.

Nagy, W. E., and R. Anderson. "How Many Words Are There in Printed English?" *Reading Research Quarterly* 19, 1984, pp. 304–330.

National Education Association. "Parental Involvement Improves Student Achievement" (Sept. 10, 2002). (http://www.nea.org/parents/). Retrieved January 31, 2003.

National Institute for Literacy. *National Reading Panel Report: Teaching Children to Read: An Evidence-Based Assessment of the Scientific Research Literature on Reading and Its Implications for Reading Instruction.* Washington, DC: U.S. Department of Health and Human Services, 2000, Publication No. 00-4754.

———. *Put Reading First: The Research Building Blocks for Teaching Children to Read.* Washington, DC: National Institute of Child Health and Human Development, 2001.

National Research Council. *Starting Out Right: A Guide to Promoting Children's Reading Success.* Washington, DC: National Academy Press, 1999.

Neuman, S. B., and D. Celano. "Access to Print in Low-Income and Middle-Income Communities: An Ecological Study of Four Neighborhoods." *Reading Research Quarterly* 36 (1), 2001, pp. 8–26.

New Zealand Reading Recovery. www.readingrecovery.ac.nz/index.php. 2007.

Nichols, C. M. *Evidenced Based Reading Instruction: Putting the National Reading Panel Report into Practice.* Newark, DE: International Reading Association, 2002.

North American Reading Recovery. www.readinrecovery.com/reading_recovery/index.asp. 2007.

Ogle, D. "K–W–L: A Teaching Model That Develops Active Reading of Expository Text." *The Reading Teacher* 39, 1986, pp. 564–570.

Osborn, A. F. *Applied Imagination: Principles and Procedures of Creating Thinking.* New York: Scribner, 1953.

Palinscar, A. S., and A. I. Brown. "Interactive Teaching to Promote Independent Learning from Text." *The Reading Teacher* 39, 1986, pp. 771–777.

Palmatier, R. A. "Comprehension of Four Notetaking Procedures." *Journal of Reading* 17, 1971, pp. 72–78.

Pauk, W. *How to Study in College,* 2nd ed. Boston: Houghton Mifflin, 1974.

———. "Preparing for Exams." *Reading World* 23, 1974, pp. 286–287.

———. "The New SQ3R." *Reading World* 23, 1984, pp. 274–275.

Pavio, A. *Imagery and Verbal Processes.* New York: Holt, Rinehart & Winston, 1971.

Pinnell, G. S., and I. C. Fountas. *Word Matters.* Portsmouth, NH: Heinemann, 1998.

Pressley, M. "What Should Comprehension Instruction Be the Instruction of?" In M. L. Kamil; P. B. Mosenthal; P. D. Pearson; and R. Barr (eds.), *Handbook of Reading Research, Vol. III.* Mahwah, NJ: Lawrence Erlbaum Associates, 2000, pp. 545–561.

Raphael, T. E. "Question-Answering Strategies for Children." *The Reading Teacher* 39, 1982, pp. 186–190.

———. "Teaching Learners about Sources of Information for Answering Comprehension Questions." *Journal of Reading* 27, 1984, pp. 303–311.

———. "Teaching Question Answer Relationships, Revised." *The Reading Teacher* 39, 1986, pp. 516–522.

———. "Teaching Question Answer Relationships, Revisited." *The Reading Teacher* 39, 1986, pp. 515–522.

Rasinksi, T. V., and N. D. Padak. *From Phonics to Fluency.* New York: Addison Wesley Longman, 2001.

Reutzel, D. R.; P. C. Fawson; J. R. Young; T. G. Morrison; and B. Wilcox. "Reading Environmental Print: The Role of Concepts of Print in Discriminating Young Readers' Responses." *Reading Psycology* 24 (2), 2003, pp. 123–162.

Reynolds, A. G.; and Flagg, P. W. *Cognitive Psychology.* Cambridge, MA: Winthrop, 1977.

Ruddell, M. R. "Teaching Content Reading and Writing." In R. B. Ruddell, *Teaching Children to Read and Write: Becoming an Effective Literacy Teacher,* 3rd ed. Boston: Allyn & Bacon, 2002, p. 263.

Rundus, D. J. "Analysis of Rehearsal Processes in Free Recall." *Journal of Experimental Psychology* 89, 1971, pp. 63–77.

Rupley, W. H.; J. W. Logan; and W. D. Nichols. "Vocabulary Instruction in a Balanced Reading Program." *The Reading Teacher* 52, 1998–1999, pp. 336–346.

Samuels, S. J. "Method of Repeated Reading." *The Reading Teacher* 32, 1979, pp. 403–408.

Schreiber, P. "On the Acquisition of Reading Fluency." *Journal of Reading Behavior* 12, 1980, pp. 177–186.

Schwartz, R. M., and T. E. Raphael. "Concept of Definition: A Key to Improving Students' Vocabulary." *The Reading Teacher* 39, 1985, pp. 198–205.

Searfoss, L. "Radio Reading." *The Reading Teacher* 29, 1975, pp. 295–296.

Snow, C. E.; M. S. Burns; and P. Griffin (eds.). *Preventing Reading Difficulties in Young Children.* Washington, DC: National Academy Press, 1998.

Smith, M. K. "Measurement of the Size of General English Vocabulary through the Elementary Grades and High School." *Genetic Psychology Monographs* 24, 1991, pp. 313–324.

Stanovich, K. E.; A. E. Cunningham; and B. B. Cramer. "Assessing Phonological Awareness in Kindergarten Children: Issues of Task Comparability." *Journal of Experimental Child Psychology* 38, 1984, pp. 175–190.

Stauffer, R. G. *The Language-Experience Approach to the Teaching of Reading.* New York: Harper & Row, 1970.

———. *Reading–Thinking Skills.* Paper presented at the annual reading conference at Temple University, Philadelphia. Cited in T. G. Gunning, *Creating Literacy Instruction for All Children.* Boston: Allyn & Bacon, 2000, p. 274.

Taba, H. *Teacher's Handbook for Elementary Social Studies.* Reading, MA: Addison-Wesley, 1967.

Taylor, B. M. "Looking beyond Ourselves to Help All Children Learn to Read." In M. G. Graves, P. van den Broek, and B. M. Taylor (eds.), *The First R: Every Child's Right to Read.* New York: Teachers College Press, 1996, pp. 62–69.

Tierney, R. J.; J. E. Readence; and K. E. Dishner. *Reading Strategies and Practices: A Compendium* (3rd ed.). Boston: Allyn and Bacon, 1980.

Tompkins, G. E. *Literacy for the 21st Century.* Columbus, OH: Merrill Prentice Hall, 2003.

Topping, K. "Paired Reading: A Powerful Technique for Parent Use." *The Reading Teacher* 40, 1987a, pp. 608–614.

———. "Peer Tutored Paired Reading: Outcome Data from Ten Projects." *Educational Psychology* 7, 1987b, pp. 604–614.

Torgesen, J. K., and P. G. Mathes. *Assessment and Instruction in Phonological Awareness.* Tallahassee, FL: Florida Department of Education, 1999, pp. 36–37.

Traxler, A. E. "Improvement of Vocabulary through Drill." *Language Arts* 53, 1938, pp. 319–322.

Trelease, J. *The Read-Aloud Handbook,* 5th ed. New York: Penguin, 2001.

Vacca, R. T., and J. A. L. Vacca. *Content Area Reading: Literacy and Learning across the Curriculum,* 7th ed. Boston: Allyn & Bacon, 2002.

Walsh, D. S.; G. G. Prince; and M. G. Gillingham. "The Critical but Transitory Importance of Letter Naming." *Reading Research Quarterly* 23, 1988, pp. 108–122.

Wisconsin Literacy Education and Reading Network Source (WILEARNS). "Think Aloud Prompts." Retrieved June 10, 2007, http://wilearns.state. wi.us/apps/Print.asp?ap=&cid=609.

Wolpert, E. "Length, Imagery Values and Word Recognition." *The Reading Teacher* 26, 1972, pp. 180–186.

Wylie, R., and D. Durrell. "Teaching Vowels through Phonograms." *Elementary Education* 47, 1970.

Yopp, H. K. "Developing Phonemic Awareness in Young Children." *The Reading Teacher* 45, 1992, pp. 696–703.

Young, T. A., and S. Vardell. "Weaving Readers Theatre and Nonfiction into the Curriculum." *The Reading Teacher* 46, 1993, pp. 396–406.

INDEX